Praise for

Redeemed

"Penny Lane's memoir of childhood trauma is engrossing and terrifying. Carefully crafted and beautifully written, this memoir is a tribute to resilience and, in the end, to family and love and belonging."

—ELLEN BARKER, author of *East of Troost* and *Still Needs Work*

"The author had me from the start and kept me riveted throughout her harrowing story. Few among us can not only survive a painful and emotionally abusive childhood but also go on to thrive and make deep meaning of our lives. Penny Lane has done that, and has written a tour de force that will resonate with so many people. This is a book that will be spoken of for a long time."

—JOANNE GREENE, author of *By Accident*

"I found myself incredibly inspired by this author's resilience and ability to overcome circumstances that were beyond her control. Much like *The Glass Castle* by Jeannette Walls, this memoir almost reads like a thriller."

—CORRINE PRITCHETT, Publicist, Books Forward

"The narrative will stir strong emotions in the reader and hopefully prompt more people to speak out and report abuse. A compelling, gripping story that ends in redemption."

—LINDA MOORE, author of *Attribution* and *Five Days in Bogota*

"I was hooked from the first words of this engaging memoir—I strongly recommend it."

—LALLY PIA, MD, author of *The Fortune Seeker's Prophecy*

"Penny Lane's memoir confronts the stark realities of childhood trauma with unflinching honesty. Though it may be triggering for some, I found myself drawn into Penny's world. This memoir is a poignant reminder that while scars may linger, they need not define us, and that true redemption lies in the courage to reclaim one's own story."

—JUDE BERMAN, author of *The Healing Zone* and *The Die*

"Penny Lane's gripping memoir is both heartbreaking and heartening, a testament to resilience and hope. This is a page-turning journey that maintains hope through the bleakest of circumstances, and ends on a tremendously satisfying note. I highly recommend this book!"

—ANN BANCROFT, author of *Almost Family*

"What a spectacular read; I could hardly put it down. Lane's writing is eloquent and intimate, easily drawing the reader into her world. You are in for a real treat with this remarkable book."

—CLAUDIA MARSEILLE, author of *But You Look So Normal*

"*Redeemed* will grab you and wrap you into a forty-eight-hour whirlwind! Be prepared to start this book and not put it down. It pulls you into an unbelievable story of trauma, sacrifice, and a true testament of a woman surviving in this patriarchal and pained world. Penny tells her story with precision, bravery, and honesty. Do yourself a favor and read it."

—ERICA TANAMACHI, award-winning director/producer

Redeemed

Redeemed

A Memoir of a
Stolen Childhood

Penny Lane

SHE WRITES PRESS

Published 2024
Printed in the United States of America
Print ISBN: 978-1-64742-700-9
E-ISBN: 978-1-64742-701-6
Library of Congress Control Number: 2023921753

For information, address:
She Writes Press
1569 Solano Ave #546
Berkeley, CA 94707

Interior design by Stacey Aaronson

She Writes Press is a division of SparkPoint Studio, LLC.

Names and identifying characteristics have been changed to protect the privacy of certain individuals.

Author's Note

Some of the names and other identifying characteristics of the people included in this memoir have been changed. Memories are imperfect, and each person has a perspective. The following memoir is accurate to the best of my ability.

For my mother, Patricia Ann,
and for my Aunt Charlotte

Redeemed:

verb. To free from what distresses or harms

PART ONE

Losing Home

The man kissing me told me he was my father, but I did not know him. His face was rough and scratchy, and his smell unfamiliar. His sloppy kisses soon turned into hugs as he babbled away in a foreign accent that I did not recognize, acting as if he knew me. I didn't want him to kiss me but did not know how to tell him to stop. I tried to pull away, but he was too big, and I didn't stand a chance. My throat closed up, and I couldn't talk.

The year was 1963. I was four years old. Before this strange man walked down my driveway, I had been plum happy sitting on my red tricycle, scanning the neighborhood for someone to play with. I had a great life in a big, brown two-story house in Linden, New Jersey, with lots of yard on a shady, tree-lined street. We had a long, wide driveway on which I could ride back and forth all day or play hopscotch with my cousins. I lived with my aunt Charlotte and uncle George and their kids, Georgie and Alex. Living downstairs were my uncle Buddy and aunt Mary and their brood, Maggie, Rebecca, and Ted. We had neighbors next door who were old but still nice, and there were lots of kids and fun on our street. I fit right in.

"Penniké," the new man called out enthusiastically, grinning with his funny teeth. He kept calling me Penniké, though my name was Penny, and he called me another funny word, *csillagom*.

Just then, Aunt Charlotte came outside in her going-to-town dress and began talking to this man like she knew him. She did not seem surprised by his presence, or his odd words, which made my stomach queasy. She looked at me with eyes I could not read, then quickly looked away.

The street was quiet, except for the grown-ups talking, and it was hot. My clothes were starting to itch and stick to my back, making me even more uncomfortable. After a while, my aunt hunched down to me, her soft, tender eyes at my level. She smiled as she stroked my cheek, but I could sense that she was having a hard time of it, her smile cracking into a sad face.

"Precious," she said, "this is your father, and he's come to take you home."

What? I thought to myself. I had never seen him before in my life.

Home? I was already home. This was where we had birthday parties and ice cream, where we kids played hide-and-seek and chased fireflies in the backyard at night. I had always lived here, and I did not like this stranger. Aunt Charlotte held my hand as she and the man started walking way too fast toward a car parked at the curb. I dragged my feet and pulled back, but Aunt Charlotte tugged me along with a force that I had not experienced with her before. I let go of my tricycle and hoped it would not tip over. What was going on? And why was this man carrying the suitcase I had seen in the kitchen that morning? As I looked back at the house, I saw my cousins Georgie and Alex in the front window, watching. I looked up at the adults talking to each other over my head, but I could not make out the words. Something was very wrong.

In the car, a man waited for us in the driver's seat. He smiled and handed me a beautiful teddy bear, which calmed me down a little. Maybe this was not so bad. The driver's eyes were kind, and he held my gaze for a few moments, as if to communicate some sort of comfort, but did not say anything. As we got in the car, the driver spoke to my father, but their words were in a funny language, and I did not get any of it.

I sat in the back seat with Aunt Charlotte, who continued holding my hand. She told me we were going to see Uncle George at the train station. My uncle George was a ticket agent for the Pennsylvania Railroad, a glamorous-sounding job to me. But we'd never visited him at the train station before.

As we pulled away from my home, I looked back at my tricycle left in the driveway. Aunt Charlotte held me close, her arm around my back. The two men in the front seat were still conversing in their strange language. Sometimes I heard them mention that name, Penniké.

I could tell by the struggle on her face that my aunt was getting ready to say something and was choosing her words carefully. "Precious, your mother died when you were a baby," she told me gently. She said she had taken me in, and I had been living with her and her family ever since.

"You were too young to remember," she said.

My head and throat were starting to hurt, and I became dizzy. I had always thought that Aunt Charlotte was my mother and that Uncle George was my father and that I was part of their family. Why hadn't anyone told me?

I kept quiet. There was a lot of chatting among the adults the rest of the way to the train station, but I was still reeling from what Aunt Charlotte had told me. Why did my mother die? Would Aunt Charlotte die? Would I die too? I held on to Aunt Charlotte's hand for dear life. I looked at the two men in the front of the car as if in a dream, wondering how they got there. My eyes filled up. I could not speak.

When I gazed up toward Aunt Charlotte, I noticed that she was biting her lip as she looked out the window, and there were tears in her eyes too. Soon, we got to the station, and she squeezed my hand.

"I'll be right back, Precious," she said, not looking back at me. In a flash, she was out the door, disappearing into the crowd before I could say anything or muster the courage to run after her. She never looked back.

In that moment, I had no way of knowing that my carefree, happy life was about to turn into a nightmare I could never have imagined. That I was being ripped from my loving home and thrust into a world full of fear, neglect, and abuse that would take decades to escape. That I was about to become an unwanted alien, lost in a cold, foreign home, and a powerless scapegoat lacking any sense of self or worth, one that not even God could save.

Until I finally broke free and found a way to stand on my own.

In the car, the two men in the front seat remained silent as we drove away. I waited nervously for Aunt Charlotte to come back. But it would be more than fifty years before I saw her again.

2

Budapest, California

W e drove away from the train station in silence, me waiting for the driver to pull over and for Aunt Charlotte to miraculously step back into the car. But it didn't happen. I was cold and scared, trembling, and feeling alone with these strangers. I stared out the window as a storm of cars rushed by to and fro, and we arrived at a busy set of buildings. People and cars were everywhere. But where was my aunt? I was too shaken and confused to ask. The man at the steering wheel dropped us off quickly, as if trying to get away, calling after us with his kind eyes.

"*Jó von, viszontlátása Penniké.*"

My new father and I were at an airport. The terminal was the biggest building I had ever seen—loud, crowded, and frightening. My father held my hand firmly, and I held on to it as if my life depended on it as we ran to catch our plane. My short legs struggled to keep up, and my head hurt from the noise and my confusion. Once we boarded our flight, I thought about running away but soon realized I couldn't get very far in the enclosed airplane. My aunt was not here. I was alone with this man I did not know. Deflated and again anxious, I took my seat.

"Would you like some crayons, sugar?" a beautiful stewardess asked in a sweet southern drawl. I nodded, doe-eyed, momen-tarily distracted from missing my aunt, and smitten. She buckled me into my window seat in the first row and tucked a blanket on my lap. Smelling like flowers and dripping with kindness, she made me feel like it was all going to be okay. My fears ticked away as I took in her glamorous blue dress, high heels, fancy hairdo, and red, lacquered nails, which matched her glossy lips. I thought she was the nicest, prettiest woman I'd ever seen. She was pleasant with all the passengers but extra kind to me. She winked at me whenever she passed by and made me smile. In addition to a coloring book and crayons, she gave me an airline pin, just like the one she had on her dress. I relaxed back into my seat. I would tell my aunt Charlotte about this nice lady.

My father sat next to me as if I wasn't there, with a beer in hand, grinning, joking, and chatting with the stewardess in his thick accent. He didn't say much to me at all. He didn't tell me where we were going, and I was too shy to ask. I wanted to know when I was going home to Georgie and Alex, but I couldn't ask that either. When the stewardess served us dessert with dinner on little dishes like my tea set, I forgot about ever being afraid and settled into being treated like a real princess. I loved dessert but had never had it served with dinner before.

After we landed in California, my father and I took a taxi to a house in the desert. He maintained his silence. The house was unlike anything I had seen before. It was small and flat and white, with no upstairs. There were awnings over the windows, and a big US flag that hung limply from a pole by the front door. There was no grass, bushes, or trees anywhere, and no breeze. Just sand and odd-looking plants with pins sticking out called cactus. Everything was pale and strange. This was not like Aunt Charlotte's.

"Welcome home," my father said.

I noticed that no one was on the street, which I thought was very strange. It was so hot that I started sweating as soon as I stepped out of the taxi, and there was a haze over the horizon that made me rub my eyes to straighten them out. Exhausted from our long journey, I squinted into the blinding sun as we trudged to the house, only to jump when a little green lizard skittered in front of me. My father laughed.

"This is Desert Hot Springs, Penniké," he snickered. "We have lizards here, big ones and little ones."

I never did get used to those lizards. Nothing was the same in California. I knew we were still in America because of the flag out front, but it did not feel that way.

At the house, a stern woman approached and immediately started talking to my father in that funny language that I did not understand. The tone sounded frustrated, as if we were late or something. She ignored me even though I was standing next to my father, holding his hand. I watched her face, trying to make out her words. She did not look happy, and sounded put out. I looked up at her, longing to be seen, when she finally addressed me.

"Hello," she said in perfect English, but nothing more.

I was surprised and relieved that she spoke my language and told her so. She laughed at me and explained that they spoke Hungarian at home and that I'd have to learn it too. Why was she laughing at me? Had I done something wrong? What was Hungarian? And what was I doing with these people who spoke this funny language? It still did not make sense. I felt lost again, holding back tears. I missed my aunt Charlotte, but something in my gut told me it would not do to mention it.

As the days passed, I tried my hardest to fit into this new family. I figured out that this woman was married to my father, and she was going to be my new mother. I was not sure what to make of this situation—or her. No one was telling me anything.

My stepmother was pretty but reserved, almost aloof. She looked a little bit like Elizabeth Taylor with a rounder face and less makeup. She wasn't tall but wasn't short either. She wasn't fat or skinny. The air was always chilly around her, and I could not feel at ease. She didn't speak to me much, but when she did, she just called me Penny.

There wasn't much to my new home. The living room and kitchen were both small, but I had my own room. I couldn't find any toys, and no dollhouse like I'd had in Linden, only coloring books. There was some shade in the backyard, which was a small square surrounded by a chain-link fence. I thought looking into other people's backyards was a strange thing to do, though it didn't matter. No one was out anyway. I couldn't see or hear any kids, which caused that creeping feeling to come back to my stomach. I was alone here. Who would I play with? Who would be my friend? Who would hug me like Aunt Charlotte used to?

The house smelled different too, maybe because my stepmother cooked weird things, made with a strong spice that she called *paprika.* She put it in everything, even eggs. We ate food that I had never tasted before, things made with cabbage, onions, green peppers, and sour cream, which was disgusting. But I did like the things called *palacsinta,* flat, thin pancakes rolled up with jam.

The food was the least of my problems, though. This place was different, and so were the rules. My new parents spoke Hungarian all the time, and I had to work hard to make out what they were saying by guessing what was going on. I learned that *menj enni* meant go eat, and *menj aludni* meant go to bed. Did the other kids in the neighborhood speak this way? I had no idea. I could not shake the feeling that I did not belong here, and I did not really feel wanted either.

It was always very quiet in the house, except when my step-mother played opera, Elvis Presley, or Glenn Miller on the record player. At least it was in English, except for the opera. I did not ask a lot of questions, like I had done with Aunt Charlotte. I quickly understood in this foreign place that I was to be seen, not heard. I was not exactly scared, but I existed under an odd cloud of not fitting in, of boredom and silence. My stepmother seemed nice enough, and Father appeared to be a jolly guy, whistling all the time and joking with my stepmother. But none of us had much to say to each other like I was used to back in Linden. Nothing was like back in New Jersey. I missed my real family, but we never talked about them.

Sometimes my father would break up the boredom by taking us for drives. He loved to drive. But those brief trips could not dispel a nagging question: Why had my father gone to so much trouble to bring me all the way out here, when he was never around, and never talked to me when he was? He worked all the time, even Saturdays, and liked to sleep in on Sundays while I just had to be quiet.

Eventually, I was allowed to wander around the neighborhood, but only if I asked. It was too hot to stay out for long, and I didn't make any friends. At Aunt Charlotte's I'd had the run of the neighborhood, as I'd had my cousins around me and my aunt was so friendly, I knew everyone on the street. My stepmother didn't seem to have any friends either. We were always in our house by ourselves. I just colored in my room and waited for my father to come home. I felt empty inside, like something was missing, but I did not know why.

My father never mentioned my aunt Charlotte again, and as I

settled into my new life, I started to forget about her and my cousins Georgie and Alex. That life seemed like an old dream, distant and vague, like something that hadn't really happened. I barely remembered the plane ride, but when anyone asked what I wanted to be, I always answered, "Stewardess."

My stepmother and I coexisted, but we didn't always get each other, and I don't mean just the Hungarian, which I was picking up with each passing day. Things were different between us in a way I did not understand.

"I'm hungry," I told her often.

"You just ate," she'd reply.

"But I'm still hungry."

She would put her chin up and walk away, as if I did not deserve an answer. I knew that I would have to wait for the next meal to get more food. It seemed like I was always hungry in California, yet another thing I did not understand.

There was no warmth between us. No love, though I wanted to be loved like I knew Aunt Charlotte had once loved me. I could not approach my stepmother. I wasn't afraid exactly, but her air made me too timid to even try. My stepmother looked at me funny sometimes, like she was trying to figure out whether she could change my looks, to see whether there was another way to do my hair, which she said was straight and ugly.

Things changed a few months later when my half brother Steven was born. No one told me we were having a baby, so it was a big surprise to me. His fancy white crib covered in a beautiful quilt sat in my parents' bedroom, a shelf of stuffed animals nearby. Because the house was small, I heard his cries wherever I was, but I did not mind. I loved having a baby brother. The house became alive with his arrival.

Steven was truly a cute baby and soon became the light of my life. Everyone was a lot happier when he came home, even though there was a lot of work to do. We were always changing, feeding, washing, or burping him. I got to swish his diapers in the toilet and rock him to sleep by shaking his crib. My stepmother fussed and fawned over him, and was always on guard whenever anyone else held him. She was constantly on the phone to her family in New York telling them his every detail, and sending them pictures of him from our black box camera. He was the first male grandchild, and firstborn son, which I found out was a big deal to Hungarians, a much bigger deal than girls. At least now I got to help, which made me less invisible.

Steven was chubby and round, with beautiful olive skin and curly brown hair, which we wove around our fingers into a roll of hair on top of his head. That was how they did it with babies in Hungary, my stepmother said. With the arrival of Steven, my father was home more, which made me happy. He whistled and joked with me as he helped me fetch diapers and bottles. He bought my stepmother flowers and brought stuffed animals for Steven. I held my half brother with real, deep joy when my stepmother wasn't around, but nervously when she was.

Even better than getting a baby brother was starting kindergarten a few months later. I had played school with my cousins back in New Jersey but had never been to a real one. Now, I finally had other kids to play with, and we could run around on the playground and make as much noise as we wanted. I made friends quickly, and had lots of them. Something else was different at school, a feeling inside that was hard to pinpoint. Like I mattered to people. Like I was as good as everyone else there. There were crafts and books and music and snacks. It was pure fun, and I fit right in from day one. The teacher let each kid have a turn talking, and I got to say what I liked. There was no Hungarian spoken in the classroom, or on the playground, or anywhere, which was a welcome change. The kids at school seemed more like me.

I loved school and hated when we had a day off. And, best of all, I never got in trouble there, and seemed to do everything right. Instead of raising your hand to be called on by your teacher, the rule was to sit up straight to be noticed or picked, which I did, straining to sit taller and straighter so I'd get chosen. I could tell the teacher liked me, and before long, she told me I was so bright that she was going to move me up to first grade early. With this promotion, I could stay in school all day. I was overjoyed.

But after my initial week in first grade, my bubble burst. My parents told me that we were moving to New York. I had no idea where that was, but I knew for sure I did not want to go.

3

The Bronx Zoo

Standing next to my metal trash bin, I rode the clanging old elevator down to the basement of our Bronx apartment building. The ride always took forever, but I didn't mind. Sometimes I would bump into the super, Hector, who would smile at me with his gold-covered teeth, or Mrs. Laski, who would get on from the third floor.

As soon as the door opened into the basement, I saw Marci Lieberman and her father emptying their own trash.

"What are you doing down here all alone?"

Mr. Lieberman always asked me that, saying it wasn't safe for a little girl to be in the basement alone, but I never thought anything of it. Instead, I just tapped Marci on the arm and we started playing tag, laughing as we ran around the dozens of big black barrels in the dank cavern of a room. I wasn't afraid. I loved taking out the trash and doing other errands because I had fun and I felt free.

It was a relief not to be trapped indoors all the time, like I had been in California. Six months earlier, my parents had decided to move to New York to be closer to my stepmother's family, and in 1965, the Bronx was the most affordable of the city's five boroughs. My stepmother and my baby brother had flown back on their own, while my father and I had driven a U-Haul with our meager belongings across the country. The trip was long, hot, and boring, and seemed to go on forever, the only relief being our infrequent stops for gas and the bathroom or food. My father didn't talk to me much. He liked to whistle or listen to the radio. Eventually, after many days on the road, he announced that we were looking at the lights of New York City. It was big and tall and bright and crowded. And loud.

My life in the bustling Bronx was far different from the barrenness of the California desert, but somehow it suited me just fine. My family and I lived on the top floor, at the far end of an echoing hallway in an Edwardian brick building. There were ten apartments to a floor, and six floors to slide down the banisters on, until you were dumped into a tiny marble lobby. A whole village nestled into an old, creaking building. Our block was lined with a few trees and many more buildings just like mine, holding their residents in until their errands and children sent them teeming into the street.

There was always something going on in our little corner of the South Bronx, a decent, working-class neighborhood of mostly Eastern European immigrants. Inside our apartment, I felt like one of those immigrants. I kept to myself and spoke only Hungarian. On the streets, though, I became more of the outgoing American I was, one who spoke English well and didn't know a stranger. The girl in Linden who laughed all the time and rode around carefree on her tricycle. The girl who used to be me.

The sidewalks were busy with people carrying bags of food or running to catch a train, kids jumping rope or playing hopscotch, or boys playing handball against the buildings. In the mornings, the shopkeepers in long white aprons swept the bits of sidewalk in front of their businesses before setting out their cardboard-box displays of fruit, cheap radios, or pots and pans. Above me, airplanes crisscrossed the sky and window air conditioners hummed loudly, while mothers shook out rugs and called down to their children or husbands with reminders to get milk on the way home. There was always something happening on Boynton Avenue, and it filled me with energy and life.

On the other side of Westchester Avenue, the street that carried the elevated subway that we just called the El, lived the Puerto Ricans, Jamaicans, and Blacks, who erupted onto the street with an energy like the pulse of a party. On that side, there was always music playing, people calling out in all kinds of languages, kids on bikes or roller skates, and fancy cars blaring salsa music, honking for children to get out of the way. Bright fabric shops, fragrant food stalls, and crowded hardware shops were abundant on the avenue, the wares and aromas spilling onto the sidewalks, which were scorching in the summer and frigid in the winter. Yet the weather never bothered me. I could breathe in the Bronx, and loved being out and about in its frenzy.

I usually skipped instead of walking as I ran errands, and sometimes I acted out little plays I had learned at school with arm gestures and dance steps, the music chorusing in my head. I saw no reason to keep it all to myself, and couldn't if I tried. Exuberance and song bubbled out of me.

I knew most of the people on my block, if not by name, then enough to say hello, or to join in on a game of double Dutch for a few minutes on the way to the vegetable stand to get soup greens. I had fun on these walks. There was never anything to be afraid of. The shopkeepers smiled at me if they were out for a smoke, and I always said hello to Mr. Chan sitting inside his laundry. His daughter Mary was in my grade, the only Chinese girl in my school.

Invigorating as the neighborhood was, school was the place I loved the most. Public School 77, or PS 77 for short, was much bigger than the one in California, and the schoolyard was the length of an entire city block. The teachers were mostly young, happy, and easygoing. It was *the* place where I mattered, did well, and could be myself. I had friends and I had fun, and I loved to learn. I clamored to sit at the front of the class, with my hand strained up in the air to be seen and chosen to give the right answer, which I always had. I read well, even at a young age, and was not shy about reading out loud like others were. I was first in line, rushing to hold the teacher's hand as we walked back from recess, hoping for a compliment, which I usually got.

At home, there were no compliments, only orders and rules. It seemed there were rules about everything, including what I could eat and when. I constantly ran errands, taking out the trash, going to the market, and helping take care of Steven— whatever my stepmother told me to do. She rarely said more than a few words to me, but she somehow made clear that she thought I was ugly and stupid. My father was hardly ever around and barely spoke to me when he was. Though I had lived with my new parents for almost three years, I still didn't know very much about them, where they came from, or why I was with them. And they never asked me about anything.

In the Bronx, I did not have my own room like I had in California. My family's apartment was a smallish one-bedroom, whose saving graces were its tall ceilings and large windows. Our place on a sixth-floor corner exposed large swaths of light, sky and cloud rarely seen on lower floors in the tightly packed buildings.

Right off the entry was a short, wide hallway between the living room and kitchen, leading off to the bedroom, where my father, stepmother, and brother slept. The hallway was my space. It was lit from the kitchen window on one end and the parlor on the other, the dimmest place in the apartment. I was not usually allowed in the living room or bedroom unless I was watching my brother. "*Maradj a helyedben, lány*," she'd say to me if I forgot. "Go to your place, girl."

My stepmother didn't explain this rule to me, and yet somehow I knew better than to ask. Her face wore a permanent frown when she spoke to me, smiling only for my brother. My stomach began to quake when she was near, and I involuntarily backed away. I ended up spending most of my free time in the hallway when I wasn't running errands, or doing homework or chores in the kitchen. The hallway was painted antique white, the same dreary color as every other apartment in New York at the time, a color not so much white as a dull, diluted gray. My metal folding cot was against one wall, and a small wooden table and two chairs against the other. My clothes were in the closet by the front door, and my book bag leaned against the wall. But there was not much else. The few toys I had did not make it from California, and I was too old for coloring books.

My favorite time at home was being alone in our bright living room on the warm carpet with my brother. He was a good baby and always happy to see me. I was fluent in Hungarian by then, so I could teach him little nursery rhymes like "Debrecenbe kéne menni," about going to the town of Debrecen to buy a fat turkey. I had memorized the words but had no idea what they meant. It made him laugh, and that's all that mattered. We spoke to Steven only in Hungarian, so I had to keep thinking of songs and words he could understand. I'd build him a tower with his wooden blocks, and I'd say, "*Üsd le*," and he would squeal with joy as he knocked them down, over and over again.

I loved my brother. He was easy to please and not bothered by much, the opposite of my stepmother, who seemed to be annoyed by everything. Being around him was my joy, a joy that quickly dissipated when my stepmother appeared. Whatever I did was not good enough. I was not holding him right. I was not watching him closely enough. If she asked me to sweep the kitchen, she always found a spot I missed. When she sent me to the store, I somehow got the wrong brand of flour, forgot something, or took too long.

One day, I was sitting in my hallway not really doing anything when I was surprised by sounds coming from the bedroom. It was laughter. It was very unusual because my stepmother always insisted on quiet. I thought about creeping to the door to look but was afraid I might be seen and get in trouble. Steven was still a baby, not yet walking, but I was almost seven. I remember hearing all three of them, a tickly, joyous, bubbling-over laughter, over and over again. It sounded so happy. I smiled as I heard my brother's laugh, such a sweet, sweet sound, followed by my father and step-mother's. I listened closely, hoping to hear them call me in, but they did not. Soon I began feeling a weight in my chest. It started out small, and at first, I didn't pay attention to it. But it kept getting worse until I realized it hurt. A dull, numbing pain that slowly spread and made heavy tears drop from my eyes. The hallway was supposed to be my own personal space, but in that moment, it felt more like a cage that I could not break out of. I wanted to join the family's fun. I wanted to belong to them! I wanted to laugh with them, but they didn't seem to be aware that I existed. I still wondered whether they would call me in, but a long stretch of time passed, and then things got quiet. I was still alone.

I was six years old. And suddenly, I understood something. I was not really wanted. My stepmother would never want me, and my father couldn't make her. I was not part of that family—or its laughter. And I never would be.

4

***

Bread and Blood

School was my favorite place, and my favorite escape was being sent to the bakery. It was an excursion I loved, not only for the free cookie I usually got but also for the chance to be away from a dreary and cold home. I knew I was not really part of the family, but I still had school and my errands in our lively Bronx neighborhood, and they kept me quite happy.

The bakery had a huge glass window filled with beautiful, airy cakes of all flavors that looked more like fine works of art than things to eat. My face brightened and my mouth watered before I even entered the crowded shop. It was always busy with harried people coming and going, ordering things I could only dream of tasting, sometimes in languages I could not make out. I always paused to take in the aroma of apple cake, burnt sugar, and baking bread, and thought it must be the best fragrance in the world. I gazed longingly into the rows of glass cases, savoring the sight of the strudel, Danish, rugelach, babka, and jelly doughnuts with table sugar on the outside.

The shop had an important feeling of urgency as patrons clamored for their desired loaves, rolls, and pastries before the bakery ran out for the day. As the patrons jostled for their turn, they ignored the young child in their midst. I took a number from a machine that I could barely reach and then waited to be called. Their heads covered with kerchiefs, the bakery ladies were short, stout women with thick arms and accents not unlike my parents' yet different in a way I could not figure out. They were always kind and generous.

On this particular day, the wait was longer than usual, making my stomach signal its emptiness with audible grumbles. When my number was finally called, I ordered the usual. "Seedless rye bread, sliced, please."

My father would only eat bakery-made rye bread, which he had at every meal. But he wouldn't eat it if it was more than a day old. Hungarians, I was learning, were obsessed with food. Whether the meal was fancy or simple, it was discussed and fussed over in detail. Ingredients were shopped for with very specific instructions, as if the world would fall apart if they were not followed: meat only from certain butchers, cold cuts only from Schaller & Weber, fruit and vegetables only from select produce stands. The shopping was done daily, not only because we did not have money for a big weekly shopping trip but also because that was how it was done in Hungary, and there was no reason to change. If company was coming, things were even more precise. My father would be dispatched to the Hungarian neighborhood on Second Avenue in Manhattan for the best cuts of meat, authentic Hungarian paprika, or old-world pastries. Each step in a recipe had to be done in a certain way, to exacting standards, or it would not turn out, which was a fate worse than not having food at all. Hungarians were different, I was finding out.

At the bakery, I watched one of the lady workers pick an oval loaf from the shelf and put it in the slicing machine, which looked like the silver rib cage of a whale, scissoring through the loaf while leaving it aligned. I reached up to the counter with my thirty-five cents and smiled as the woman handed me a butter cookie with a half cherry in the middle. It was gone in seconds as I clutched the still-warm, fragrant bread wrapped in a waxed paper bag to my chest. Oh, it felt so good!

Being in the bakery had made me hungry, which was not unusual. What was unusual was that I was hungry enough to ignore the warnings to never eat anything without asking. I was usually hypervigilant of my stepmother's rules, as her slaps were swift and sharp. Without thinking it through, giddy from my cookie and the aroma of the bakery, I carefully selected a slice from the center of the loaf where I thought it would not be missed. It was still warm, soft, chewy, tasting of yeast and salt, the crust tough, crunchy, and satisfying. It was a heartwarming snack, and I skipped back home, obliviously happy.

When I returned to the apartment, my stepmother took the bread and a moment later asked whether I had eaten any. My heart dropped to my feet and a chill crept up my arms as I remembered the rule. Realizing I would be in trouble if I said yes, I did the only logical thing for a seven-year-old: I lied. My terror made me stutter.

"N-n-n-no, I didn't touch it."

In a flash, before I knew what was happening, my stepmother pulled out a wooden dowel from my brother's crib, lifted it high over her head, and started beating me with it. I cowered in a shaking ball as near to the floor as I could manage.

"Thief! Liar!" she yelled with an unimaginable fury.

I crouched down, my hands over my head, choking out cries of pain, gasping for air, begging for forgiveness. After many blows to every part of my little body, the wood struck my forehead, breaking the skin, and blood squirted in every direction. It splattered all over, on me, her, the linoleum, and the dirty white walls.

My stepmother continued screaming at me, lashing out, now about getting blood everywhere. I cried out, stumbling on my words, my nose running, snot mixing with blood and tears, promising to clean up the mess. At some point, she stopped long enough to push a rag into my hand so I could hold it to my bleeding head. Yet instead of tending to my wounds, she left me alone in the hallway, grumbling about how she had to look after her husband's bastard child. I had no idea what a bastard was, though I knew it had to be something bad. I held the rag to my forehead while spraying Formula 409 on the walls and floor, and trying with a shaking hand to clean up the mess as best I could to avoid her further wrath. I hurt all over, and feared I had more to come.

When I finally got all the blood cleaned up, the bread seemed to be forgotten. I crept into the bathroom and stood on the edge of the tub to look in the mirror. There was a huge gash on my forehead, almost an inch long, with pink-white stuff sticking out. My insides, I guessed. My face was red, battered, bloated, and bloody. It didn't look like the face of any little girl I knew.

Eventually, my stepmother came into the bathroom and cleaned me up in silence, pouting angrily with her usual down-turned frown and putting a Band-Aid on my head. She said nothing to me but muttered in Hungarian to herself with words I could not make out. When it was all over, the atmosphere in the apartment was like the calm after a storm: eerie, quiet, and foreboding; a sort of silent truce where no one speaks and no one admits wrong but no one was mean to me either. I never went to a doctor or got stitches, and I don't remember a "sorry." My father never said a word about it when he got home, if he even noticed me at all. At least my stepmother didn't tell him that I had stolen a slice of bread and lied about it, which was good, as I did not have a good explanation for what I had done. Being hungry didn't count in my house.

The next day there was no hiding the incident. Much to my horror, I woke with two black eyes, surrounded by all shades of yellow and blue, making what I thought of as my already ugly face much worse. I cried when I looked in the bathroom mirror, but I got no solace. My father was already gone, and my stepmother was not yet awake to see it. So off I went to school, not knowing what to expect. I walked slowly, crying because of how I looked and trying to hide my face in my short pixie cut. But it was impossible. I hoped that one of my kind teachers would notice my face and do something. Maybe they would call the police, who would knock on the door and demand that my stepmother explain her actions. Then they'd take me somewhere safe to live with nice people, in a pretty house with lots of food and books and warmth.

But I soon realized that it was not going to happen. Even though my black eyes lasted for weeks and everyone stared with some suspicion at my scars, not a single person at school or in the neighborhood asked me what had happened or whether I was okay.

It took a few days, but my father finally noticed my face.

"*Mi történt?*" he angrily asked my stepmother, demanding to know what had happened.

Apparently, he didn't like her answer, so he pulled me aside in front of her to ask me directly, holding my shoulder and making me look into his eyes. My cunning stepmother had prepared me for this, and had told me to say that I had fallen off the bathroom window and hit my head on the toilet pipes. It would have been conceivable, I guess. The bathroom had a high window with a wide sill directly over the toilet. But my father did not buy my story for a second, squeezing my arm and shaking me, now making me fear them both.

"*Miért hazudsz?*"—"Why are you lying to me?" he yelled.

I was too scared to speak. My stepmother was watching me, the disdain on her face palpable, and I knew she would beat me again later if I told him. I decided to stay quiet, even though his yelling and shaking me was making my head hurt even more. I struggled to hold down the vomit growing in my gut and to keep my body upright.

It finally came to an end when we drove to my uncle Joe's in Englewood, New Jersey, that weekend. My parents had been silent the whole hour-long drive. When we arrived, my father got out and told me to come with him while the others stayed in the car. My stepmother stared at me pointedly as my father and I walked away. He pulled me aside in the front yard, out of eyeshot, and said:

"Look, I'm the only one who loves you. No one else in the world loves you like I do, so you better tell me what happened."

I could not take the pressure any longer. Breaking into tears, I told him what my stepmother—his wife—had done. I told him I was afraid of her. That she had not said she was sorry. That she was always angry at me, and I did not know what to do about it.

He didn't say a thing. Instead, he dragged me roughly by the arm and tromped to the car. He shoved me into the back seat, and we started the long, silent drive home without seeing my uncle Joe. I never heard my parents discuss the beating, and it was never mentioned again.

Although not a word was spoken, I learned a lot on that ride home. I already knew I was a foreigner in my own home. That no one really wanted me. But now, at seven, I knew no one was going to protect me either. My stepmother felt no guilt or remorse, and my father continued to look the other way and take no action on my behalf. I wondered whether I'd be safe if I just stopped taking bread. But somehow I knew that could not be true. I needed to figure out how to survive. Not in the neighborhood or at school but at home. Back at the apartment, I began to shrink even more than before, becoming awkward, hesitant, withdrawn, and pre-occupied, cowering to take up as little space in the room as I could. I tried to make myself so small that I would not instigate her anger. I tried not to be there at all.

5

The Library Card

Books were my very first friends. One day, during reading hour in class, I eagerly turned the pages of *The Adventures of Pippi Longstocking*, a tale about a fearless girl whose mother had also died. Since the beating incident with the bread, reading had taken on an even greater meaning. Books were an escape from my bleak life into another time and place. They were the allies I did not have. They made sense to me, as my family life did not. They were real and predictable to me in a way that people were not, and I developed feelings for the characters. They "spoke" to me, as my parents didn't. The few books we had at home were Hungarian children's books, but I did not know how to read Hungarian. At school, the books broadened my narrow, closed world, and I looked forward to them with excitement and without reservation.

My third-grade class was a colorful mishmash, just like the neighborhood. Many of the students were immigrant children like me, including my first crush, a Czech boy named Olaf, from a country near Hungary. He was smart and very good-looking, with a round face, white-blond hair, and piercing blue eyes. He and I competed for the most correct answers when the teachers called out questions, and for our teachers' praise.

In the class, there were also the pretty girls with dainty dresses, turned-down white lace ankle socks, and shiny patent-leather shoes. None of them would play with me during recess. One of the fancy girls was Annie, whose mother, Mrs. Freundlich, happened to be my teacher. Annie's father, Mr. Freundlich, also worked at the school. They were a beautiful couple, stylishly dressed, cheerful, and always looking at each other with smiling eyes in the hallways. They had to be in love.

I wondered why the pretty girls wouldn't hang out with me. Perhaps it was my clothes, which were functional at best. I didn't like feeling excluded—or understand why they didn't want to be my friends. But my clothes didn't seem to bother the Black girls, and after a while, I started playing with them. They always had lots of fun and seemed happy to have me around. They were my only friends at school, or anywhere, and I was very grateful for them. They were willing to share their lunches too, which brightened the worst part of the school day.

Lunchtime was always an embarrassing ordeal because my sandwiches were made of dried-out bread. The day-old rye, which my father would not eat, would start curling up in its waxed paper bag as it sat on the kitchen counter at home. That was the bread that I was ordered to take with me to school. Along with a piece of bologna, it was supposed to be my entire school lunch. At home, the rule was that I could eat only what was presented to me, so I never looked in the kitchen for anything else to add to my lunch. I dared not anyway, lest my stepmother beat me again. My stepmother kept track of the food like a hawk. And even if I had been allowed to look for food at home, we didn't have much to choose from. There was not a lot of extra food around, and virtually no snacks.

Sometimes the rye bread was still bendable, so I would try to straighten it out by holding it with two hands as I ate. Most of the time, though, it was hopelessly dry and curled up, and I was too ashamed to eat it. I would just throw the bread away and tell people that I had forgotten my lunch. The Black girls always seemed to have nice sandwiches and lots of extra treats, so I sat with them longingly, hoping they would give me some. Often they did, at least at first.

Sometimes, if I was really hungry, I would use my best poor-girl face to tell one of the cafeteria aides that I had lost my lunch on the way to school—and they would give me a hot lunch for free. Those warm meals made me so happy, even though most of the kids hated the cafeteria food and complained about whatever was being served. I knew I couldn't pull off this stunt very often, but it got me through lunch from time to time. The Black girls were happy to share until their mothers found out, and then that was the end of that.

Still, I loved school. It was the one place where I excelled and didn't do anything wrong. Since I did the homework and the assigned reading, I always knew the answers in class and eagerly raised my hand when asked. I was not afraid to speak up or write on the chalkboard, and the teachers loved that. School got me out of the house, where it was getting harder and harder to be happy and stay out of trouble. At home, I tried hard to please my stepmother, but inevitably I cut the carrots wrong, didn't wash the dishes clean enough, or missed a spot when I vacuumed. In her eyes, I missed the mark every time. Were all Hungarians this demanding? I wondered.

The most exciting day in third grade was our field trip to the local public library. We lined up in two rows, and of course I had to be first in line so I could hold Mrs. Freundlich's hand during the four-block walk. She was young and pretty, and pleasant to everyone. I dreamed of having a mother like her.

The library was a squat brick building like all the other buildings in the neighborhood, but with large picture windows. At the massive front desk, there was a smart-looking woman with cat-eye glasses who greeted us with a welcoming smile. She wore high heels that clicked on the marble floor as she gave us a tour. My eyes lit up as she told us amazing things about the library, such as how people used it to learn about new things, people, and places. Best of all, the library was free and anyone could use it.

After the tour, she gave each of the students a special card that would let us use the library anytime we wanted. She told us how we could travel the world of books and take ten books home at a time. Ten books! I had never had ten books at a time before and was thrilled to my spine. My new little library card had my name typed on it, and I clutched it to my chest like gold. It was the best gift I had ever received. I skipped all the way home from school that day, all six blocks.

But when I got home, the atmosphere in the house felt ghostly, and there was a chill in the air that I felt on the back of my neck. My stomach began to roil nervously as soon as I saw my stepmother. It seemed she was lying in wait for me, and for the first time ever, she wanted to know what I had done in school that day. I started shaking, frantically thinking about what I could have missed, and what I might have done to warrant this much scrutiny.

I described my day, instinctively stepping as far back from her as I could, listing the phonics, math, and science, before adding the library at the end, almost as an afterthought. Suddenly, my stepmother violently grabbed my book bag and looked at me with cold, bitter eyes. By this time, I was sweating, though I still had no idea what I had done. Her very presence made me quake.

When she found the library card, she looked at me smugly and tore it to pieces.

"No!" I begged, crying uncontrollably. "I love the library! Please, no!"

She yelled things in Hungarian that I did not understand. But the best I could figure out was that she was angry that she had not signed the permission slip for me to go on the library field trip. Had she purposely not signed it? The teachers at school hadn't seemed to care about the permission slip. But in my stepmother's mind, I had gone to the library anyway—against her approval.

I could not speak. My precious library card was gone. But more than that, I could not grasp *why* she was doing this to me, or why she was so angry with me. If I could just figure that out, then maybe I could make it stop. I understood why she had been mad about the bread, even if I couldn't comprehend why I had been beaten for it. But why didn't she want me to go to the library? Why tear up my card? Did Hungarian mothers not want their children to read?

6

The Little Prince

S teven and I were playing in our tiny bedroom when suddenly
he snuck to the door and closed it. The impish expression
on his face told me that he was up to something. Something
bad.

"Where did you get those?" I hissed.

Steven had just flashed a book of matches in front of me. We
both knew that we were not allowed to have matches—and especially not in the bedroom. But at six, Steven loved playing with
fire and tried to get his hands on matches whenever he could.

"Shut up," he said. "Paulie gave them to me so I could make
some players for Skelzy."

Skelzy was a street game that our whole block played. To prepare
for Skelzy, you melted different-colored crayons or candles into
bottle caps. During the game, you flicked your bottle cap—using your
index finger and thumb—to shoot the cap to numbered squares that
were drawn with chalk on the asphalt. The competition was fierce,
as was the desire to have the most colorful cap. Steven had decided
that our bedroom, which we shared, was the perfect place to create a
winning cap.

When he was a baby, I had spent all my free time with him, at
first because it was fun, and later because it was my job to watch

him. Now that he could walk and talk—and create trouble—it was my responsibility to make sure that he did not get hurt. For an eleven-year-old girl, trying to watch a headstrong child was a tall order.

Near Steven's bed, I tried to take his matches away, reminding him that he was not allowed to play with them. But as usual, he ignored me. He said we would melt the crayons quickly—and do it under the bed—so that his mother would not get a whiff of the awful rubbery-wax smell.

"We're going to get in trouble," I warned.

"No, we won't," he said.

These days, Steven was often doing stuff that he knew we weren't supposed to do, totally disregarding my warnings at every turn. He was not afraid of his mother like I was. He had not felt her wrath himself. He handed me a red crayon.

"Hold this while I light the match."

We were so absorbed with melting crayons that we did not see the small flame that caught on the thin, filmy cloth hanging from the underside of the bed. Within seconds, my stepmother burst into our bedroom, yelling at the top of her lungs, and when we looked up, we started to cough. My stepmother grabbed my brother and shooed him out of the room, then pushed me violently toward the window, demanding that I open it. I thought she might push me out of it.

"*Idióta!*" she screamed at me.

In a matter of seconds, she flipped my brother's twin mattress and beat out the low flames with a pillow. I was still coughing by the window when she grabbed me by the hair and slapped my face. She then dragged me by the hair to show me the mattress. I was afraid of fire, but more afraid of her anger.

"*Hogy történhetett ez?*"

She wanted to know what had happened. I tried to explain, but it didn't matter.

"*Hülye, jó semmiért!*"—Hungarian for "You're good for nothing!"—she spat at me before leaving the room and slamming the door behind her.

This was not the first time that something like this had happened. At a picnic by a lake once, Steven had been poking the smoldering charcoals in the barbecue grill with a long stick when he flipped one of the briquettes to the grass. Knowing he was not supposed to play with fire, he quickly ran to pick up the briquette and put it back before I could tell him to stop. Too late—he burned the palm of his hand. I got into huge trouble for that, as if I had not tried to stop him from playing with fire in the first place.

And on it went.

When Steven was first born, he had been easy for me to love, because he was a good distraction and a fun playmate. I read to him every chance I got. Our favorites were Richard Scarry's *Best Word Book Ever* and *Cars and Trucks and Things That Go*. As Steven got older, we'd make up our own stories as we played with his Fisher-Price farm or playhouse, with their little round people that sat in the tiny chairs or cars that we pushed around making *zoom-zoom* noises. Eventually, the Fisher-Price toys gave way to Hot Wheels, miniature cars that raced along orange plastic tracks that we set up against a dresser. We played with his toys because I didn't have any of my own.

I was always by my brother's side. I was his babysitter and playmate. I walked him to school before going off to my own and stayed with him whenever he went out to play. Steven was a bright kid, supremely confident, energetic, and bossy. He had a vivid imagination, a great thing to have in a playmate. He was full of ideas for games we'd play, such as school or store or little farm scenes with his Fisher-Price animals—quite funny for two city kids. He put on magic and dance shows that the grown-ups loved, and I'd be the helper. Once he even got on the TV show *Wonderama*, where he danced on a little raised platform. We spent weeks practicing dance moves for the show.

But things changed when Steven started getting a mind of his own and stopped listening to me, like the time he got hurt racing his Go-Kart downhill too fast, or the time he skinned his knees after running out of control on the sidewalk. Since I was older and in charge of watching him, I was always the one who got in trouble. Even when he was a toddler and fell down, I was to blame. He never got reprimanded for not minding me, or for anything. It was always my fault, and I got punished for it. Eventually, I started to resent him. I knew his mother would always take his side, so I had to be cautious around him. We had our fun, and once had been close, but incidents like the bed fire were making us bicker and become more distant.

Steven was the prince of the family, and he was treated like one. He was the first male child born to an all-girl family. In Hungarian culture, people valued boys over girls. To say that my stepmother adored him would be a monumental understatement. He was her whole life, her treasure, and literally everything in our home revolved around him. Steven was showered with affection and praise, and in the absence of any restraint, he became quite spoiled. He got whatever he asked for. He was always getting new toys, books, or whatever—even though we barely had enough money for food and rent. He got lovely little Hungarian outfits and had his portrait taken. He never had any chores like I did, and instead of telling him what do to, my stepmother would plead with him, as in "Please, Steven, please don't eat any more cookies," or "Please turn off the TV and do your homework." She always spoke to him in a beseeching tone, as if he had all the power, and he did. Steven was not outright rude to my mother; he just ignored her—with absolutely no consequence, short of the frown that my stepmother always wore in her defeat, like the upside-down U-shaped mouth embroidered on the teddy bear Steven got from Hungary.

Sometimes Steven got me in trouble just for spite. As we grew up, the balance of power changed and he used it against me. Because he was the prince, he decided the games we played, and he set the rules. We did what he wanted, and my ideas didn't count. He was allowed to order me around, and I had to comply. On some occasions, he would taunt me by threatening to tell on me, knowing Mama would take his side whether he was telling the truth or not. His power trip got so incessant that I used to mock him in a baby voice, saying, "Tellin' Mama, tellin' Mama."

Though that tactic infuriated him, it did not stop him from blabbing to my stepmother, which only got me into more trouble. Now I had two people to live in fear of.

Steven was often lying prone on the living room carpet watching TV while I was in the kitchen cooking or doing homework. He'd yell, "Penny, get me some ginger ale," and I'd have to stop what I was doing to get it. Of course, the favor was never returned. To get back at him, I'd purposely walk in front of him on the way to the bathroom, which he hated, because my toes crackled when I walked, and it grossed him out.

Despite it all, Steven was still a bright spot in my life. We spent so much time together that we were soulmates on some level. We had our own little code words, phrases, and jokes that we exchanged with only a look. We adapted the soundtrack of Bugs Bunny cartoons, like the *doop doop doop* of a bass used to signal people tiptoeing through a scene. Most important, he kept me busy and away from my stepmother.

She had a special nickname for Steven, "öcsiké," which roughly means "junior" in Hungarian. The food we shopped for was food he liked. The things we bought were mainly for him. My stepmother loved to take him to special places, just the two of them, both dressed in beautiful clothes. Before they would head off for a glorious day together, my stepmother would give me a list of chores that included washing the kitchen floor or dusting the living room, and warnings not to touch the food or watch the television, which she checked for heat when she got home. They would leave me alone without so much as a goodbye. My stomach would sink as I closed the door behind them, dreading the long hours alone, wishing I could be part of their adventure. My father was usually at work at his auto repair shop, or he'd be away hunting for days on end. I could be alone for most of a day.

Together, my stepmother and Steven went to see the Rockettes at Radio City Music Hall and the Ice Capades at Madison Square Garden. Sometimes they attended special events at St. Stephen's, the Hungarian church we sometimes went to in Manhattan, where my stepmother could show Steven off to her acquaintances from the old country. Leaving me behind at home not only got her special time with Steven, but she also didn't have to spend anything on me. My stepmother once made me walk dozens of blocks while she and Steven rode the bus—a savings of thirty-five cents.

One day, I'd been home alone in our apartment for a long time. At first, I was bored more than anything. I had finished all my chores, making sure to sweep first before I washed the floors— my stepmother could always tell when I didn't. Sitting at the kitchen table, I could see from our window huge expanses of blue sky, unmarred by any buildings. But as I sat and waited, the sky turned purple, then dark. I could feel the night creeping up on me. I didn't know how long I'd been alone, but it seemed like days, and I started to get anxious. I had a nervous feeling that something bad might happen and there would be no one to help me.

Suddenly, the phone started ringing. I was under strict orders never to answer the phone when my stepmother was gone. The ringing stopped, then started again, over and over. Finally, I thought that perhaps I was meant to answer it, even though I remained afraid that my stepmother would find out.

"Hello?"

On the other end of the line was Nagyi, my step-grandmother. She sounded mad.

"*Miért nem válaszoltál?!*"

She didn't understand why I wasn't answering the phone if I was home. I told her that I wasn't allowed—and that I didn't know where my stepmother was. I begged her not to tell my stepmother that I had picked up the phone. I was not afraid of Nagyi, but if she told my stepmother, I knew I would be beaten.

Nagyi promised not to say a word, which was good. But she never did anything about me being left home alone either. Eventually I got used to it, but I did not like it. It was often dark when my stepmother and Steven would come home. And, as with most things, my father never found out.

My stepmother even arranged family vacations with just her, Steven, and my father. They would drop me off with my aunt Veronka and uncle Joe in New Jersey and go off on some adventure of their own.

Once, when we stopped for gas on the way there and my father was out of the car, my mother asked Steven whether he was excited about their trip to the Catskills.

"Is Penny coming?" he asked, looking at me sideways in the back seat.

"No, she's going to visit her aunt and uncle. We're going to have our own special vacation, just the three of us. *Te vagy az egyetlen édes fiam.—*You're my only sweet boy, the only one I ever wanted."

Steven kept looking at me, maybe waiting for my response, but neither of us knew what to say after that. The rest of the trip to New Jersey was quiet, and I was relieved when we arrived at Uncle Joe's house.

Uncle Joe was my father's oldest brother, the first of the thirteen siblings of which my father was the youngest. Joe was my father's only relative in the United States. He was much older than my father, and his daughters—my cousins—were older than my parents. Uncle Joe was the patriarch of the family and carried that status in his large, upright frame with authority and pride. He was the first of the clan to immigrate to the United States in 1919, after World War I. With just the shirt on his back and a set of tools in a wooden box, he left his little town of Putnok, Hungary, and boarded a ship that brought him to New York Harbor.

Back in Hungary, the Farkases were well-respected coopers, or barrel makers. Uncle Joe brought the family trade with him to the States, working most of his life for the Anheuser-Busch brewing company in New York. He settled in Englewood, New Jersey, to be close to work and bought a four-bedroom house on a tree-lined street of modest homes and new families like his. He learned English fast, and by the time I came on the scene in the 1960s, his family all spoke English at home, with no accent at all.

He was a man's man who stood tall, didn't joke around, and defended his place in the world with a confidence that I did not see in my father. Uncle Joe was a hard worker, a hunter, and good with his hands. He could make anything out of wood and often made beautiful wood cabinets that held TVs, stereos, or Aunt Veronka's sewing machine. He proudly showed off his gun collection and basement full of professional woodworking tools. His gun cabinet stood in a prominent place in the dining room, and the walls were decorated with the heads of buck that he had shot.

Uncle Joe once told me a great story. After he'd come to America and started a family, he was laid off because of Prohibition, a word that I did not understand. There were no legitimate jobs for barrel makers during Prohibition, and that was all he knew how to do. But as he told it, his kids "didn't know no Prohibition." They still needed to eat, so what could he do? He went to work for the bootleggers. I didn't understand what bootleggers were either, but I could tell that he was proud of his work—and I was proud of him too.

Aunt Veronka was the kindest, most loving person I had ever met. Where Uncle Joe was tall and thin, towering over six feet, she was short and plump, and smelled clean like freshly ironed cotton. She was always up before I was, fully done up in a dress and hose even in the summer, and old-fashioned lace-up shoes. Her hair was neatly pinned in place. She was always ready for me with a warm smile and a great full-body hug. In my young mind, she was the ultimate mother: She cooked wonderful meals, baked cakes from scratch, sewed, crocheted, gardened. And she loved me and told me so—something I never got at home.

Aunt Veronka called Uncle Joe "Daddy," and she was "Mommy" to him. I never saw them embrace, but they spoke to each other in quiet, respectful tones, and although I imagined he could be harsh, he was never anything less than loving and kind to me. They had three grown daughters, one out in California, one nearby, and one we called Violet who still lived at home.

Their home was always spotlessly clean and smelled of floor wax and sun-dried linen. The house was a wood-paneled Edwardian, with warm brown shingles and a big porch. The stained-glass windows in the foyer refracted color onto the gleaming wood floors. The house had a small formal dining room, a pantry, a basement, an attic to play in, and, best of all, a sewing room. Aunt Veronka could make anything, and the walls held her needlepoint, the sofa her handmade pillows, and tabletops her crocheted doilies. Their home reflected my aunt's warmth, and I loved it.

The kitchen smelled of coffee and fresh-baked cinnamon cake. I loved the pantry, which had windowed cupboards with glassware and pretty dishes, and boxes of cookies and treats. It was where my crayons were stored for me and brought out for each visit. Sometimes Aunt Veronka decided it was time for "fresh" crayons and coloring books, which she let me pick out. I'd grin like a hyena as we walked the neighborhood hand in hand to the little town center, where my cousin Violet worked in the bank, and we bought supplies at the five-and-dime. Violet had never married and was more like an aunt herself than a cousin. My parents called her a spinster, which sounded bad, but Violet didn't seem to mind at all. She was not around much, just enough to say hello when she came home before she locked herself in her room for the night to sew or read or who knows what.

The house had a huge, well-kept yard with a manicured lawn and big trees, which to a city kid was like the Garden of Eden. Uncle Joe and Aunt Veronka had rows of flowers, and an actual vegetable garden where they grew peppers and tomatoes, cucumbers, and vegetables I had never heard of, like pole beans, which Aunt Veronka would can and turn into supper. I loved everything about the house—and them—and I knew beyond a doubt that they loved me. It was my version of heaven.

There were neighborhood kids I could ride bikes with. Uncle Joe kept a two-wheeler ready for me, oiled, pumped, and tuned so that it flew down the street as I laughed out loud. Unlike my parents, who never spoke to anyone in our building, Aunt Veronka and Uncle Joe were friends with all their neighbors, who sometimes stopped by to say hello to me, remembering my visits from the years before. Sometimes we would go to their houses, where they would serve cookies and tea. New Jersey seemed to be full of normal, happy people. Although Aunt Veronka and Uncle Joe spoke Hungarian to my parents, they always spoke English when I was around.

My parents didn't send me there as a treat, but that was okay by me. My stepmother hated my uncle and aunt, and came up with the idea of dumping me off in New Jersey so that she, Steven, and my father could vacation as a family. And for his part, my father pretty much went along with anything my stepmother wanted. I never revealed even to my brother how much I loved going to Englewood for fear that if my stepmother found out, she would put an end to it, even if it meant having me tag along on vacations. While Steven bragged about the dude ranch they went to, I stored up the sweet memories that carried me through the year, and eagerly awaited my next trip to see Uncle Joe and Aunt Veronka. Visiting their welcoming home kept me sane, knowing that happiness was out there.

7

The Baby

One day, my father woke my brother and me in the middle of the night to drive us to our grandmother's house. Steven and I went in our pajamas and without an explanation, but being half asleep, we didn't question it. Besides, going to Nagyi's was usually fun. My grandmother had a gorgeous apartment with chandeliers, marble tables, and artwork, and even if she was strict about some things, like not eating in the living room, she was kind and always had lots of treats. She met us in her robe and ushered us into comfy beds that she had made up for us on the couch.

For the next few days, Steven and I just hung out with Nagyi. We had no idea what was going on, and no one told us. Hungarians, or at least my family, did not explain things to kids. The mystery was solved when our smiling parents showed up—with our new baby sister tightly wrapped in a pink blanket. She was a total surprise to me. I hadn't noticed from my stepmother's figure that she was pregnant, because she'd looked about the same. She had been holding her lower back and complaining more than normal, using a word in Hungarian I'd never heard before, *állapotos*. Once she arrived with the baby, I figured out that the word meant "pregnant."

Kitti was tiny and beautiful, and she was fussed over and passed around to all the grown-ups in Nagyi's living room—until she burst into a bloodcurdling wail, and the adults all scurried to make a bottle for her from some powdered stuff in a tin box. Neither Steven nor I knew exactly what to say. Beyond the shock of a new sister, I was struck that my stepmother and father seemed unusually close and tender with each other, something that I had not seen in a long time.

Shortly after my sister was born, we moved to a huge apartment building in Jackson Heights, a busy neighborhood in Queens. Our second-floor apartment was simple but had many windows and beautiful hardwood floors, and was a good size by city standards. It included a small dining room that served as a foyer, a galley kitchen, a spacious living room, and two bedrooms.

I was impressed at how nice the new place turned out to be. The apartment was decorated with many heirlooms from Hungary, gifts from relatives collected over the years, which we had not had room to display before. There were colorful hand-embroidered doilies under ornate cut-crystal vases and numerous large oil paintings in heavy gilt frames. One wall in the living room was taken up by a lacquered display case called a vitrine, full of rare Herend porcelain from a world-renowned factory in Hungary that had been around since the 1820s. All the women in the family collected and treasured these figurines depicting stories from Hungarian folklore as if they were their dowries. Each time a relative came or someone went to Hungary, a figurine was requested and carefully padded and smuggled in a suitcase to avoid tariffs or breakage, giving every piece a story about who'd brought it and the elaborate ways they'd avoided detection. I always wondered how we could afford our ostentatious furnishings when we struggled to keep groceries in the house.

Our new building was quiet, elegant, and inviting. It was an old Edwardian with ancient elevators and ten apartments to a floor. It had a large marble lobby reminiscent of a more graceful time, with a high vaulted ceiling, a huge trundle table that might have come from a castle, and marble stairs with majestic balustrades going up to the second floor on either side. I felt special when I walked into the lobby, as if I had walked into a bygone era, but that feeling disappeared as soon as I left the building.

Just one block away was the pulsing commercial hub of Jackson Heights. The No. 33 bus ran down our street day and night, and from our second-story window, I could look into the lighted bus at night, at the weary commuters clutching their packages on their laps, lost in their thoughts. There were always people walking by, and the area seemed constantly busy. Nagyi lived around the corner, and Aunt Sári, my stepmother's sister, and our cousins were only five blocks away. We had arrived! I welcomed the change and hoped that my life would improve.

At our corner was a Jahn's restaurant, a wonderful little diner that served rice pudding with raspberry sauce. Kitty-corner from Jahn's was the newsstand/candy store, a tiny shop crammed full of newspapers and magazines in many languages, and shelves of candy like Ice Cubes chocolates, Good & Plenty, Sugar Daddies, and Bazooka gum. I could get something for a penny or two. Next door, there was a butcher shop, where you could buy a pound of chicken livers or bones for soup.

The Fields department store on the corner, which took up a whole city block, was my entrée into the world of fashion. Every chance I got, I used the Eighty-First Street store entrance to check out the women's clothing section and to savor the perfume, cosmetics, and jewelry. As I made my way to the Eighty-Second

Street exit, I would stare at the gorgeous saleswomen, all smiling and extravagantly made-up and bejeweled, with long painted nails and big blingy rings. I so wanted to be like them, I'd spend as much time in there as I could.

Up Eighty-Second Street, toward Roosevelt Avenue, was the elevated 7 line, the subway that brought people home from Manhattan or took them out to Flushing. Both sides of the street were crammed with people and shops big and small. Barton's chocolates on the corner, the Jackson cinema, Clarks shoes, Genovese Drugs, Woolworth's, and a record shop displaying the racy Farah Fawcett poster and the Rolling Stones' *Sticky Fingers* album cover. It was an amazing neighborhood, full of promise and life—and I thought it might save me.

This was one of those rare times when the family seemed content. My dad was in a good mood, perhaps because his work at his auto repair shop seemed to be going well. At home, in the first few months, even my stepmother appeared to be happy. Relatives were around constantly to help care for the baby and attend to my stepmother's every whim. The truth was, Kitti made everyone happy, and she brightened up the house the way babies do. We had a huge gathering of relatives for her christening. We even had relatives come visit us from Hungary—Magda néni, Aunt Margaret—to help with the housework and make delicious Hungarian specialties like *töltött káposzta* (stuffed cabbage) and *mogyorótorta* (hazelnut cake).

But as the novelty of the baby wore off and the relatives left, we settled into a new routine that was not so upbeat. Since my stepmother had given birth, her arthritis had gotten worse, and I had to take on more and more of the baby's care. At first, I loved it, because I loved babies and had always wanted to be a mother. Kitti was adorable and smelled so good. I could always make her smile and laugh, which gave me a bit of a triumph over my mother, who did not have the same soothing effect on her. But soon, Kitti became a heavy burden that wore me out.

When I got home from school, I would get Kitti up from her nap in my parents' room, change her, feed her, and bathe her. After taking care of the baby, I would go to the store for groceries, chop vegetables for dinner, and tidy up the house before getting to my homework.

I was twelve.

Even though I took on almost all of the work when I was home, my stepmother was miserable all the time, which was worse than the workload itself. I dreaded displeasing her but lived in fear of it. It seemed that her medication was no longer working. She told people she'd even considered ending the pregnancy in the first place, out of fear that having another baby would make her arthritis worse. Now she was spending more and more time in her recliner, calling out directions to me.

"*Adj Kitti-nek tejet.*"—"Give Kitti her bottle."

"*Keverje hozzá a paprikát.*"—"Stir in the paprika."

"*Menj, takarítsd ki a fürd őszobát.*"—"Go clean the bathroom."

We did not have medical insurance, so my stepmother's doctor visits depended on us having the money, which we usually didn't. She also needed someone to drive her to the appointments in Manhattan because hiring a taxi for regular visits was way beyond our means. The only solution, from what I could tell, was to increase the dosage and frequency of her medication, which meant more trips to the pharmacy in our old neighborhood a mile away— lots of walking and less time for my homework.

When I came home from school, the chores were constant, with hardly time to breathe. Change Kitti, get groceries, start dinner. Laundry, which was done in the basement, had to be done more often with a baby, with special detergent for her clothes, and watched over so no one took them. For his part, Steven spent his afternoons parked in front of the television, watching *Gilligan's Island* and *Lost in Space* reruns. He was still the Little Prince, without a care in the world.

Kitti always needed something: changing, washing, feeding, burping, high-chair cleaning, sheet changing, nipple sterilizing, etc. On top of that, she adored me and wanted me to hold her constantly. I was forced to haul her around on my left hip like an appendage while doing chores. I carried her way longer than she should have been carried, because she did not want to be with anyone else. When she started talking, she took to calling me "Mama," which is what we called my stepmother. My stepmother did not like that one bit. I would have happily given up the title, but I couldn't shake it.

Despite all the work and childcare I did, I still could not please my stepmother. When we were alone at home, she called me horrible names like *kurva*, "whore" in Hungarian. I did not know what a *kurva* was, but I knew it had to be an insult. She beat me and pulled my hair if I came home late from school, took too long at the supermarket, or didn't hear her calling me when I was in the other room.

As my stepmother's mood got darker, my father was gone more and more—and his drinking got worse. He was coming home later and later each night, keeping me in a constant state of trepidation. Making matters worse, his business was making less and less money, forcing my stepmother to borrow money from her mother at least once a week. It was clear to me that Nagyi did not like my father from the way she looked at him and made remarks about his drinking, or about his being a liar and a good-for-nothing.

When we first moved to the new building, I had hoped that the energy of the neighborhood would somehow enliven my parents. But as the months passed by, it was obvious that they favored a life of seclusion, never speaking to or meeting any of our neighbors. They got together only with family or other Hungarians, and even that, rarely. Worse, my parents were fighting all the time.

"You're always at work, but we never have money," my stepmother would sling at him.

"I can never please you, can I?" my father would respond.

My father usually closed his shop around six and spent a few hours every night at the dive bar around the corner, having just "one drink," as he put it, which meant four: a few beers and Hennessy chasers. Sometimes my irritated stepmother would call the bar to see where he was. I couldn't understand why he would spend more time in the bar with strangers instead of coming home to his wife and kids, and to protect me.

I was used to no one speaking to me, and the television being on all the time, but now the apartment was invariably tense at night. Even when my parents were not fighting, the air was charged with sarcasm and contempt.

I was always emotionally on high alert, listening and creeping around to avoid doing anything to attract attention, since any I got was never good. Steven seemed oblivious to anything that went on . . . or he just did not get involved. When my father was home, he was distant and easily irritated. When I served him dinner in the living room, he would eat his meal in silence, without joy, before falling asleep in front of the television. Even when he was home, he was never really there.

8

In the Fog

My stepmother was in her recliner, as usual when I came home from school, like a queen reigning from her throne. The apartment was quiet except for the strains of *Days of Our Lives* coming from the old television. My sister was asleep, and my brother in his room. I was glad to catch my stepmother alone. I knew I had to plan my words carefully. She could get upset at anything, even when I did something right.

Earlier that day, my sixth-grade teacher had pulled me aside at lunch to tell me that I had been accepted into the Accelerated Progress Program for junior high school. My last marker of elementary school and childhood was the crown of getting into the revered AP program. The honors curriculum allowed students to take college prep classes or work toward a commercial degree that taught secretarial skills such as stenography and typing. Students in the commercial program could graduate a year early. My teacher was very proud of me, and I was thrilled to be one of only three kids in her class of thirty—and the only girl—to get in.

"Do you know what you want to do?" my teacher asked.

"I want to go to college," I answered, with no hesitation.

In the living room, during a commercial break in the soap

opera, I approached my stepmother and took a deep breath. I needed her to sign the most important form of my life—a form that would get me to college.

No one in either of my parents' families had graduated from college. My stepmother had started a semester at Hunter College in Manhattan before she'd quit to marry my father. Her sister had married before finishing high school, as had their mother. Most Hungarian women I knew did not work, and none of them I knew had graduated from college. Those who did have jobs worked part-time as hairdressers or waitresses to make a few extra dollars to save for a house. The men went to trade school if they could, apprenticed somewhere, or learned the family trade. They were watchmakers, mechanics, machinists, or tradesmen. None had a formal education past high school. We did not talk about college in my house. But because I loved school, and most of my classmates talked about going, I naturally assumed that I would do the same thing.

I handed my stepmother the AP form. "My teacher says I'm one of her best students. She thinks I should go to college."

As I explained the situation, my mother looked over the form. I tried to quell my shaking legs. Then she looked up at me with mean, spiteful eyes and laughed out loud. I had never heard her laugh quite that way, and I did not understand what was funny.

"You're too stupid for college," she spat, with a smug expression that had the look of someone who'd won something. "*Dolgozni fogsz.* You are going to *work* when you graduate, and earn your keep," she growled at me, as if going to work was punishment for even thinking about college.

I felt violently slapped, although this time she hadn't touched me. I was too stunned to say a word, let alone to understand what had gone wrong. A cold dread swept over me. At school, I'd been applauded for achieving this honor. Now, at home, it was just another thing to get me in trouble. I guessed that my stepmother wanted me to get a job after high school so that I could start earning money—which she would then take from me, just as she did when relatives gave me money as gifts for my birthday.

My stepmother quickly signed the form and shoved it back into my trembling hand. She was forcing me, at twelve, onto the commercial-secretarial track, deciding something for the next six years of my life that I did not want. *Why?* I kept asking myself with tears in my eyes. *Why?* She often told me that I was a cheat who could not be trusted. I wish I had been clever enough to just fill out the form and sign it myself, but like other children in Hungarian families, I did what I was told. I did not negotiate with my parents like my American classmates did. She had trained me well never to question her decrees.

This dark cloud hung over me as I started my first day of junior high school. Looking around for new friends, I noticed that most of the kids appeared to know everyone else. They seemed happy and at ease, with the casual self-assurance of people who were at home in their milieu. They were confident. They fit in. They belonged.

Most of my fellow students joined school clubs such as chorus or band or took part in school plays, but I didn't even try to participate, although I loved to sing and would have loved to be in a play. My stepmother would never have allowed it. I was reduced to listening vicariously in the hallways as students talked excitedly about their activities.

As the routine of junior high settled in, friendships and cliques began to form, and hangouts, sleepovers, and birthday parties were planned. I was not part of any group, but some of the girls were nice enough to invite me a few times—before they tired of my excuses and stopped asking. I didn't ask my step-mother if I could go over to friends' houses, meet them at a park, or go to their birthday parties. I did not have the proper clothes for a sleepover or the money for a gift, even if my stepmother would have let me go. After a few months of not being able to so-cialize after school, I became an outsider there too, just as I was at home.

I did not get to make choices or pursue activities of my own. No one asked what I wanted or needed. My life, for all practical purposes, belonged to the family to use as they wished. I had ab-solutely no say. The AP program was the first time I had asked for something, and the message was clear: Don't do it again.

More and more people ignored me at school, and I didn't have the clothes or trendy hairstyles to attract attention. Among the girls, the most important topics were boys, dating, and getting one's period, and I had absolutely nothing I could talk about.

Boys barely acknowledged my presence. My stepmother had convinced me that I was dreadfully ugly, so I did not expect any-thing different. I was thin and had no shape to speak of. I wasn't cool, pretty, or interesting. Those who did talk about me made fun of my flat chest or dated clothes. My stepmother never bought me more than she had to, and I was too beaten down to even know what to ask for when it came to clothes or fashion. I wasn't menstruating like most of the girls, who were developing wom-anly figures right in front of my eyes. Those girls got the most attention from the prepubescent boys, who were painfully rude to those of us still in young girls' bodies. Some of the girls had boyfriends and discussed them in minute detail. I didn't have a boyfriend, of course, and had never been to a hairdresser, both crucial milestones for a girl. My stepmother cut my hair herself. She seemed to prefer an unattractive shoulder length that I could just put behind my ears, and doing so became a nervous tic that my father hated and that only added to my awkwardness at school. I kept my head lowered, trying to hide my face with the hair that fell over my right eye. I attempted to ignore the boys, even though they were always on my mind.

Clothes also seemed to be of the utmost importance to the girls, and in the 1970s, faded bell-bottoms and platform sandals were the uniform of the day. The brand, color, and style mattered greatly. My classmates looked casually dressed in jeans, Converse or Keds, and T-shirts or pretty sweaters, but each item was carefully planned and shopped for with their mothers or older sisters. Most girls at school had highlighted hair, long and straight, or cut into fashionable shag styles. Some wore makeup and had coveted military surplus jackets and the ubiquitous army-green backpacks. I did not own makeup, and my few clothes were bought once a year from the bargain bin at Alexander's by my aunt or grandmother, who never bothered to ask what I wanted or liked. The Hungarian generation that survived the war in Europe didn't think about how clothes could affect the self-esteem of a young teenager. Because I was tall and thin at five foot six, with flat size 11's that looked more like paddles than feet, I always got old-lady shoes, frumpy tops, and pants too big or high-waters too short. This made me the butt of jokes at school, but I had no choice but to wear the embarrassing outfits. I so badly wanted to fit in, but everything seemed to take me further and further from that dream.

The close attention I did get at school was not the kind I wanted. A few tough girls who were bused in from Corona would corner me in the stairwells and ask me for a nickel or a dime, which I never had. They seemed to sense that I was an outcast, someone they could bully. They didn't believe that I didn't have money until they searched my pockets and book bag more than once. At first, I was defiant, as in "No, I'm not giving you any money," with a false bravado gleaned from my total disgust with my life. But that strident tactic inspired only more bullying: a few shoves to the wall and names like "Henny Penny" and "Skinny Bitch."

One time, the Corona girls followed me into the bathroom and watched me over the top of the stall. I was nearly in tears, wanting my privacy to do my business—and just to be left alone. When I came out, they held out my arms and asked why I was so dirty. I had never noticed it before, but my arms were indeed covered in grayish . . . dirt. None of my family members had seemed to notice it either. No one had ever told me to wash, take a bath, or brush my teeth, so I guess I rarely did. My arms were truly filthy, as if I were a vagrant person on the street. The dirt had almost become one with my skin, part of the coloring. When confronted with my filthiness, I lied and told the girls that it was a skin disease, and although I could tell they didn't believe me, they never bothered me again.

For many years, school and learning had been my refuge and joy, but now it was a torment. All the pressure of my demanding baby sister, angry stepmother, and adult workload threw me into a fog. I was always exhausted. It was excruciating to sit in classes I hated day after day, while in homeroom my classmates were discussing which colleges were better: Columbia, Barnard, or CUNY. These students were in art, music, and English lit classes, all things I longed for, while I struggled to keep up with the daily speed drills in typing. The college-bound students got to go on field trips to museums and concerts, while I stayed behind in stenography class.

I was supposed to be preparing to be a secretary, but I honestly did not know what a secretary was. Once I found out, I did not want to be one. Who wanted to sit in an office all day typing and taking orders from someone else? I wanted to be my own person.

More important, what used to come easily was becoming really hard. School, which had been fun for me, was becoming a burden. Homework was harder in my AP program, and there was more of it. As the demands at home were increasing and I had less time and ability to focus, I started falling behind. I was awkward and uncoordinated, unable to keep up in either typing or steno, where you had to learn many new jots or squiggles an hour. Zoning out for even a second meant you missed something, and I was zoning out a lot.

Through the fog of all this, I was beginning to see that my stepmother was deliberately trying to obstruct any effort I made to educate or better myself, yet I was so terrified of her, I could not think of what to do about it. I remembered when I was eight and she tore up my library card. She had disciplined me for not getting permission for the library field trip. But that didn't explain why my stepmother wouldn't let me read in my rare free time, forcing me to read by streetlight after she went to bed.

Now, her antagonism was getting even worse. At night, when I was finally able to get to my homework—after housework—my stepmother would call out from the living room, *"Befejezte az iskolai munkát."*—"You are done with homework." Even though I would meekly tell her that I was not finished or that I had a test to study for, she would respond angrily: *"Azt mondtam, végeztél!"*—"I said you were done!" Hungarian parents did not accept talking back.

She was ordering me to pack up my books, even when no household chores remained to be done. Kitti was asleep, the family fed, the dishes washed. Again, why? Didn't she want me to learn? What did it matter to her if I did homework all night? Or was she just trying to keep me in my place?

I didn't think that anyone could possibly understand what I was going through. I felt like I was slowly going crazy. I knew the way I was being treated was wrong, but I felt powerless to do anything about it, which only made my angst worse. I couldn't tell anyone about this at school. I could not tell anyone in my family, because I knew they would take my stepmother's side. And I couldn't tell my father, because he was there and could not see it. But I felt something inside me change—even if I did not know what—and I was beginning to have more questions than answers.

9

The Hungarians

"*Gyerekek, menj játszani!*" Aunt Sári yelled over the noise of laughing and music. "*Hagyja békén a feln őtteket!*"

It was New Year's Eve of 1972, and Aunt Sári was ordering my cousins, my siblings, and me to go play—leaving the grown-ups alone for nostalgia and a lot of alcohol. We kids ran through her living room in Yonkers to grab some more *langos*, a deliciously salty Hungarian fried bread, before retreating to the children's area. Hungarians love to eat, and there was always plenty at Aunt Sári's place. Even so, I was careful before I took any food from the buffet table, making sure to avoid my stepmother's miserly eye.

I looked forward to these parties, and not only because of the treats. These gatherings also provided a rare opportunity to pick up details about my family. I wanted to know why my stepmother acted so cruelly toward me. What made her like this? No one else I knew from these parties seemed mean. Whenever we kids would ask our parents anything about their past, we would get only snippets, and then only grudgingly. Desperate to make sense of my life, I would listen and observe at parties like these as the adults let down their guard.

Hungarians love to dress up. All the friends and relatives arrived in high heels, fancy low-cut dresses, or suits, with the children in outfits saved for special occasions. The kids' job at these parties was to run to the door when the bell rang, taking the guests' coats, hats, and scarves and greeting each newcomer. The women all came from the hairdressers, smelling of hair spray and perfume, with teased updos and lots of elaborate jewelry. Hungarian women loved to show off their jewels.

Despite the fancy dress and festive air, the party eventually became a collective mourning of the loss of the country they had fled for their lives. The United States had granted asylum to about thirty thousand Hungarians as a guilt offering for not helping them during their 1956 revolution against the Soviets, who had been running the country since World War II.

Whenever my Hungarian relatives got together, they told stories of how good life was "before," of abundant grape harvests and the superb wine called Egri Bikavér (Bull's Blood), which they made and drank all night. Everyone made Hungary sound like the best place on the planet: the food was tastier, the soil richer, the wine much better.

There were also the tales of relatives and friends left behind. As the night wore on, everyone would break into old patriotic songs of the empire before the Soviets had come, when Hungarians ruled their own country and life was grand. The later it got, the louder the singing and the more morose the theme. The loudest in the group was always my father.

My father loved to hold court in any gathering, and New Year's Eve was no exception. He was the thirteenth child born to what was considered a wealthy family in his tiny hometown of Putnok, Hungary. Everyone knew the Farkases. He was from a well-known clan in a rural town where the undulating land was covered in grapevines, and the family business making wine barrels was the main employer. Roles in the large family, as in most Eastern European families, were divided along traditional lines. His mother raised the children, kept house, and cooked sit-down lunches for all twenty or so of the workers in the family business. His father and brothers, meanwhile, ran the business and made all the rules. The boys went to school, hung out with buddies, and worked. They were given freedoms that were never allowed the girls. My father's sisters were kept at home, destined to help their mothers with the chores and to be married off. My father got special treatment because he was the baby and the apple of his mother's eye.

My father missed his mother back in Hungary and referred to her as "*édes anya*"— "my sweet mother." At the parties, he mourned the fact that he could not go back to visit, because he was a wanted man in Hungary. My father had fought against the Soviets during the Hungarian Revolution and had barely escaped after being tipped off that the authorities were coming for him. I did not understand much about this part of his life, and he never talked to me about it.

He came to America at the end of 1956 at the age of twenty-three as an asylum seeker, sponsored by members of the Hungarian Catholic Church in Manhattan. My father started his new life socializing only with those he knew from back home, because he understood their language and habits. He never mixed much with Americans, not having the language or cultural references to discuss the topics of the day, the news, the stock market, or baseball. Finding work as a mechanic, he lived with his sponsor, Olive, and her family on the East Side of Manhattan. During that time, he got to know his sponsor's vivacious teenage daughter, Patricia, whom everyone affectionately called Patsy.

She was my mother.

Patsy was warm and cheerful, full of life and laughter. She was a voluptuous, radiant girl, at a time when a full figure was the standard of beauty. Her smile filled a room. Patsy was everyone's best friend, and a bright light in my father's new world. They soon married and had me eighteen months later. In photos, my parents both glowed and seemed very much in love.

As I looked at the loud, overdressed people at Aunt Sári's party, I wondered whether any of them had known my real mother, but most of the time, I was afraid to ask. It might get back to my stepmother, who was hostile to any mention of my mother, my father's first wife, or my life before I had come to live with her. I used to ponder what it would have been like to grow up with my own mother and father as my parents, but I could not imagine it at all. I searched for a party guest who might know her, but everyone was a friend of my aunt and stepmother. No one from my father's side was ever invited.

My father never talked about my mother, and on the rare occasions I had him alone, I would try to ask about her, but his face always turned gray.

"*Majd beszélünk róla néhánydsay.*"—"Someday we'll talk about it."

When I did secretly ask my stepmother's family about Patsy, they would respond, "*Ki?*"—"Who?" My real mother was some-one who never occurred to them. We did not discuss her at all. In fact, we never mentioned her name, as if she had never existed. As if my past had never existed.

Instead, my relatives had Hungary on their minds, all the time. The old country was still "home." It was always glorious, as if it weren't the place they had fled at gunpoint, swimming danger-ous rivers, abandoning their homes and businesses, and leaving everything they knew behind. In their new country, they were insular and assimilated only as much as necessary to survive, find work, and send their kids to school.

Most of my relatives had few friends and did not go out of their way to make any. They attended Hungarian churches, ate at Hungarian restaurants, and shopped in Hungarian markets. They even went to a hotel in the Catskills owned by a Hungarian couple that served Hungarian food. There, they could gossip with old friends and play Magyar kártya, an old country card game that featured four suits: acorns, hearts, leaves, and bells.

My relatives spoke Hungarian all the time, causing some issues in kindergarten for my brother, Steven, when he did not know English despite having been born here. If my family socialized, it was only with other Hungarians. Since I had moved in with my father and stepmother, not one non-Hungarian had visited our home.

Gazing at the drunken men and overheated women at the party, I asked myself whether all Hungarian immigrant families were this devoted to the old country and shared the view that their country and culture were superior to the one they now lived in. It wasn't like my family had room to be so snobbish: only a few of them were shop owners, and none had a formal education. Yet they felt themselves above everyone else in the United States. They were xenophobic, racist, and anti-Semitic, unless in the company of a Semite who was wealthy. When that happened, my family would be envious and respectful, while speculating how such a Semite must have cheated the IRS or gotten a lucky break to have made so much money. Money was always a high priority to my relatives, and they talked about it constantly.

At my relatives' parties, I saw a side of my father that I never saw at home. He came to life at these gatherings, comfortable around friends who knew him from before he'd married my stepmother. My father liked to take up space, especially when he had an audience, something he did not often have at home. And he had a beautiful voice that could carry a room. He never heard when people grumbled that he was too loud, and it wouldn't have bothered him if he had.

In my aunt's kitchen, while I was getting Hawaiian Punch for my sister, one relative chuckled at my father's loud voice and told me that my dad was a charmer.

"*Nagyon jól nézett ki a maga idejében.*"—"He was very good-looking in his day," she said as she patted my cheek. "He is always the life of the party."

Funny, I thought. At home, he was so quiet. And even on those rare occasions when he was in the mood for fun, my stepmother never seemed to respond. "Let's go for a walk," he'd say when he came home from work. "*Menjünk egy meghajtóra.*"—"Let's go for a drive," he'd say on a Sunday when we had no plans. But my stepmother wasn't interested. When I first moved in with them, I remember my father swaying and snapping his fingers to big-band music playing on our stereo. Now, he never touched the stereo. He had married a woman with no joy, who could barely walk, let alone dance.

My father was a rough man's man, with grease under his nails and a proud stance, although he did not have much to his name. He loved dogs, although my stepmother would not allow one in the house. He kept one named Yago at his shop, and we swore that he loved the guard dog more than us, as my father went there on Sundays to feed him while we waited at home. Yago was a fierce German shepherd who would lunge at anyone who tried to come near him. Luckily, Dad kept him chained up.

My father never did any housework, although his wife was

almost completely immobile. In fact, he never asked whether she needed help, not giving a thought to how everything in a household was supposed to get done. He just worked for a living, and my stepmother was supposed to figure out the rest. He loved manly things like guns and hunting, and often went off for a few days at a time with his brother, Uncle Joe, or other Hungarian pals. He'd come home with a deer on the roof of his car and smelling of blood and trees and dirt.

He never bothered to learn much English, just enough to get by. He often mispronounced things, such as saying "sneak" for "snake" in pointing one out in the park. The mispronunciation did not bother him, but we kids thought it was hilarious and laughed at him when he did it. My father made his way in the world with his overwhelming confidence and did not worry about the rest. He did not read much, if at all. We never got a newspaper at home, and he never picked up a book. But he seemed to have an opinion about everything, which he defended to the death, loudly, right or wrong, and he was usually wrong.

My father and I didn't talk at all, except in greeting. The lines were clearly drawn: parents talked, kids listened, the old "be seen and not heard" alive and well in Hungarian households. Our daily conversation when he came home, smelling of alcohol and car grease, was the same: "How you doing, Chicken?" "Fine, Papa." And with maybe two or three exceptions in my lifetime, that was all I got. He called me Chicken because he said I was so skinny that my bones rattled.

"Penny, hol van a húgod?"—"Where is your sister?"

My stepmother's snappish tone jolted me back to reality at the New Year's Eve party. She had just appeared in the playroom, not bothering to hide her contempt for me from the other children as she did in front of the grown-ups. She did not greet me or the other children and did not show any of the warmth people usually did around kids.

"*Nagyi elvitte, hogy megmutassák az embereknek.*"—"Grandma took her to show off to people," I meekly answered, as the other kids paused in our game of Twister to watch us. If they were surprised by her tone, they did not show it. I was supposed to be watching Kitti, and my stepmother did not like me having fun, even though Kitti was in good hands.

For the most part, my stepmother seemed happier at these big family events. She could show off the few elaborate jewels that her father had given her and display her ample figure in low-cut dresses. But she always found a reason to be unhappy, particularly when I was around.

My stepmother also had escaped Hungary during the 1956 revolution, with her parents, Nagyi and Nagyi-papa, and her sister, Sári, with a few clothes and some money they had squirreled away. Nagyi-papa, a business owner, had been constantly hassled and arrested for being "bourgeois" and for having money.

Nagyi was the boss of the whole family. Nagyi-papa openly adored her. She was a serious person and held herself with authority. She was confident, opinionated, and outspoken. The whole family was opinionated, and everyone thought they were right, but Nagyi always got the final word. She did not emote, was not affectionate, and gave you a good telling off if you didn't mind her. But she was generous with food and little gifts.

Nagyi babied my stepmother, giving her extra care because of my stepmother's arthritis, permanently putting the word *poor* before her name when referring to my stepmother, and making sure she had every comfort wherever we were. The whole extended family pivoted around what was best for my stepmother. The rest of the family members always took second place after her and my brother, the firstborn male and Nagyi-papa's favorite.

Nagyi-papa was kind, funny, and wonderful in every way. I liked him from the moment I met him, when he came with my father to pick me up from Aunt Charlotte's. He was the family peacemaker-diplomat to Nagyi's authoritarian rule. He was a gentleman and dressed like one in vests or waistcoats and suit jackets, and smelled faintly of soap and aftershave. He was soft-spoken and of few words, except to make jokes or try to get the reluctant Nagyi to kiss him. He calmed arguments and advised family members in times of crisis. He made us kids laugh by calling us over, then popping his dentures out to scare us. He gave us little gifts that he made himself, and let us "help" in his store when we were older. He was the only one of my stepmother's relatives who tried to engage my father, jokingly asking each time they met, *"Hogyan istenverte csavar esztergálás?"*—"How does the goddamn screw turn?"—mimicking my father's vernacular. The rest of my stepmother's family ignored my father past the customary greeting, barely hiding their contempt. Nagyi-papa would check in with me sometimes, out of my stepmother's earshot, and although I didn't dare tell him much, I felt his care as he patted my head with a *"Jó van, Penniké, jó van."*—"It's good, Penny."

My grandparents did a lot for the grandkids, taking us places and giving us gifts. Although they always told me, *"Penniké, olyan vagy, mint a többi unoka,"*—"We treat you like all the other grand-kids," I wondered why they said it so much. It was always in the face of the other kids getting more money or more gifts, but at least they gave me more than I ever got at home.

When they arrived in America as teenagers, my stepmother and her sister were kept close to home, sent to Catholic school, and given very few freedoms. My stepmother desperately wanted to get out of her house and her mother's rules, and my father, good-looking and charming in an Arnold Schwarzenegger sort of way, came calling.

Aunt Sári was two years younger than my stepmother and was her polar opposite: sweet, kind, warm, outgoing, and full of life. Perhaps because Aunt Sári was only fourteen when she arrived from Hungary, she was the most Americanized of all my older relatives. She would play Aretha Franklin records at the parties, jumping up and singing along. She had made some American friends. She sometimes prepared American food, like shrimp, cupcakes, or macaroni and cheese, which we kids loved. She always looked at me with love, and although she could not say much, I could tell that she cared about me. Her daughter—my cousin—once told me that Aunt Sári had tried to adopt me when I first came to live with my parents, but my dad would not allow it. I always wondered why not. I would have loved being her daughter.

My father and stepmother came from different worlds and were as dissimilar as could be, yet as is common with recent immigrants, the familiar brought them together, and they thought it would be enough. My stepmother was from a tony city south of Budapest, the daughter of a well-connected and fun-loving couple. She was brought up middle-class, was educated in private schools, listened to opera, took piano lessons, vacationed on Lake Balaton, and had hired help to do the ironing. My father was from a remote, rural village where people worked with their hands and there was little sophisticated culture.

My father and stepmother met in the 1960s at St. Stephen's Catholic Church, the same Hungarian community in Manhattan where my father had met my mother and his sponsor. By the time he met my stepmother, he had already known love and loss.

The childhood friend he had come to America with had committed suicide, and my father's young wife had died less than two years after they'd married, leaving me, a six-month-old daughter, to raise.

My stepmother had only known her sheltered childhood in Hungary and her parents' small apartment in Manhattan. Before meeting my father, she had never lived on her own, dated, traveled, or held a job. He was young, charming, and good-looking, super confident. My grandparents never liked him. They thought he was a liar, his Swiss bank accounts, and other stories, a sham, and they were right. They were against the marriage, her first proposal, and strongly warned her not to go through with it.

But my stepmother was always very sure of herself. Like the emperor with no clothes, she was unwavering in how she saw the world. She never questioned her own thinking but always distrusted others and dismissed anything not already in her worldview. Hers was the air of a much older, more erudite, and accomplished person. If she thought it so, so it was, and nothing anyone said could change her point of view. I never saw her as being young, although she was probably only twenty when she married my father and I came into her life.

She was what we call in Hungarian *doondy*, or pleasantly plump, and was a small person, maybe five feet tall. But she somehow managed to command a lot of space in a room, giving off the air of authority, of being in charge and in control. She wore her short brown hair away from her face, which was unusually bloated from all the medications she took. Big eyeglasses gave her a learned air, and she was, relatively speaking.

Everyone in my stepmother's family had a solid immigrant work ethic. They saved money to open a business and buy a house, or, in Aunt Sári's case, a duplex in Yonkers. But my father never cared very much about getting ahead. My stepmother wanted more money for our family, but her arthritis prevented her from earning extra cash.

Even when she was a young woman, my stepmother's fingers were already bent and gnarled from the arthritis. One of her legs swung out, and she walked with a limp because of the pain in her knees. She did not venture out much due to her difficulty walking, which made her somewhat of a shut-in by the time I was a teenager. Yet being mostly confined to her recliner didn't make her any less imposing. I involuntarily trembled whenever I was near her.

Though my father was not ambitious, he shared my stepmother's desire to keep up appearances. To compensate for their lack of upward mobility and money, my parents had trinkets of wealth. Besides amassing their collection of dozens of expensive Herend porcelain figurines, my father kept us in used Cadillacs—the "I have arrived" car of the times—even if they regularly broke down and were always dirty from being parked on the street. He liked to brag that he drove my stepmother around in the ultimate American luxury car, something no one else in our circle of hardworking, saving immigrants had or saw as a thing of value. But values are funny things, and my father valued making my stepmother happy. In the middle of a recession, he bought her a full-length mink coat, something I couldn't understand since we could barely make the rent. But getting the coat did make her happy, and she got to show it off at parties like the one at Aunt Sári's place.

The people at the New Year's Eve party were kind to me, patting my head and telling me, "*Jó testvér vagy*,"—"You're a good sister,"—and "*Jó kislány vagy*,"—"You're a good daughter,"—as they watched me caring for Kitti while my stepmother sat with her legs up. My stepmother hated when I received compliments. She would not comment, just draw her lips into a forced line or change the subject. It seemed hers was a zero-sum game: if I got something, it somehow took away from her or her children.

When I first started living with her, it was merely awkward. I was essentially an American kid, she a haughty European, and we were very different. I was ugly to her Hungarian idea of beauty, and she told me so. With my skinny body, knobby knees and elbows, straight pixie-cut hair, and freckles, I was not the European picture of a cute, curly-haired Shirley Temple, whom my stepmother adored. We didn't hug or talk, which I found strange because everyone else in the family greeted each other with a kiss on the cheek.

At the party, she watched the crowd from her central spot and did not show her cunning side to anyone but me. As I looked around at the various families at the party, I tried to picture myself in them. I longed to find out more about my mother, to make sense of my life. But no one here could help me. The little I did know of my mother, I got by chance.

One day before my sister was born, we went as a family to see *Love Story*, a movie about love and class, romance, and heartbreak. A lot for a young girl to take in, watching the young and beautiful Ali MacGraw die of a terminal illness soon after she marries the rich and handsome Ryan O'Neal against his family's wishes. During the deathbed scene, my father leaned over to me in the dark theater and whispered, "That's how your mother died."

Shocked, I looked up at him for more details. But he focused on the screen, his jaw tight, while I sat in the dark and processed this bombshell. I assumed this meant that my real mother had died of leukemia, although that specific disease was not mentioned in the film. I had asked him many times what had happened to my mother, knowing he was the only one who could tell me. "Someday we'll talk about it, Chicken," was always his answer. When our family left the theater, it was night, and my father immediately ran off to get the car.

We never spoke of it again.

10

Cold Guilt

*W*haap!

In the dead of the night, a slap in the face jolted me awake in my bed. My ears rang and my face stung. Instinctively, I edged as far back on the bed as I could. What was happening?

In the dim shadows, I could just make out the form of my stepmother, who repeatedly lunged to strike my face, my head, or any part of me she could connect with in the darkness. The air whooshed by my head as she swung again and missed. She hadn't said a word, so I did not know what I had done to deserve this new punishment. I was so shocked, I couldn't think straight. I caught my breath and started mumbling, "I'm sorry, I'm sorry," not really sure what I was sorry for, but it came out without thinking.

"*Fogd be a szád.*"—"Shut your mouth," she hissed through her teeth. She attacked me again but could only scratch me with her sharp nails as I clung to the wall, away from her grasp. Failing to land another substantial slap, she grabbed my blanket and pulled it away, leaving me to shiver against the dank wall. Because our radiators were so noisy, my stepmother constantly had the heat off at night, so it was cold in the house during the winter. Quietly hobbling out of the room, she dragged the blanket behind her, leaving it by the open door.

I held my breath, waiting for her to return. On full alert, I sat up in bed, my knees drawn into my chest, my heart pounding. I wasn't sure if my shivering was because of the cold or my fear. I listened to my stepmother leave the bathroom and braced for the worst—but she walked past my room back to her own bed. Gradually my heartbeat slowed enough so that I could hear my brother's breath as he slept soundly. I heard the creak of my stepmother's bed as she got in, and my father's snoring.

I began rehashing the day to figure out what I had done wrong. Her attacking me was not new, but she had never done so in the middle of the night, while I was sleeping. Over and over, I replayed the events of the day, but nothing stood out. My stepmother had been mad at me for taking too long at the store, but it had been rush hour, and I could not help it. I had done everything right with baby Kitti, and even fetched my father's dinner—without being asked—when he'd come home later than usual. My stepmother had stared at me coldly as I served him, but she always did that.

I looked around from the shadows of the large room that I shared with my brother. His bed was close to the door, on the inner wall bordering my parents' room, the warmest spot available. His was a new twin bed ordered from Sears. Mine was against the wall, to the left of the tall windows, and it had been given to us by Aunt Sári to replace my saggy folding cot, which had fallen apart. Apparently, someone had died in my bed, so Aunt Sári had been happy to part with it, even though she had three kids of her own who needed beds.

I was so cold. Even though it was dark, the outside streetlight made it possible for me to see my blanket by the door. But I was afraid to get it. I knew that my stepmother would hear me, and I could not imagine what she would do to me this time. It never occurred to me to call out to my father, or to wake my brother. So I slept curled in a ball and uncovered the rest of the night.

No reason for this abuse was provided the next day, and dread had trained me not to question any punishment meted out to me. No one seemed to notice the scratches on my face. I spent the day wondering what I had done and trying as hard as I could to outdo anything she asked of me. I assumed that I was responsible for her ill treatment of me, and therefore, if I was responsible, I could make it stop. But it did not stop. Nighttime became a time of terror. She came again, and again, and again.

From that time on, I tried to stay awake in bed every night, keeping one ear uncovered to listen for her step so I could protect my head with my hands. But I was so spent by bedtime, from household chores and babysitting, that I could rarely stay awake for long. My stepmother's nocturnal visits always ended up surprising me. My joints hurt from sleeping knees to chest, huddling into a ball to keep warm, covering myself with my thin sheet on the mattress. I woke up tired every morning, red-eyed and overwhelmed by a sense of hopelessness. Why couldn't I make it stop?

It had to be my fault. More and more, I was being plagued by guilt. The Catholic Church seemed to talk about guilt a lot, as I had recently learned at catechism class for my First Holy Communion. Most kids, including my brother, had their First Holy Communions at six or seven, but my stepmother had never bothered to sign me up. She sent out announcements for my brother's Communion party to all our relatives—even those back in Hungary, where First Holy Communion was considered a big event.

But then our relatives called out my stepmother, asking her why I hadn't received my Communion. Against her will, she permitted me to take classes and accept the sacrament with my brother. The aunts in Hungary sent me a traditional Hungarian dress for the occasion, a thick white tunic of heavy material with colorful traditional flowers embroidered down the front, like those typically seen on peasant blouses. It was at least two sizes too big and hung on my lanky frame. It was the total opposite of the bright-white, frilly lace dresses that the rest of the girls wore, making me stand out even more than my height and age already did.

My stepmother was also forced to include me as an honoree at the Communion party, where I was supposed to share the limelight with my brother—an injustice, in her mind, that made her furious just to think about. It made me dread my First Holy Communion.

"*Menj a konyhába!*" During the party, she repeatedly told me to get back in the kitchen to tidy up. Unsuspecting relatives kept pulling me back into the festivities, telling me not to worry about cleaning up on my special day.

Before the party, the Communion ceremony had taken place at St. Joan of Arc, around the corner from us on Eighty-Second Street. I had walked by the imposing structure for years, wondering about God without ever going in. I had often questioned whether God could help me, but I didn't know how to get to this person that I heard people mention. No one in my family talked about God. The church was a stately redbrick building that took up a whole block. It had rows of wide steps leading up to three massive wooden doors with ornate black metal hinges, and crowned with stained-glass windows depicting St. Joan, Christ, and his disciples. The building had authority. It was mysterious. Its school and rectory were a big part of the neighborhood.

Inside the building, I felt something I had not felt before . . .

holy. The church smelled of incense and floor polish. The music
was solemn and quiet. Footsteps echoed. People walked slowly,
with reverence. They whispered and bent to cross themselves
with virtue. They dipped their fingers in the holy water and
touched their foreheads and lips as if transformed by it. I looked
forward to the Communion lessons, which I took to heart as I did
everything, hoping to finally understand God. But instead, I
learned only that I would not measure up. At our last class, the
nun told me that unless I made my Confirmation, I would not be
right in the eyes of God and could never marry in the church. She
acted like it was urgent. Maybe she thought I was too old already.
Because of the fuss my stepmother had kicked up at my Communion party, I knew she would never let me get confirmed. I took
that to mean that I was damned, or worse, could never get married.

The guilt gnawed at me. Not guilt about my soul, which I
soon forgot about in my daily battle for survival, but guilt as to
why I could not do anything right. Why I could not make the in-
explicable punishments stop. Why I made my stepmother call me
terrible names. Why I made her so angry. Why I had to be so
afraid all the time.

Sometimes my brother and sister and I would be waiting
with my stepmother for the elevator, chatting and laughing with
each other, when out of the blue, my stepmother would claw me
in the neck and face with her nails. My brother and sister never
said a word during these encounters, either to her or to me. It
was as if nothing had happened. On one occasion, I was in our
narrow kitchen doing chores when my stepmother walked in, put
her hand on my face, and pushed my head into the wall. She did
it with such force that the back of my head broke the paint, creat-
ing a shallow crater in the soft old plaster. As usual, there was no
explanation. For me, the crater became a constant reminder of

what could happen at any minute. Apparently, no one else noticed the dent, and it was never fixed. But my angst continued.

The cold reality of my powerlessness plagued me. I thought about it constantly as I walked to school or ran errands for the family. When I was fourteen, we had some bitter winter days in New York, and people avoided going out if they could. The wind pierced the warmest coats like knives. It seemed to be dark by three thirty when school got out, and I always shivered on the way home. We had snow days and school closures because of the cold and the poor heating in some of the older schools.

My stepmother rarely went out in winter, and a foul cabin fever set in. My brother had chronic ear infections, which came with fevers and crying, and the baby had a constant runny nose, both of which put my stepmother on edge. I was as healthy as an ox and never sick, but my stepmother was sure that I was carrying the germs home from school and infecting my siblings. My parents' relationship was also becoming more frigid. My father was drinking more and staying out late all the time. It only added to the bleakness.

Because I blamed myself for not being good enough to stop my stepmother's anger and abuse, I exhausted myself thinking about it. I started to contemplate suicide as my only out. I reasoned that it was a sound answer, a simple solution. The problem was I had no access to drugs or poison, so my options were limited. I went up to the roof once with thoughts of jumping, but our apartment building was lined with privet bushes, and I was not sure they wouldn't break my fall and spare me. I couldn't chance a broken arm or leg if I didn't die outright.

Then an idea came to me: maybe the cold could be a solution. When we went out as a family with my father to visit any of the relatives, or to school, I wore a decent winter coat. I was thin, so

I was always freezing. One day after school, when being sent on an errand, I reached into the closet for my coat, and my stepmother said no, not that one. Instead, she gave me a long, loose-knit sweater that a relative had given me but I had never worn. It offered no solid protection from the cold or the biting wind.

"*Viselje ezt.*"—"You're wearing this," my stepmother said. I was confounded. It was below freezing out, and so windy that people could not walk upright. I took the sweater and put it on, and started crying as soon as the apartment door closed behind me. For weeks, this routine continued. Over and over again, I'd wear a good coat to school or to Nagyi's place but be told to wear my thin sweater for errands. I walked the streets in tears from the cold, huddled into myself as much as I could and still keep walking. Sometimes I'd happen to be waiting at a street corner when a classmate or neighbor would ask why I was out in a sweater when it was so cold.

"Oh no," I'd lie. "I'm not cold. I like it."

By the look in people's eyes, I could tell that I was not fooling anyone, but I didn't care. I was tapped out. I had no energy left to even care. I just wanted it to be over. I wanted to die.

On my way to the pharmacy to get my stepmother's pain medicine, I came to a decision. Entering a deserted playground on Seventy-Eighth Street, I sat down on an icy bench. I concluded that freezing to death would be easy and a painless way to go. I could just stay there and fall asleep, and all my troubles would be over. As the wind whistled through me, the idea of taking my own life actually made me happy, something I hadn't felt in a long while.

No one was around in the park. The trees were bare, and the birds were gone. Sandboxes and slides were empty. The wind blew the sand through the air in small twisters, and the swing sets clanged back and forth. The sounds of the horns and buses were distant and quiet. A few dogs barked, then the silence of real cold.

As I sat on the bench waiting to die, I thought of how sorry they'd all be. I had no real concept of heaven, despite my Communion, so I did not consider spiritual issues. I just thought of who might miss me. I thought of how they would regret treating me as they had, and how embarrassed they would be, and that it would serve them right to suffer without me. But the longer I sat, the darker the sky got, and the colder I got. I was alert and no closer to dead, still thinking my thoughts, just much stiffer. More miserable by the minute, I decided this plan wouldn't work. I had better hurry to the pharmacy before it closed, or I'd get in trouble for being late.

I continued to live in a dark funk, and no one in my family noticed. Except Aunt Hanna. Aunt Hanna was part of my extended stepfamily, an uncle's sister. She was a loving and kind woman, and very pretty, married to a wonderfully elegant Italian man named Uncle Victor who spoke with a singsong Italian accent that I loved. When Aunt Hanna noticed my angst, she tried to do what she could about it without upsetting the family applecart. She thought that she could cheer me up with some new clothes.

Most of the women in my family were large. Not quite obese, but big, which in their Hungarian culture was totally acceptable, admired even. Skinny, flat-chested people like me were the abnormal, weird ones. What made Aunt Hanna different was that she was slim, one of the very few Hungarians in my life who were. She was beautiful in every way and very shapely, and with her husband being a tailor, she wore gorgeous, fitted clothes, and looked great in them.

By the time I got to high school, I was used to being singled out as strange because I rode my bike to school while others rode the bus. And because I didn't have the right clothes, no one considered me worth talking to. The uniform of the day was bell-bottom jeans by Jordache or Faded Glory and some sort of skimpy, clingy top, preferably braless if you had something to show off, or with a padded training bra, which would have been useful in my case. But I had none of these things and no way to get them. I had to survive on my bargain-bin rags.

Being kindhearted, Aunt Hanna had a pants outfit that she thought would suit me, and she gave it to me. It was a super-baggy polyester set, in mint condition, perfect for a grandmother. I was aghast. What fourteen-year-old wanted to wear old-lady clothes? But my stepmother insisted that I accept the gift. When I got it home, I quickly hid the outfit in the back of my closet, hoping my stepmother would forget about it. But I knew it was only a matter of time before she remembered.

The time came up sooner than I thought. One night a few weeks later, my stepmother decreed that I would wear the outfit to school the next morning. I was sick to my stomach. My body began to tremble and sweat. There was no way I could show up at school in those clothes.

For ten years, I had survived the neglect, the punishments, the physical abuse, the deprivations, the name-calling, and the anger, but the prospect of being thoroughly humiliated at high school pushed me over the edge. These old-lady clothes were an atrocity I could not live down.

I had to think of a way around it. I went through my options. There was not enough room in my backpack to hide other clothes in, and no place to change in the morning before I got to school. In my stupor, I could barely think, so it was difficult to devise a way out. Around and around my thoughts spun in my exhausted brain. There was only one thing to do. Something that had never occurred to me before.

I would run away.

11

Hicksville

On a gray November morning in 1973, I pedaled my bicycle under the El on Roosevelt Avenue toward Flushing Meadow Park. Dodging potholes, people, cars, and double-parked delivery trucks, I was headed for Long Island.

Dressed in my aunt's frumpy clothes, I had left the house at my usual time of 10 a.m. Newtown High School had split shifts, and I was on the 11 a.m. start. I had tried to act normal before I left the apartment, but I was shaking inside at what I was about to do. I closed the door behind me, not saying goodbye as I headed for the basement to retrieve my bike.

During the night, I had formed my getaway plan so that I could avoid being humiliated at school in my ridiculous outfit. I had tiptoed around the apartment and managed to sneak a few dollars out of my father's pants pockets in the dining room, where he kept his work clothes. With some singles from Nagyi, I had a total of seven dollars.

Outside, it was a crisp forty degrees, warm by New York winter standards. I felt fortunate that the weather was dry because I had no hat, gloves, or helmet. There were a few schoolbooks in my backpack—I still wanted to keep up with my studies—but I had no plan on how I'd ever get back in school. I could not think about that now.

The furthest I'd ever cycled was to my school, a mile and a half from my apartment building. Yet despite my terrible sense of direction, I miraculously managed to recall the streets we had driven through for years and cobbled together a route to Long Island. My bike, a rusty relic that my father had brought home from work, was stored in the common area of our basement. It was not in great shape, but I could not let that stop me.

As I rode, Jackson Heights turned into Corona, which was scary with its boarded-up businesses and people hanging out on stoops and storefronts, watching the lone girl riding a bike in winter. I mostly stuck to residential areas until I got to Flushing. After Kissena Park, the city thinned out. I paralleled the Jericho Turnpike until I got to Hicksville, Long Island. I had been pedaling about six hours.

By the time I arrived at the Hicksville Shopping Center, it was already dark and starting to get bitterly cold. I could barely feel my hands. I remembered this landmark because I'd seen it from the Long Island Expressway on our many drives to our summer place in Ronkonkoma, an old shack that my parents had bought when they had more money. I hated the place, so I dreaded the summer journey, but I had passed the time by taking in the sights, including the shopping center. With its big white cement building and its oversized "Sears" sign, the shopping center always stood out among the tiny neighborhoods, parks, and gas stations that we passed from the highway. We had driven by dozens of times but had never stopped.

Near the shopping center, I found a secluded spot and locked my bike to a metal pole. I began walking around. Just getting to these stores was as far as I had planned. I knew I needed to find a place to sleep for the night. Maybe I would sleep behind the building, or in the woods that surrounded the stores.

Because the shopping center was so lit up, I could make out the main shops. There was a large supermarket, a Korvettes department store, a pizza place and a few other little restaurants, a movie theater, a bank, and a Sears. I went inside the grocery store to get something to eat and kill some time. While I walked the aisles, I realized that my parents would know that I was missing by now, and I angrily hoped they were worried. I wondered whether they would call the police or just wait for me to come home. Would they go to my school and find out that I didn't go today at all? As I was paying for a few bagels and apples, both cheap and easy to carry, I saw some postcards of Long Island beaches. I bought one of Fire Island. I decided that I would write my parents to let them know I was safe but lie to throw them off my trail by telling them not to look there, as I had really gone north.

Then I headed over to Sears. The store was brilliantly lit up for Christmas. I could feel the warmth of the heater blowing down on the store entrance—a great comfort after my long, cold ride. The store was busy with couples and families, kids running around, and distracted salespeople. Holiday music played softly in the background, and men on ladders were hanging up decorations. The store felt festive, cheery, and safe.

I tried to take it all in, but the store was so large that I could not see to the other end of it. I took my time walking past the displays, first men's clothing, then boys, then jewelry and accessories. I became aware of the smell of chocolate, making my stomach grumble. There was a little candy stand with fancy chocolates, which they sold by the pound in dainty little bags. I came upon an escalator. The second floor beckoned.

When I arrived on the next level to a sea of living rooms and bedrooms, it hit me how tired I was. I had sunk into one comfortable armchair after the other, before moving on to the sofas and beds. I liked looking at furniture, and was starting to enjoy myself, taking in the glamour of it all, smelling the new fabric, leather, and wood. The second floor was less crowded than the first, and I relaxed on a bed, gazing at the ceiling lights. My rest didn't last long—a salesperson started walking toward me. I grabbed my backpack and scurried down the escalator.

Back on the first level, I found myself in the tool department with hardly a customer in sight. I walked the aisles, slowly taking in the table saws, drills, hand tools, hammers, screwdrivers, and nails. It felt strange that there was no one around. The next aisle was garden equipment: rakes, shovels, lawn mowers, barbecue grills, patio sets, and lawn furniture. Next came irons, ironing boards, and sewing machines, followed by an aisle of thread, needles, buttons, and elastic in every color. I did not know that there was this much stuff to be had for a home. Next, I ventured into what I thought was the garage section. It was full of metal shelving, storage bins, and tall metal cabinets. That's when I heard the announcement, "The store will be closing in ten minutes."

I was standing next to a tall, white wardrobe cabinet that was at least a foot taller than me. One of its two front doors was wide open, displaying a roomy space, with lots of headroom inside. I could easily stand up in it and close the door.

I looked around, my stomach tingling with excitement. Nobody was around. Just to be sure, I walked a loop around the tool department, but I could see no one any which way I looked. I went back to the wardrobe cabinet, quickly checked left and right again, got in, and closed the door behind me. My heart beat wildly. I had to catch my breath. I had found my bed for the night.

I did not move for what seemed like a very long time. I strained to listen to every sound. No one walked by. After what seemed like hours, the light that seeped in the frame of the door became darker. Silence. After waiting even longer, I opened the door very slowly, inch by inch, to a dark and silent store. I left my coat and backpack inside and crept out slowly from the cabinet to see whether anyone was around. I waited for my eyes to adjust to the dark. I stood still for a few moments to see whether I heard anyone. With the coast apparently clear, I took off my sneakers and left them with my pack as I started walking around. I was totally alone in the nearly dark department store at night. It was exhilarating!

Slowly I looped around the first floor, through the men's and children's clothes, shoes, jewelry, and handbags. I stopped at the chocolate stand, a rare treat for me, but for some reason I was afraid to take some. When I finished my loop, I walked back up the now-still escalator to the second floor. It was much darker there, probably because there were no windows. The other half of the floor was the women's and teen girl clothing. My pulse started to quicken as I looked around. I moved slowly, in case anyone might show up. But no one was around. Rack after rack of new girls' clothes! I knew stealing was wrong, and I had stolen before, when I was hungry, or in a warped attempt to please my stepmother with something I had lifted from the drugstore. But I could easily justify those incidents because I had done what I needed to do, and no real harm was done.

At Sears, the temptation was overwhelming, though I could not find any of the brand names that the kids wore at school. Even at the age of fourteen, I knew nothing about what size I wore, or how to find the right size, so I grabbed a pair of jeans at random and held them up to my waist. They were soft and had that great new clothes' smell. I took off my aunt's ugly polyester pants and tried the new jeans on. They were long enough, which was usually an issue, as I was tall and skinny for my age. But they were inches too big at the waist. No problem, I thought. I knew how to sew and had seen the notions department downstairs.

Now it was time to look around for a belt. As I scanned the aisles in the dark, I found pretty little tops here and there, and took a few of those as well. I found the belts and chose one with flower appliqués and a gold buckle. I slipped off Aunt Hanna's ugly top and put on a new, blue flowered one. After throwing another pair of jeans and a few tops over my shoulder, I scrunched up Aunt Hanna's old clothes and threw them into a nearby trash bin.

It was the most freedom and fun that I had ever had. I loved being in the store at night. I felt alive, free, and happy. It was as though I didn't have a care in the world. I continued walking around, exploring every corner of the store. Though I remained quiet, I was starting to feel more relaxed, believing that I was alone for the night. I even rested on one of the beds, beginning to drift off. But I shot up quickly to wake myself up. Sleeping on one of the beds was too risky, because I might not wake up before the store opened. I tiptoed back down the escalator and made my way to the notions department for some thread to take in my new pants.

My energy was starting to wane. It had been a long and victorious day. I felt I had outsmarted my stepmother, and I had some nice new clothes! I was happy to be gone and didn't think about the future. After finding some dark blue thread and a package of needles, I packed my new clothes into my over-loaded backpack and crawled back into my wardrobe cabinet. Sleep came quickly.

I awoke to the sound of wheels rolling across the floor,

maybe from a dolly, followed by metal scraping on the floor and boxes being cut open. I did not have a watch, so I had no idea what time it was. I also had no idea whether the store was open or just being stocked up by employees. I tried to breathe as softly as I could when I heard the sound of voices nearby, but those sounds eventually faded away. I was not sure what to do. As I waited in the cabinet, I put my sneakers on and counted to one hundred to make myself wait a bit longer. Quietly, I crept out of the cabinet, and walked out of the store.

I had a whole day to kill before I could hunker down in my wardrobe cabinet again. I explored the shopping center a few times. For money, I thought I could bag groceries at the super-market for tips—which I'd seen kids do at our neighborhood market. But when I scoped out the scene, there were no kids around, and cashiers were doing the bagging. I forgot that it was a Wednesday during a school week and realized that I better make myself scarce before someone asked why I was there.

Now that I had been gone for almost a day, the guilt over leaving my home was getting to me. I knew that my parents would be angry but also worried. I found the post office and mailed my parents the postcard. I wrote that I was fine, and not to look for me on Fire Island, as I had gone the other way. I hoped that it worked.

I decided to check out the movie theater. It was an older building, off the beaten path, and a bit scabby, but beggars couldn't be choosy. It surprised me that they let a teenager in alone during school hours, but everybody seemed to be minding their own business, and no one said a thing. I had found my refuge for the day!

The theater was playing *Billy Jack*, a movie that I had not heard of. It was about an American Indian who was a Vietnam veteran, working with mixed-raced kids who the townspeople didn't like for some reason. I didn't understand much of the movie, but it was entertaining to look at, and the theater was warm. Too warm, actually, and I fell asleep several times during the movie.

When I got up to go to the bathroom, it was past six o'clock. The movie was already a blur, but the music and lyrics to its theme song, "One Tin Soldier," stuck with me, and I sang it over and over to myself like a lullaby.

Somehow I managed to pass four days like this, hiding in my wardrobe cabinet at Sears at night, leaving at the right time each morning, foraging around the shopping center during the day, finding a place to read, and sneaking back into the cabinet at night without arousing any suspicion. I was not bored, scared, or hungry. I was content, even happy, in my vagabond state, naively not thinking of the future or how long I could sustain my little adventure.

On the fifth day, I made a big mistake. On previous mornings, I had managed to time my morning appearances just right, even without knowing the time. There were watches in the store, but for some reason, I did not think of taking one. On this particular day, I thought I had waited long enough, but I came out too early. Because I had repeatedly heard people speaking, I assumed that the store had opened. But it had not. As soon as I stepped into the main aisle of the store, an employee saw me and asked what I was doing there.

I tried to talk my way out of it, but it was way before opening time, and the store clerk didn't believe that I had wandered in with my mother. He looked kind, and almost sorry that he had to turn me in, but he said we had to go to the office.

As a runaway, the word *office* held a special dread, just as it did at school. I knew it would involve calling my parents and was certain that I would be arrested on charges of sleeping in the store and shoplifting. I was petrified and shaking. I did not want to go, but the clerk gently took my arm, and I was too scared to resist.

The security manager in the office was a woman of average mother-age, not young but not yet old, and was very gracious to me. She was not at all angry as I had expected. She wanted to know what I was doing in the store and asked whether she could look through my backpack. She rifled through my things, item by item. Although I tried to lie at every turn, she gently refuted my story by questioning each item in my bag: the bagels, the clothes, a recent test I had in one of the books. She also wondered why I had books from a school in Elmhurst when I was in Long Island.

The manager assured me that I was not in trouble, and that kids hid in stores all the time. I didn't dare ask whether kids typically hid for five days. She was so kind to me. I could not believe that she was not harsh or mean. Again, I lied and said I had not hidden in the store. I pretended to not know what she was talking about, all the while sinking into a deeper despair that I was going to be sent home, and that my stepmother would make me pay for this dearly.

Finally, after about half an hour of me trying to convince her of my innocence, the manager told me that the motion sensor had gone off a few nights, so they knew I had slept in the store. I had no choice but to confess that I had run away. When she asked why, I said it was because my parents were mean to me, and that I could not go back. I started crying. She questioned the nice clothes I was wearing, and the new clothes in my bag. It seemed like she believed my lie that I had come in with them, that my grandmother had bought them.

But my lying did me no favors. I could see that because of my new clothes, the store manager did not believe that I was mistreated at home. And I could not confess to stealing the clothes, as I did not want to get locked up for shoplifting. I wanted the manager to call child protective services instead of my parents. I hung my head, knowing that I had blown my only chance of rescue by stealing nice clothes. They called my father.

An hour or so later, my father arrived in a huff, looking stressed and angry. He glared at me once before signing some papers. He didn't say a word to me. We collected my bike from the side of the mall and drove the forty minutes home in silence. I sat as far away from him as I could in the front seat. I was afraid to say a thing. Yet I knew I'd get worse from my stepmother. Finally, as we got closer to home, my father asked in an angry tone, *"Miért tette ezt?"*—"Why did you do this?"

I started sobbing. I was literally blubbering over my words. I told him how cruel my stepmother was to me all the time. How she threatened me, how she beat me with wooden spoons, belts, pots. How she made me go out without a coat when I ran errands. I pleaded with him to let me go somewhere else to live, anywhere. I told him I'd go to an orphanage or reform school, both places idle threats that Hungarian parents used on their kids, and my father probably used on me under duress from my stepmother. To my knowledge, neither place really existed, but I was desperate, and I wanted him to know it.

I begged him not to take me home, but he gave me his standard answer, one I had heard a hundred times before. "I'll take care of it," he said.

He never did, and worse, I knew he never would.

My father dropped me off at home unceremoniously and left for work. The apartment was cold and quiet. My stepmother sat as she always did in her recliner with her feet up. She did not get up when I came home. If she noticed that I was wearing new clothes, she didn't let on. She told me to sit down on the couch, something I was not usually allowed to do. I stared at the carpet, awaiting my fate. I was certain that she would beat me.

But to my shock, she didn't. There was no yelling, curses, or name-calling. No bringing up how much trouble I had caused the family, or how bad I made them look to people. There was no expression of worry or gladness in me being home safely. She simply asked me, in a low, humbled voice that I had never heard before, "*Miért szöktél el?*" Why had I run away?

I didn't say much, but I didn't have to. I lifted my head and, unflinching, looked her in the eye. She already knew the answer.

PART TWO

12

Sweet Sixteen

I could not believe my eyes or ears when I opened the door to our apartment.

"*Boldog szülinapot!*"—"Happy Birthday!" Uncle Joe, Aunt Veronka, and cousin Violet shouted, each giving me a hug. I was truly surprised. They made a big deal out of me turning sixteen, how tall I was, and how beautiful I looked. Even though I didn't believe their compliments, it made me blush and feel good. Then Uncle Joe handed me flowers and a card that he was trying to hide behind his back.

"*Ne mondd el az anyádnak.*"—"Don't tell your mother," he whispered as he handed me the card.

Following close behind were Nagyi and Nagyi-papa, who had just gotten off the elevator. Nagyi-papa was in a good mood. "*Boldog szülinapot! Milyen idős vagy, Penniké?*" Nagyi-papa knew how old I was, but he loved to joke around with us kids, pretending he could not remember. Smiling, I hugged him and gave Nagyi the customary kiss on the cheek. It felt like a real party, and we were just getting started. I could not believe it was for me.

The surprise party also explained why my stepmother had seemed more agitated than usual during the past week. She'd been busy enlisting the extended family to pick things up for her from Paprikas Weiss, the Hungarian importer, and the Magyar butchers in Manhattan. She had never mentioned what it was all about, but had been cursing me under her breath, as if I were to blame for her trouble. All the while, I had been running even more errands and doing more cleaning than my typical load. To top it off, she ordered me to cook up big pots of *csirkepaprikas* and *töltött káposzta*. The house had been tense, and she'd acted put-upon. Finally, I understood why.

In the twelve years I lived with my family, my stepmother had never acknowledged my birthday. Relatives may have given me presents when they saw me around my birthday, but I had never had a dinner, a party, or a cake just for me. Apparently, my aunt and uncle had called my stepmother and asked why they weren't invited for my sixteenth birthday, and she felt obligated to do something. No wonder my stepmother was so upset. She hated having to acknowledge me as a real part of the family.

After the party guests left, my father departed to feed Yago, the dog he kept at his gas station. Alone with my stepmother, I set about cleaning up under the full brunt of her wrath. She was furious at all the attention that I had gotten and began calling me every unsavory name in the book. But that was not all.

"*Adja ide az ajándékait!*"—"Let me see the gifts they gave you!" she ordered. *Oh, no,* I cringed. I knew what was coming. I had gotten some money in the cards, and I knew that my step-mother would take it, as she always took any cash that was given to me. My father never objected, because he never knew, and I never had the guts to tell him. Some Sweet Sixteen.

In the two years since I had run away to Sears, my home life had not gotten any better. But something inside me was changing, even if I was not sure what it was. I was still afraid of my stepmother, but I was less submissive, less obsequious to my stepmother's every whim and declaration.

Though she had been initially sheepish after I had run away, she eventually began openly resenting me. She let on that in her mind, I was the one at fault for leaving the family in a lurch and confusing my poor two-year-old sister by fleeing. She thought I was the "*önző fattyú*" (selfish bastard) who got away with everything, and who deserved reprimands instead of any sympathy.

Neither my father nor the rest of the family ever talked about me running away. It was like it never happened. My brother, who was nine at the time, never mentioned it at all, and at two, my sister was just happy to see me. My stepmother's sister, Aunt Sári, looked at me with understanding in her eyes, but because of the family's perpetual deference to my stepmother, she didn't ask why I'd run away. She let me know that she was unhappy I had stolen the clothes, and that she would tell her kids, my cousins, that I had gotten them as gifts. Aunt Sári was something of a mother figure in my eyes, and even though she knew I was in the wrong for stealing, I could see something like love in her eyes toward me. Something she did not let my stepmother see. Something I did not see from others.

Even Nagyi never brought up my running away, and she had strong opinions about everything, letting people know when she thought they were in the wrong. I guess everyone was just glad that I was back and that my stepmother had someone to help her around the house. When I was at Sears, I had never really thought of how they would have managed if I had not come back.

Much to my surprise, my father had searched for me himself when I'd turned up missing. He had gone to the school and looked in every room. He had talked to people in our building, people on our block, but none of them had seen me. A few mentioned my forays out in the cold in the thin white sweater. Knowing he knew about this had given me the liberty to stop wearing the sweater, without even asking. By my family's standards, this in itself was a rebellion.

None of my teachers said anything about my running away. At school, I threw myself into my studies as a distraction from the stress at home. The one thing I had learned from running away, and everyone's reaction to it, was that no one would help me. No one really cared why I ran away, or whether I was unhappy, unsafe, or desperate. Not the school, not my father, not the extended family. This was sobering. But I found a bright side. Because I had combined seventh and eighth grade in the Advanced Placement program, I could graduate high school a year early. If I was careful with my electives, and chose classes that I needed to graduate, I could carve off an additional six months—and graduate at sixteen and a half.

That's exactly what I set myself up to do.

Underneath my resolve, I was still a teenager, and badly wanted normal teenage things. I wanted to fit in, to have friends, a boyfriend maybe. I wanted some freedom, and respect, and the ability to have my own life. I felt like an indentured servant, while people around me looked like they were having a good time. The kids on my block were constantly inviting me to parties, to the park, to the cemetery—a hangout place for young people in the city—but I was not allowed to go. The girls around my age had boyfriends, and clothes. They were dropping acid, smoking pot, and listening to great music. It all sounded so fun, except for the drugs. They never appealed to me because I had seen what drinking had done to my dad. The last thing I wanted was to be anything like him.

One day soon after my party, I was coming home from getting groceries and noticed a "Help Wanted" sign in a tiny travel agency on Thirty-Seventh Avenue. It wasn't a very inviting place—sterile, narrow, with industrial desks like teachers had at school, covered with piles of papers, with posters of faraway places on the walls. But when I ventured into the establishment, I felt like I was walking onto a cruise ship, my eyes aglow with possibility. There was a lone man working behind one of the desks, and he motioned for me to wait as he finished his phone call. I waited nervously, as I had no idea what I'd say, or how I could possibly be allowed to work. But I at least had to try.

I mumbled something about being a senior at Newtown High, and having taken a travel agency class, and loving to travel. He shook my hand, treating me like I was a real job applicant, even though I was clutching a bag of groceries to my chest. He had me sit, and he explained the business, none of which made any sense to me. But I perked up when he explained that he needed someone just part-time, maybe ten to fifteen hours a week, to call on retired people for the bus tour that they did to Atlantic City. He told me that the pay was two dollars an hour and that I could start Saturday. I could not believe it. Was it that easy to get a job? I promised to speak to my parents and get back to him the next day.

I went home walking on air and grinning from cheek to cheek. I could not believe my luck. I now had to figure out how to get my stepmother to allow it. She regularly put the kibosh on anything that was fun for me unless it benefited her in some way. I could go to someone's house, if I took my brother, or I could visit Uncle Joe, if my stepmother would be at Nagyi's summer house at the same time. I knew that my stepmother would not like it if I wasn't at her disposal to watch my sister after school or during summer vacation, but I did not care. I had to do this.

That night, my father came home early, while it was still light. I could hear him whistling down the long hallway to our apartment, which told me he was in a good mood. He hung his hat in the dining room and came into the kitchen to greet me with his usual, "How are you, Chicken?"

That's when I pounced. "Dad, there's a travel agency on Thirty-Seventh that needs a part-time clerk a few hours a week. I'd really like to work there. Is it okay with you?"

"Fine, Chicken," he said, "if you want to work, work. Work is good for you," or something like that. With that, he left the kitchen to greet my stepmother and siblings, and I smiled to myself as I warmed up his dinner. I had never gone around my stepmother like this before, getting permission from him when I knew that she wouldn't approve. That was bold for me. Certainly, there was no turning back now.

I took the job, and I was ecstatic. Not only did I have employment, but it also looked like I could graduate in just one more semester. I had no idea what I'd do after graduation . . . I could not see that far ahead. I had no role models, and no one spoke to me about possible careers. Nonetheless, I was excited about finishing school.

I was done with classes at noon and started at the travel agency right after school. It was easy work, and I caught on in no time. The job itself was not that interesting, but being out of the house and doing something on my own, out from under my stepmother's thumb, was liberating. It turned out that I was good at talking to people on the phone. They liked me at that little agency, and I was so proud of myself. When I got my first paycheck, I walked right across the street and opened a bank account, depositing my whole check. I didn't wait for parental permission and take a chance that my stepmother would abscond with my paycheck. It was mine, and I was not letting it go.

Even though I was home every day by five, and it was still light enough to take my sister out or get groceries, my stepmother soon went on a tirade about my new job. I was not there when she needed me. Kitti had no one to play with. Steven did not have food after school. The laundry did not get done. I did not get her medicine before the pharmacy closed, blah, blah, blah. Her complaining went on for a few weeks, but my father kept brushing it off.

While my parents fought, my brother and sister took no notice. They just lay down on the living room rug, watching the TV as if nothing was going on around them. They were both loved and coddled, and got everything they needed. They never did anything wrong, and never had to help around the house. They managed to ignore everything else that did not concern them.

My stepmother kept bringing up reasons why I should quit my job. My father would bat them away with easy answers that showed he didn't want to be bothered by the topic and didn't see why it was a problem. It wasn't quite that he approved of my job. He just wanted peace. There was no real problem, but as usual, my stepmother was bound and determined to create one.

One night, the air in the apartment reverberated with tension. My stepmother was in a foul mood, and I tried to stay out of her way. My father was later than usual getting home. When he finally arrived, he was quiet and irritable, answering my stepmother with one-word, evasive answers. They started arguing, their voices rising. She started complaining about all the things I was doing wrong and what a good-for-nothing I was. The whole time, I was hiding in the kitchen, hoping not to be noticed. Then my stepmother threw out an astute argument that I had never thought of before.

"*Megórültél?*"—"Are you crazy?" she said to my father. "Why are you letting her work? So she can save up some money and run away again?"

My father started yelling at my stepmother, "*Mit akarsz nó?*"—"What do you want, woman? Do you want me to beat her to death, is that what you want?"

This time, my brother and sister started yelling back at them to quiet down. My father jumped up, stomped into the kitchen, and pulled me by the hair into the living room. He dragged me right in front of my mother, and asked, "*Ez az, amit akarsz?*"—"Is that what you want?" "*Hogy halálra verjem?*"—"You want me to beat her to death, would that make you happy?"

Soon, he started slapping me across the face, still holding me by the hair. During his rampage, my stepmother, brother, and sister all screamed at him and tried to make him stop. My stepmother was trying to get up from her chair but couldn't do so fast enough. For me, the room seemed to be spinning. I could not hear, and I felt like I could not breathe. He slapped my face with his big, rough hands, and held me up by my hair as I tried to get away. He disgusting breath was sour on my tear-stained face. The din reached a new crescendo as everyone was yelling but no one could hear.

In a flash, it was over. I was crying and shaking, hurting from my hair being pulled and my face slapped. Dizzy, I held my throbbing head. I knew that I could not go on like this. I just could not. It was not getting better. It was getting worse.

When I calmed down enough to think, I realized that my stepmother was totally dependent on me to take care of my four-year-old sister and the house—and this was the closest that she would come to admitting it. I had never thought of running away again, because I considered the Sears misadventure an epic failure. But I was wrong. I had accomplished a lot—I just hadn't seen it. That I had successfully figured out a place to go, and a means to get there, and survived on my own for five days—safely. That even though school was a grind, I was almost through—with decent grades, no less. That I had found a job on my first try.

My stepmother won the battle that night, and I was forced to quit my job. But she had planted a seed in my mind. I would win this war if it killed me.

13

The Sykes

My brother and I ran through the scraggly backyards and alleyways of the tall buildings that lined our neighborhood, jumping fences to avoid being caught. It was good to be outside and horsing around. There were not many places to play in the city, so we amused ourselves where we could, even if it might result in a telling-off by the tenants or building supers. When my brother wanted to go out to play, I was tasked with tagging along to "watch" him and keep him safe. We did whatever he wanted, which was inevitably boy stuff. Sometimes we were joined by a couple of other kids who lived in a basement apartment directly across the street from us.

They were a ragtag bunch and usually traveled in a pack, two boys and a teenage sister. Niven Sykes was about my brother's age, eleven, and reminded me of the Artful Dodger character from Dickens's *Oliver Twist* in his demeanor and mannerisms. He was streetwise, filthy, and rough around the edges. Short for his age, hardened and chunky, Niven had long, oily hair that obscured half his face. A lit cigarette usually hung out of the other half. He seemed to be always scheming, and always had something that he'd gotten for free. He traveled with his little brother, Shane, who was around five or six, and equally urchin-like and dirty.

Sometimes Fiona, the thirteen-year-old sister, came with them. She seemed much older, and far too seasoned for her young age. She was shorter than me, at maybe five feet, and thinly built, with wavy shoulder-length hair cut into a trendy shag. With her large gold hoop earrings and big green, mascaraed eyes and a sly smile, she always looked like she was getting away with something. She was quiet when Niven was around but loquacious and in charge when it was just us girls.

The Sykes kids had two older sisters who lived at home. The oldest sister, who was nineteen, worked at the A&P on Northern Boulevard. The next-oldest sister, Molly, was the pretty one, always smiling and happy, and didn't appear to do much. She went out a lot, and always seemed to have a new boyfriend. There was no father in the Sykes family, not even in reference, and the mother was rarely around. The kids seemed to be running things.

Whenever they saw my brother and me, the Sykes kids would cross over to our side of the street, and the boys would start in on some game. Fiona and I were usually left to ourselves. At first, I was a bit afraid of her. She was outgoing, worldly, and confident—and had a boyfriend. She had a knowing look about her, like she'd been around the world and maybe had already had sex. She was unlike anyone I knew. I, on the other hand, was timid, downcast, and afraid to open up. I was ashamed of my clothes, my shabby looks, and of how uncool I was. I kept my eyes on the ground and my hair in my face, hoping to hide from her and the world. I would have never initiated a conversation, let alone a friendship, with anyone cool like her, for fear of rejection. I was also afraid to engage with others who might find out about my horrid "secret" home life. Little did I know that anyone could have read my secrets in my burdened walk and on my sad face.

Fiona was not the least bit reticent in asking about our family, already implying that it was not normal. She asked why I had to perpetually watch my brother, who was older than her brother, who did what he wanted. She wanted to know why I had to do whatever my brother wanted, and why we spoke a funny language. She wanted to know why I couldn't hang out without him, why I couldn't go to the park with her. She wanted to know about my cold stepmother, whom Fiona sometimes saw scowling at the world as she limped down the street.

The Sykes kids were fun to be with because they were so totally free, completely unsupervised and unrestrained by rules, manners, or right and wrong. They laughed riotously all the time. With them, my brother and I did things that we were not allowed to do: scale rooftops, explore basements, and climb fences into shut-off backyards and alleys. The older Sykes kids smoked, and all the siblings cursed habitually like drunken sailors, even little Shane. They were out all hours of the night. They stole milk from the trucks that were double-parked for milk deliveries in the buildings. They took newspapers from apartment lobbies, and whole brown bags of bread left outside delis in the dawn hours. Nothing scared them.

I was reticent to divulge my home situation to Fiona because I was embarrassed and afraid. I figured that because my home life was so unbelievable, one of the Sykes kids would surely ask my stepmother whether the fantastical stories were true. That would be a disaster, as my stepmother would both deny it and retaliate against me fiercely. Also, I continued to carry shame that my home life was somehow my fault, and that I should be able to do something about it. I also did not want the Sykes kids to make fun of me if they found out the truth.

As it turned out, the Sykeses' family situation was no picnic either. They had a single mother and lived on welfare, something my family had always looked down upon. We probably would have qualified for welfare ourselves, and I would have welcomed it. But it was not something that my parents would have ever considered. In fact, they were arrogant about it. They considered people on welfare to be trash who could not work for a living and provide for their families.

The Sykeses' apartment was usually reserved for the super of the building, and it seemed barely livable. It had tiny, dark rooms, few windows, and bare floors. The windows were cracked and did not close all the way, and the door had no lock. The Sykes clan did not have much, and what they had was old and ratty. I had no idea where they all slept, as they did not have enough beds to go around.

When I finally did get to meet Mrs. Sykes, I found that she was a kind, sweet, loving person. She was also a drinker and looked much older than she was. I knew they were Irish, which was hard to miss, as they all had similar dark reddish-auburn hair, freckled skin, and green eyes. But the family members never discussed their past. Mrs. Sykes disappeared for weeks at a time when the welfare check came. Only Niven knew where she was, so he could get some money from her for dinner or take Shane to her when he cried for his mother. If someone needed to get a message to Mrs. Sykes, they sent Niven. He seemed to be the man about the place. The kids never mentioned their father.

Mrs. Sykes was always pleasant when she was around, but it was rare. She would show up with Niven and a few bags of groceries . . . milk, cornflakes, macaroni, a big block of Velveeta cheese, a few loaves of white bread. She was happy to see everyone, chatting to us in her raspy, smoker's voice and coughing up a storm. She laughed easily at the boys' shenanigans and delighted in the girls' new clothes or dance moves. She made mouthwatering meals out of nothing at all, ground beef and Worcestershire sauce in a cast-iron skillet, and always shared what little the family had. Mrs. Sykes made me feel welcome.

The girls were so much fun and had a life in them that belied their scarce means. They talked about boys and clothes and showed off their pretty new bras and how to push things around in them for greater effect. They knew all the new dance moves and taught me "The Hustle." The girls told stories and laughed about people and incidents like a real family. They chatted about makeup and new earrings, and dainty tops that showed off midriffs and cleavage.

Gradually, my longing to be open—and be accepted—got the better of me, and I slowly started telling Fiona some details of my story. Her many questions made clear that she did not get it. Why didn't my dad do anything? Why didn't my brother defend me? Why didn't Steven have to do chores or run errands? If I did all the work, why did my stepmother still hit me? Why didn't I tell anyone?

Fiona was challenging the only life I knew, as if I had a choice. As if I wanted it that way. Didn't she remember that I had tried to run away? I didn't really have answers for her, because there weren't any. That was the agony of it. I was afraid to do anything. Living in terror made it harder to even *dare* to tell anyone, even when asked. It was why I had never told anyone before. I never imagined that someone like Fiona would become such an important influence in my life.

Although I begged Fiona not to tell anyone, she did. The next time I saw her brother Niven, he didn't even pretend not to know my story. He told me straight out that I should just leave home. "Leave?" I asked. "And go where?" He shrugged. "Anywhere." His world was so much bigger than mine, and he acted as if he feared nothing. My world was so tiny, and I feared everything. I especially feared that Niven would tell my brother that he knew about our family situation. If Niven did so, my brother would surely tell my stepmother, and it would bring down her wrath in ways that made me shudder. I felt worse off for speaking up, wishing there was a way to turn back the clock. I quite literally shook with despair.

But as far as I knew, no one told my stepmother, and life went on. But after hanging out with Fiona, I was having a harder time with the isolation and drudgery at home—things that I had just accepted before. After the big fight about my job, I knew I had to do something, but I did not quite know a way out. Something was brewing inside me, though. I could feel it.

One hot, languid August night, I sat reading on the bedroom windowsill by the streetlight, as I liked to do, when Fiona, Niven, and a few others I knew from the neighborhood approached from down the street. They were going to the cemetery, one of their frequent after-dark hangouts. I whispered down to them as they called up to me, laughing at their jokes and relaxing into a smile at their cheer and freedom. It was fun to just be included, although I feared being found out at any moment.

After a while, they said to me, "Come with us."

"No, no, I can't. I'm not allowed out."

"Just walk out the door," they said. "What's the worst that can happen?"

I laughed. They obviously didn't know my stepmother.

But they did not let it go. I kept shaking my head, even as excitement grew in my stomach. They kept at it with suggestions: "Take a key and come back before anyone gets up." No, my stepmother would see my empty bed when she came to check on my brother. They would wake up. I would be found out and punished.

"So what?" they said. "You get punished anyway." That gave me pause. They were right.

Finally, they said, "Just leave."

"Leave?" I asked. "What do you mean, leave?"

"Pack a bag and throw it down to us."

Niven and Fiona Sykes said I could live with them. I could pay them rent from my travel agency money.

"What is your mother going to say?" I asked.

"She likes you," they said. "It will be okay, we promise, and she can use the extra cash." They mapped it out for me. I could continue going to school like nothing ever happened and get a job after school to support myself. Anyway, I'd be done with school in December, which was only four and a half months away.

I sat there on my windowsill in the dead heat of the night and thought it through, while Niven and Fiona smoked cigarettes below, waiting for me to decide. They were young, and foolish, and directionless, I knew that. But they were on to something. I had nothing to gain by staying, and nothing to lose by leaving. I was too naive to know how easily girls like me could get lost on the streets of New York City—to drugs, pregnancy, gangs, shysters, rape, or sheer stupidity. But ignorance was my bliss, and the more I thought about living with the Sykes family, the happier I got.

"All right," I said, "I'm coming."

They let out a quiet cheer. But if I was going, I wanted to leave something that left no doubt about why. I began writing a note, telling my stepmother that she was a witch, and that I was tired of being her servant. My anger came boiling out, and I tried to be as mean I as could in my note. In that moment, I was not thinking of my brother, whom I had spent most of my time with, or my sister, whom I had practically raised. I was not thinking of my father either. He did not care about me anyway. That night, the only thing I thought about was becoming free.

Because I was leaving home for good, it would not have mattered if I had walked out the front door, except that maybe someone would have woken up. But I took the hard way out—the window. The problem was, I was afraid of heights, and it looked like a long way down. It was far enough to break a leg, and I did not want that. I talked back and forth with the kids, their cigarettes tips glowing in the dark. They suggested that I tie some pant legs together to the radiator, which was in front of the window, and lower myself down. That's exactly what I did.

It took me a while to make this rope, which would hold my weight and take me to freedom. My pants were thick corduroy or velvet, the fashion in the '70s and always on sale at Alexander's. The first pair to go on the rope was my purple velvet pants, which had a sequin rose on the front. I hated those pants, mostly because they were four sizes too big, and no one at my school wore anything but denim and T-shirts. The velvet pants were hard to tie up, and even harder to attach to the radiator, but I got the job done.

I was surprised that my stepmother, who had sonar hearing, did not hear any of this. Or maybe she did but was too tired or sore from her arthritis to get up. Not a peep from my brother sleeping eight feet away from the window. To me, time ticked ever so slowly during this window caper, but it was probably just fifteen minutes. I packed my book bag with some papers and clothes, leaving my life's worth of report cards and school things behind. Then I threw the bag down to my friends waiting below.

I shook with excitement and fear. Time to climb out the window.

It was harder than I thought, even with the pants-rope and

my friends promising to catch me. My flight down the rope had starts and stops as I caught my breath and pulled back onto the windowsill. Some of my friends below were getting restless and wanted to leave for the cemetery without me. We lived on a busy street, with people walking around, but no one seemed to notice me at the window above.

Finally, I had no choice. I had to get down that rope—or be found out by my stepmother and left without my friends.

Sitting on the windowsill, I slowly planted my right leg out of the window and held tightly onto the pants. Despite trembling with fear, I inched my bottom out as I clutched the rope to my chest. Then I brought my second leg out. The next thing I knew, I was completely out of the window, clutched against the coarse brick building. To my horror, I soon ran out of pants-rope—even though I was far from being all the way down. My heart was pounding in my chest, drowning out all possible thoughts or sound. When I came to my senses, I heard my friends calling out.

"Let go! Let go! We'll catch you."

But my window was over an alleyway, with two iron banisters right under me. I was afraid I'd fall on them and break my neck.

"We have you," my friends said. "We'll catch you—we promise."

My bones were shaking with fear. Life had taught me to never trust anyone. How could I trust them? I didn't. I knew who they were. They were fickle kids, out for a good time, and might not be the solid friends they made themselves out to be. I might literally be jumping from the frying pan to the fire. But I could not live this way anymore. I knew that if I was ever going to get out of my situation, if my life was ever going to get better, it had to be my doing. The short rope was the only thing stopping me.

I let go.

14

The Freedom Train

I awoke to the sound of traffic and peeked timidly out the window of Fiona Sykes's tiny bedroom. To my horror, I could see the imposing figure of my stepmother, in her blue terry cloth bathrobe, standing in my bedroom window across the street. With a scowl on her face, she was untying the pants-rope dangling from the window. I could only imagine what she might be saying: "*Semmire sem jó kurva!*"—"Good-for-nothing whore!"

It had only been several hours since I'd run away from home, and already my stepmother seemed to be looking straight down at me. Even though I was certain that she could not see me through the bushes, and the curtains framing the Sykeses' apartment window, I stepped back with a gasp. Then I quickly awakened Fiona, who hurried to the window to look for herself. "She looks mad," Fiona said. I was shaking. Fiona held my arms and looked me in the eye: "You are safe here. She cannot get you. We won't let her in, I promise."

After my escape down the window the previous night, my friends and I had run the few blocks to the park on Seventy-Eighth Street before stopping to catch our breath. We did not know whether anyone had heard us or might follow us to try to bring me back. Once we were convinced that we were in the clear, there were whoops and hollers as everyone high-fived and hugged me, welcoming me to the group. The kids were from the surrounding neighborhoods, mostly Irish American, an Armenian, a Czech, but thankfully no other Hungarians. If there had been, my whereabouts would have certainly gotten back to my stepmother.

Some of the kids I knew from middle or high school, some from just seeing them on the street. Some I had never even seen before. Most were around my age, some younger, a few older, all with nowhere else to be. It was my first time being with a group of people my age. I was overwhelmed with a range of emotions . . . fear, excitement, anticipation—I could hardly think straight. From my bedroom window, we had set off on a long trek to St. Michael's Cemetery, where we'd sat around the tombstones for hours, laughing, talking, and joking around. We got back to the Sykeses' place in the wee hours of the morning, and I fell fast asleep on one of the narrow cots in the bedroom.

I figured that my stepmother—with my brother's help—probably had a good idea where I was. The prospect of running into her terrified me, so Fiona and Niven showed me how to exit their apartment in a way that I would not be seen on our street. Their apartment had a back door to the basement, which had another door to an alley behind the building. It was sometimes dark and creepy out there, but if I exited into the backyard and climbed a short fence, I would end up behind a building on an entirely different block one street over and could weave through that alley without being seen.

Tettem magam szűkös. I was making myself scarce, as we said in Hungarian. Not being seen became my preoccupation.

Although I was still in a daze at what I had done, and unaccustomed to my new, unconventional surroundings, living with the Sykes family was fun. Despite their meager apartment, it felt like a real home. The Hungarian homes of my youth had always seemed so formal. There had been breakable stuff everywhere, so we couldn't run around. We also had to be quiet because of the neighbors, and we children had to keep to ourselves. Since the Hungarians of my youth measured wealth in the things they displayed, belongings always seemed more precious than the people in our homes. We may have been more orderly, or had nicer furniture and more space at my home, but the Sykes family had something else that I could not quite put my finger on. They seemed *normal* and happy, almost joyous when Mrs. Sykes was around. They were the closest I had felt to really belonging since I'd been taken away from Aunt Charlotte twelve years ago.

Often the Sykes family would gather in their tiny kitchen to hear what everyone had to say. No nagging or bickering, just loving acceptance and warm family banter, as if nothing else mattered, as if they weren't poor and living in a shabby apartment. They joked around with each other or played dance music while everyone sang along or moved to the beat, unlike the monotone stillness or drone of the TV at my house. Instead of ordering me around or telling me off, the Sykes family would ask my opinions and ask about my day, whom I had met, or what I thought of the pop star of the day. I felt like I mattered there.

True to Fiona's word, Mrs. Sykes was happy to have me, and I fit right in. She did not have any rules for me like my Hungarian relatives did. No one there asked me to do any housework, although being so used to it, I did the dishes and swept the kitchen without being prompted and was glad to do it. Once it was clear that my parents weren't going to try to bring me back, I felt like I could exhale for the first time.

My senior year of high school started two weeks after I left home. I wondered whether not living at home would be a problem for school officials, but it wasn't. Just like when I ran away to Sears, no one seemed to notice—and I went to classes as if nothing had ever happened. Hungarian parents didn't get involved in school. You were expected to go, and take care of anything school-related, so I was used to managing everything on my own. Classes started at 7 a.m., which was hard to wake up for now that I was going out with my new friends every night. About once a week, we would walk all the way to the cemetery, which was about twenty-five blocks away. But most of the time we just went to the park nearby until people got bored, tired, or left because of a curfew. The high school had a rule that if you were late more than five times, they would drop your first class, which I could not let happen, as I needed it to graduate. Somehow I skated by, although I'm sure that I was late more than five times. For a change, things seemed to be going my way.

The avenue that intersected my block was lined with shops and restaurants, where I went door to door looking for work after school. My school friend Asli worked in a shop called the Co-Op, run by Jacob Weck, a young guy with black-rimmed glasses and short hair. Jacob sold all sorts of new things that had slight defects, called "seconds"—the paint was nicked or a seam not straight— but otherwise were perfectly usable, and could be sold for much cheaper than Woolworths on Eighty-Second Street. He also imported household items that attracted immigrant housewives looking for a bargain. Signs and prices were hand-painted on cardboard, and the staff was made up of high school kids like me to keep the prices low and energy high. As a referral from Asli, whom Jacob had a crush on, I was hired on the spot. Only two weeks into life on my own, I seemed set. I had a place to live, a job, and I was a senior in high school with four months to go.

After a few weeks of work, I went on a shopping spree, buying cute new clothes and shoes from the little boutiques that dotted Thirty-Seventh Avenue. I favored Faded Glory jeans, skimpy little tops, and nicer shirts from Fields department store. I also had Fiona take me to get my ears pierced at a little jeweler near their house. It was nice to have money to spend on anything I wanted. In Hungarian homes, there were all kinds of rules about how girls should dress, like not showing too much flesh, or wearing jewelry and makeup. These were things I no longer had to worry about, and I didn't.

Food in the neighborhood was cheap, and I ate ice cream, bagels, Chinese rice with a red gravy, and pizza to my heart's content. I was very thin and all my clothes were loose, so I could afford to gain weight. I ate like crazy. My job was near a Dairy Queen, where I became a regular customer. I didn't miss the Hungarian food. After a month or so, one of the boys in our group said I was looking better since I had put on a few pounds. I was starting to look and feel like a regular teenager. I was having fun, and my confidence outside of school was starting to blossom.

I met my first boyfriend at Budd's, a dive bar on Thirty-Seventh Avenue where I sometimes went with Molly, Fiona's older sister, to drink tequila sunrises and dance "The Hustle." The bouncers at Budd's never proofed anyone. They were there to break up fights, not keep out the underaged. At first, it felt funny to be in a bar. Because of my stepmother's rants, not to mention my father's drinking issues, I thought bars were dark dens of depravity. "*Megy a kocsmába*"—going to the bar—was something that decent Hungarians didn't do, according to my stepmother. But the people I met at Budd's were decent, working-class, and polite, even if a little flirty.

One night, I recognized Roger standing around a group of

other young men whom I had seen at the park. He sidled over with his beer to say hello. I knew him to be "good people," a nice guy, trustworthy, always happy, always laid-back. We chatted for a bit before he asked whether he could walk me home, as I was leaving early to get up for school the next day.

By the time we walked the three blocks to the Sykeses' place, he had asked me out, which had made me smile, but his happiness was much more exuberant. He whooped a jumping "right on," ecstatic that I had said yes. Before I agreed, though, I made sure he understood that I was still in school and supporting myself, and only sixteen. Although he was twenty-three, he said he didn't mind that I was still "jailbait," as they called girls my age, or that my work and school would leave us very little time. He also didn't mind when I told him I had just left home, and that I did not want to have sex or do drugs, start smoking, or get tied down with a baby. He was fine with all this and told me I was beautiful. I'm not sure I believed him, but I liked hearing it.

Roger still lived at home with his parents in a nice apartment on Seventy-Sixth Street. He neither worked nor went to school, something that struck me as unusual. He just "hung out," and he seemed happy with that. His family's place was warm and welcoming, full of art, records, and books, which I loved, as we had few books at my old home, and none at the Sykeses' apartment. Roger's parents had a pair of comfortable wingback chairs for reading, with a big lamp between them. Roger's father was often there, reading the paper in one of the chairs when I would come over. Roger's mother, Ruth, worked for Elektra Records, which everyone considered a big deal. She gave us free concert tickets, albums, and backstage passes. We saw performers like Queen, James Taylor, The Who, Alice Cooper, and Kiss before these bands became popular.

A few months later, Roger said he loved me—in the very same scruffy bar where we had met. True to his word, he never pressured me to have sex or smoke pot, both of which we eventually did, not because he asked me to but because I wanted to fit in.

The little I knew about sex came from whispering with the girls at school and seeing the sex scene in the rock opera *Tommy*. It was more anecdotal than clinical. We never talked about sex at home, and I really didn't know much about it, except that I could get pregnant if I wasn't careful. I was not exactly sure how I was supposed to be careful, but I assumed my boyfriend would know. I wanted to do what everyone else was doing, except drugs. Roger just wanted to be with me and went along with whatever I wanted. He truly accepted me unconditionally, something I had never experienced before.

Whenever I went to their house, Mr. and Mrs. Manne were warm, welcoming, and accepting. They never asked questions about why I wasn't living at home, and I never felt judged. They were impressed that I spoke Hungarian, as they had Hungarian friends and heard it was a hard language to learn. "*Köszönöm a vacsorát*," I said to them, showing off a bit. I found myself going over there as often as I could.

Living with the Sykes had been fun at first but had become problematic once I got on my feet. Initially, they were happy with my twenty dollars a week for room and board, although there was never food in the house. But after I'd gotten a job, they were always bumming money for a Coke, or cigarettes, or milk, and never paying it back. Since I had all new clothes, and they didn't, shirts would disappear from my closet and not be returned. I would buy shampoo, but it would be gone when I went to use it.

"*Isten verje meg!*" I'd curse in Hungarian so they couldn't understand me. They thought I owed them since I was living there, and there was not much I could do. I tried putting a lock on my closet, but they quickly figured out how to open it. I started storing my stuff at Roger's place, and fortunately, his parents didn't bat an eye.

Since I lived right across the street from my family, I was always on guard about bumping into my parents. For the first few months after I left home, I managed to avoid them completely by arriving and leaving through the back alleys. But one day, I came out of the candy store at the corner, and there was my stepmother on the sidewalk, as if she were waiting for me. She glared at me and nearly spat at me in English, "If you left my house, you get out of my neighborhood." I was stunned and shaking in fear as I always did around her. "*Fattyú!*"— "Bastard!" she added. Too shocked to speak, I turned and walked the other way.

Then, three months later, as I was closing the Co-Op, I saw my father down the street, about to walk past the shop. "*Nem lát engem, nem lát engem.*"—"Don't see me," I repeated to myself as I waited for him to pass. I turned around to face the store, tugging on the metal security gate, and pretended not to see him. He walked past without stopping as my heart beat loudly in my chest. I was not sure what I would have said to him. I knew he'd be angry with me for leaving, and even angrier for not talking to him, but in my mind, he had let me down, not the other way around. I had nothing to say to him.

That December, in 1975, I completed high school. Mrs. Manne, Roger's mom, took time off work to come to my graduation with Roger and me, so I'd have a "parent" there to see me walk across the stage. I was graduating early, even though my stepmother always told me that I was "*buta*" (stupid), "*lusta*" (lazy), and "*egy senki*" (a nobody). I did not feel like any of those things that day. I felt victorious, accomplished, and for a moment, I forgot who she had always told me I was. Before the ceremony, my diploma had been withheld because of a lost textbook that I swore I'd returned. But Mrs. Manne just paid the five dollars for it, an exorbitant amount for me, so that I could go home with my diploma. I could not believe people were so kind. I was still not used to it.

I liked Roger, but I did not understand his unconditional love. All I saw was that he did not have a job, and that he was not looking for one either. That he still lived with his parents. I had also learned that it had taken him five high schools to graduate. All he did all day was pretend-play his electric guitar, tossing his Jew-fro around like Jimmy Page or Pete Townshend. I did not fully appreciate his acceptance, and his hope of a shared life. I only saw that all his friends had menial jobs, like working in a deli or driving a delivery truck, and that they chased girls or drank with every spare dollar they had, while Roger waited for me faithfully to get out of work so we could walk to the park or take the train to a concert. Somehow this was not sitting right with me.

Working and saving my earnings were of the utmost importance to me, although I wasn't sure where the drive had come from. Maybe it had come from seeing my parents' unaccomplished lives or seeing other Hungarians who had worked hard and socked away money for a rainy day. The other Hungarians I knew were industrious. Maybe it had come from seeing the dismal conditions around me at the Sykeses' place, or from my own lack of food and clothing while growing up. Wherever my drive had come from, I knew I needed a job to support myself. I no longer wanted to be the one who always got less: less food, less clothing, or less choices. Soon after I graduated high school, I broke up with Roger. I wanted more. I wanted to go places.

But little did I know that the next place I went would be the biggest mistake of my life.

15

The IHOP

Growing up in Jackson Heights, I loved to eat at the International House of Pancakes on Northern Boulevard. The women of the family adored the Americana novelty of the blue-roofed, A-frame building, the cute orange uniforms and the six flavors of pancake syrup on each table. My father wasn't quite so enthusiastic, registering his disgust at the non-Hungarian food with grunts and complaints. He hated eating anything American, unless it was steak, burned. He drove us to the IHOP grudgingly and sat stewing the whole time. My stepmother and Aunt Sári did not go for fine dining but instead for the kitschy atmosphere and large portions. Excessively American places like the IHOP, Red Lobster, and the Sizzler seemed somewhat exotic to their Hungarian senses. My stepmother also favored the IHOP because Aunt Sári had worked there part-time before my cousin Tamas was born. She had told us about all the great food on the menu and slipped us a few things for free when we'd come on her shift.

When I graduated high school, that's where I wanted to work.

The IHOP was bright and cheery, and a fun place to eat with its variety of sweet breakfast food—pancakes, waffles, and crepes. My favorite was French toast, which was made with thick-cut

"Texas" bread and grilled in butter and served with juicy pork sausage with a ball of whipped butter and powdered sugar on top. It was heaven. When I walked in on a busy Monday night in search of a job, I was told to fill out an application, which stated clearly that they did not employ anyone under eighteen. But I crossed that out. Because restaurants were always short-staffed, I was hired as a hostess right away and told to show up Friday night for the weekend night shift. I had just gotten my high school diploma, but the real schooling was about to begin.

The IHOP was a long walk from the Sykeses' place, but it was worth it. I was happy for the busy weekend shifts, where I was constantly meeting new people. I had liked belonging to the group of friends that I'd made through Fiona, but we never did much, beyond "hanging out" at the park. And that routine was getting old. No one was old enough to do anything interesting, no one worked, very few went to school, and no one seemed concerned about the future. I was outgrowing it, and my job at the IHOP was a natural excuse to break away from them.

The IHOP was usually busy, and always short-staffed, which worked in my favor, or so I thought. The patrons were always in a good mood, and I enjoyed greeting them and making them happy, which quickly ingratiated me with the boss. The job came with free food, a dream to a kid who was always hungry. I imagined eating everything on the menu, things I'd never had before, like chocolate-chip pancakes, strawberry waffles with whipped cream, and cheese omelets. The IHOP even served *palacsinta*, the thin Hungarian pancakes that Nagyi used to make, but they called them German pancakes. Most people I knew had never even heard of Hungary, so calling them Hungarian pancakes would have been a hard sell. When I'd gone to the IHOP as a kid, my stepmother had always ordered for me, and I usually had gotten the cheapest thing on the menu, a western sandwich. It seemed like I had come a long way since those days. Now I was wearing one of those cute orange uniforms—which I had shortened quite a bit—and walked around importantly seating people and pouring their coffee.

Restaurant work was hard work, but the camaraderie of the staff, particularly during rush periods, made it worthwhile. All of us labored side by side, ate meals together, heard each other's stories, and depended on each other to get the job done, as the waitresses' tips depended on good service. But there was a pecking order. An elderly Italian waitress named Mrs. Rivetti, who was heavy, and slow because of her arthritis, was said to have ties to the mob, which meant that no one messed with her. She did what she wanted, and mostly got away with it. Most of the other wait- resses were Irish, and somehow related to each other, and ranged from youngish to middle-aged, all already hardened by life.

There was Susan, in her early twenties, old to me, and a single mother of two. There was young Anita, also a single mother, who still lived at home with her parents and played tennis when not working. There was Ann, a thin, older woman with short hair and a pockmarked face who was picked up by different gentlemen at the end of her night shifts. But the most fearful and in charge was Irene. She had the seniority and had gotten five or six of the others their jobs, making them loyal and faithful to her every command. Irene was direct and bossy but called me "love" with her beautiful Irish brogue, which made it all right. "Luv, fetch me a fresh pot of coffee, wouldya now?" She made me feel like a part of the crew. She even ordered my dinner from the cooks, who tended to ignore me. I was young and new, a lowly hostess, and not worth their time.

Irene was Irish, from the old country, with a thick accent and a smoker's cough. She had a daughter in Ireland being raised by her mother and sent money back regularly. Irene taught me the rules of the road, such as not getting too friendly with a customer who was already "spoken for." Although Irene hadn't liked me at first because I was not hired through her, her mothering instincts took over and she began taking me under her wing. I loved the attention and didn't mind the mothering—something I did not get at the Sykeses' place or at my old home. With her help, the waitresses at the IHOP became my surrogate family.

All those years doing my stepmother's work had created a work ethic in me that got me noticed. I was good, I was fast, and I was happy to be there. Two weeks in, I was offered a coveted job as a waitress, put forth by Irene to the manager. It meant that I was moving up the food chain, but also that my paycheck would be cut. Hostesses made minimum wage, $2.10 an hour, but waitresses made only $1.10 an hour because they got tips. Although I saw dollar and two-dollar tips on some of the tables, I was scared that I would end up with less money. I hated to let go of that tiny bit of security. Money, which I'd never had before, was becoming very important to me. I saved everything I could after buying clothes and paying rent, eating all my meals at the IHOP. After everything I had gone through in the past few months, I was afraid of any more change. I waffled on my answer to Mr. Stanski, the manager, and told him I'd think about his offer. Again, Irene stepped in.

"What are you dallying about for, luv?" she asked, treating me more like a daughter than a coworker. She explained that I'd not only make twice as much money as a waitress, but also that it was the only way to ensure that I kept my job, as hostesses got laid off when business slowed down. Besides, she had recommended me, and she wouldn't put me forward if I couldn't do it, and now I would make her look bad if I didn't take the job. Even though I was still afraid, I took the job.

As it turned out, Irene was right. Waitressing was even harder work, but more fun, and more money. Now the cooks had to pay attention to me as I brought them orders. I felt even more important. Irene, of course, was watching me to make sure I did everything right, but she wasn't the only one keeping an eye on me. So was the manager, Mr. Stanski. People there did not like him, and Irene told me that it was best to stay out of his way. He was around only during the busiest times, and seemed distracted and distrusting, always rushing around with a cigarette hanging out of his mouth, barking out orders for people to clean things up, or bus tables faster or get off their breaks. Then he would disappear, either upstairs to his office or out the door. I took Irene's advice and stayed out of his way.

My shift was five to ten, weekend nights, and soon Mr. Stanski started asking me to stay until midnight, then later, until we closed at 2 a.m. By then, I was doing very well, making good money, which I banked. I also had my own following of customers who asked to sit at my tables. When Mr. Stanski first asked me to stay late, I hesitated. He quickly added, "Don't worry, I'll give you a ride home." Since I had nothing else to do and liked making money and the feeling of importance at being asked, I said yes. Before long, I was working most nights until midnight or 2 a.m.

Mr. Stanski looked old to my sixteen-year-old eyes. Although he was only twenty-three, the same age as Roger, they were as different as night and day. Mr. Stanski came off as a much older person, one who carried himself with authority. He had responsibilities, problems to solve, and people to corral. He wore a suit, button-down shirts, and polished dress shoes, instead of the jeans, T-shirts, and Converse sneakers that Roger and his friends favored. Mr. Stanski had a shiny new Monte Carlo coupe, not an old wreck, which was the most anyone I knew could hope for. In his pocket, he carried a large roll of bills that he took from the register when the till got too full. He ordered people around, and they acquiesced. He took no lip from anyone and was known to fire people on the spot if they displeased him. He was a real grown-up.

One night, Mr. Stanski asked me to meet him at the bar across the street for a drink before he took me home. I was surprised and flattered and tried to ignore Irene's pointed looks. Mr. Stanski had never said more than two words to me before, besides asking me to work more shifts, and had never shown any interest. "Be careful what you get involved in, luv," Irene said to me as she passed by with an armful of plates. I ignored her.

After my shift that night, I excitedly walked across the street to the bar. My eyes took a few seconds to adjust to the dark, smoky room, lit only by the drink-lights displayed behind the counter. Soon, I made out Mr. Stanski, who was at the far end of the bar, with a cigarette hanging out of his mouth. He motioned for me to join him. The patrons looked at me as I passed, the men smiling, the women sizing me up with what seemed like a laugh. Was it my age or the orange uniform? Or both? I was nervous but not sure why. I'd been in bars before, but never with people I did not know. Mr. Stanski secured a bar stool for me and asked me what I drank. "Southern Comfort," I said, trying to act like the grown-up I knew I wasn't. I had never had it before, but it was what the tough guys drank by the pint at the cemetery when they were nursing a breakup or some other slight. I was surprised by how much it stung when I tried to drink it. I was hoping that Mr. Stanski and the bar patrons didn't notice. It was dawning on me that I was out of my league.

When it was time to leave, Mr. Stanski told me to meet him

around the corner behind the bar. I thought this odd, as it was late, and I was cold and had a headache from the smoke, but I did what I was told. In the car, he drove way above the speed limit, barely stopping at the red lights on Northern Boulevard. The sounds of WBLS, the local soul station, filled the vehicle. On the way to the Sykeses' apartment, he said he picked me up at the corner because it was against IHOP policy to date people at work.

"No problem, Mr. Stanski, I didn't mind waiting," I said, not quite getting his message.

"Please, call me John, but you have to call me Mr. Stanski at work."

We drove in silence until John dropped me at the Sykeses' place. He waited for me to get in the door before he sped away.

Although I started paying more attention to how I looked at work, a whole week went by without John even acknowledging my existence with a nod or asking me to work late. I was deflated, but still, I loved the work and the crew, so I was happy to be there. Maybe I had misread the situation with John. Then one afternoon I came in during the day to get my paycheck and saw him sitting and laughing with one of the waitresses in the back booth, where we sometimes sat to eat our meals when it was slow. Her name was Annie, and she also worked at the bar across the street. Sometimes the male customers at the IHOP would ask specifically for Annie to serve them during late-night shifts. Annie looked older, maybe even middle-aged. She was petite and flirty, with big smiling eyes, gobs of mascara, a huge toothy smile that didn't look real, and short, bright red hair. It was not unusual that the manager was sitting with someone, but something about it did not feel right. When I later asked Irene about it, as casually as I could, she just looked me in the eye in her direct Irish way and said, "Now, what do you think he'd be doing with the likes of her, lassie?" I turned red with embarrassment. John had not been referring to me when he said he'd like to date someone at work. He was simply telling me that he was dating. I felt like such a dunce. I had so much to learn about this grown-up world.

A few nights later, he called me to the back booth, where he sat drinking coffee and watching us work, and asked whether I had plans after my shift. Surprised, I said, "No, Mr. Stanski, do you need me to work a double?"

"No," he laughed, looking around to make sure that no one was listening. "I want to take you out to dinner."

"What about Annie?" I asked, confused.

"Annie?" He looked taken aback, and surprised that I even knew her name. "She means nothing to me; she's just a friend."

A bit surprised that Irene had gotten it wrong, I immediately said yes. Later that night, John drove me over the Brooklyn Queens Expressway to Little Italy in Lower Manhattan. On the way, he asked me about my family. I provided him the skimpiest of details—that I was Hungarian and had left home because my family was cruel to me. I was still not sure whether he'd fire me if he knew I was a runaway, or under eighteen, so I omitted those parts. He told me he had been born in Poland, and that he'd come to the United States at eleven, with his mother, his four brothers, and a sister, after his father had died here while visiting his sister. Being Catholics, they wanted to be near their dead father. They were all citizens now, and his brothers all owned big houses in New Jersey. He grew up in the small town of Cedar Grove, where his mother still worked in a factory. They all worked from day one to help support their large family, who had no money when they arrived.

At thirteen, John had started caddying on exclusive golf courses in Montclair, cleaning golf clubs and shoes, fetching balls and earning big tips. He got very good at the game, earning the favor of the rich Italians who were in the Mafia. At the end of the season, they gave him lockers full of Izod shirts and expensive golf clubs. I could hear John's respect for these Italians in his voice and wondered whether that was why he was taking me to Little Italy. His older brother Konrad had managed an IHOP in New Jersey, where John had worked after school and had learned the business. Although he had gotten a full golf scholarship to Drexel University, he'd concluded that there was more money in the restaurant business and quit school when he was offered the IHOP job in Jackson Heights.

The restaurant in Little Italy was small, charming, and smelled glorious with garlic, cheese, and pasta. The maître d' greeted Mr. Stanski by name as he led us to a small round table in the back, lit by a candle in a wicker-wrapped wine bottle. I was completely charmed. I had never been anywhere like this before. Any hesitation I had about John got lost at the door.

A dinner or two later, we were officially dating, careful to never leave work together. Our relationship started slowly enough, with him asking me to sit next to him in the car or going to a movie. He was surprised when I told him I was only sixteen—I thought he had some idea. But he had not even read my job application. He told me that he had liked me on the spot, and needed help, so he hired me. I didn't plan to sleep with him when I did, only a few weeks after our first dinner, but somehow he talked me into it one step at a time, and I was too immature to know how to get out of it. I got sideways looks from Irene and other coworkers, but I said nothing when I showed up tired, or rushed out of work to meet John around the corner. I had overhead the cooks gossiping in their code: "The cat's been cut." I think they knew, but I did not admit anything.

One Friday, in June of 1976, when I had been seeing John for about two months, I whispered to Susan, Irene's niece, and one of the nicer waitresses there, that it was my seventeenth birthday. I really didn't hang out with Fiona's crowd anymore, and there had been no one home at the Sykeses' place when I'd left for work, so I had no one else to tell.

"What are you doing here?" Susan whispered back. She turned and hightailed it through the kitchen door before I could ask what she was doing. She came back with Mr. Stanski, who said in front of everyone, "Let's go. I'm taking you out for your birthday." I hid my surprise and smile behind my hand as I looked at Susan and slapped her arm in gratitude. John and I left quickly before the rest of the staff could object to me leaving them shorthanded. I also didn't want to look my coworkers in the eye, after repeatedly lying about the fact that he and I had been dating.

I didn't have any street clothes with me, so John drove me to the Sykeses' apartment to change. When I got inside, I found my closet door and lock open, and my best clothes gone. Again. I screamed in anger, but only Niven and Shane were home watching TV, and they didn't know anything, or wouldn't say if they did. I tore through what was left in the closet to find something decent to wear, but all my favorites were gone. I got into the car steaming and deflated that I could not look my best and told John what had happened.

"Why don't you move in with me?" he asked. "You don't need the hassle of people stealing from you. Just live with me."

By now we were going out often, to bars, restaurants, movies, and to diners that his friends ran on the other side of Queens. As John explained his offer, I listened quietly. He rented a small studio apartment, with a kitchen, about four blocks from work, a lot closer than I lived now. It would be much easier for me to come in to work if he needed me when someone else did not show up. I also could nap at his place between shifts. Plus, he said, rent was cheap, and he was already paying it, so it would not cost me a thing. Weighing all this—including my building frustration about the stolen clothes—I could not think of a good reason to turn down John's offer.

But I remained silent as he kept driving. Soon, we arrived at the Empire State Building, which I had never been in. We took the long elevator ride up, and I held my lurching stomach as we gained height. On the observation deck, we watched the lights come out all over the city. It was magical. Once it got dark, we headed down to a lower level, where there was a fancy restaurant with live music and classy, half-round red leather booths. He had taken me to a few nice places before, but I'd never been anywhere as glamorous as this. The restaurant had a huge domed ceiling, white table-clothed tables with elaborate flower arrangements, waiters in tuxes, and women in elegant evening dresses, dripping in diamonds and furs. John made me feel very special and waved it off when I worried about leaving people at work shorthanded, or the cost of the food. By the end of the night, I had agreed to move in with him.

The next time I was at work, and Irene and I sat down to count our tips and pay the busboys, she lit a cigarette and looked me in the eye. "Are you using birth control, luv?" I was shocked at her directness and looked around nervously, afraid that John would walk by and overhear us.

"Well, no, not really," was the only response I could muster.

Irene shook her head and sighed and wrote down an address on the back of a napkin.

"You go here tomorrow, luv," she said, "and you get on the pill, you hear, and no need to tell anyone."

Irene knew that I had no one to mother me, and although she had left her own daughter in Ireland for her mother to raise, she could not help but look out for me. I was grateful but too head-strong to listen most of the time. On this occasion, though, I knew she was right. We all knew that Mr. Stanski could be a jerk, short-tempered, and wasn't nice to the staff unless he wanted something out of you. I needed to protect myself.

The waitresses had all been telling me that he was using me to work all kinds of hours . . . twelve-hour shifts, double shifts, weekends. He gave me little notice and no real choice in the matter, but I still did not listen to my wise little surrogate family. I realized that John put work before everything, and I was afraid to say no. Yet after months of working so much overtime, I was getting tired of the long hours. I liked the money, and having been a nobody all my life, I liked the status of being the boss's girlfriend, even if I could not talk openly about it. But I could not see who John was as a person. I only saw that he was not a loser like my father, or Roger. John had an important job, a nice new car, an apartment, and money. He knew people, dressed well, took me to nice places and bought me things. His bar friends came to eat at the IHOP and tipped me well. More than anything, I wanted to be *wanted*. I wanted to matter to someone.

Soon, I told Niven Sykes that I was moving out of their apartment, and since he was the only one around when I left, I did not get a chance to say goodbye to the rest of the family or thank them for how they had stepped up for me when I needed it. By then, I was soured to all the girls who had taken my clothes, and Mrs. Sykes who had not been around much. It was time to move on with my life.

At first, living with John was fun. His apartment was in a

duplex on Thirtieth Avenue, way off the beaten path and much quieter than the Sykeses' noisy place. Because I worked nights, and John went in midmornings, I had the place to myself. It was a sterile bachelor pad. There was no art on the walls, no curtains on the windows, and the dishes, which were from work, were piled up dirty in the sink. I enjoyed cleaning the place up, buying a few plants and hanging curtains. I read magazines and smoked my Newport Lights on the back steps, which I really didn't like, even if they helped me pretend that I was all grown up.

As the weeks passed by, the living arrangement started to lose its luster. One day, the shrill ring of the phone woke me from a nap on my day off. It was John, telling me that someone had called in sick, and he needed me now. I had just worked three back-to-back double shifts, and it was hard on the knees running around for twelve hours.

But because John wanted only one shift from me on my two days off, I figured that I should just say yes. He would be there in five minutes to pick me up.

Unfortunately, this became a regular occurrence. Our IHOP was now open twenty-four hours on the weekends, and I was John's go-to waitress. It was a benefit to me, he said, since the big tippers came in after 2 a.m. Once the bars let out—and there were many of them in Jackson Heights—the drinkers looked for someplace open late to fill up on greasy bacon, or steak and eggs and toast. John's late-night friends at the restaurant would leave me five- or ten-dollar tips, an enormous amount of money to someone like me. The extra cash was welcome, but soon it became a noose I could not escape. I was at his beck and call, and he refused to take no for an answer.

The work that had brought us together was now driving us apart. John expected me to work anytime he asked, period. Even though I had a great work ethic, he could not accept anyone saying no to work, or to him. I tried asserting my independence and saying no to shifts when I was too tired, but he was not asking.

"You don't like it, there's the door. Take a walk," he said. John sounded like a Mafioso character from the movies we watched. And his friends acted the same way. They pranced around in their suits and gold chains, like they ruled the world, not just small chain restaurants or bars. Girlfriends were expected to do what they were told. It was never an equal relationship, nor would it have been if he weren't my boss.

Regrettably, my whole life and survival were dependent on him. I was in a trap with few doors. I lived with him, I worked for him, and all my friends were at work, and had warned me of this. I hadn't seen the Sykes clan in months and could not go back. I had nowhere to turn. I was stuck again, just like I had been with my stepmother, but this time I was truly afraid I had no out.

Then, seemingly overnight, everything took a very strange turn. John started spending more time at work instead of playing golf or drinking with buddies. He even stopped smoking. Not gradually but cold turkey. It was a relief, and we were fighting much less, but somehow I still felt uncomfortable. I banished any questions from my mind, until he tried to make all the waitresses quit smoking too, which did not go over well with the old-timers, who were having none of it.

Before long, he took to disappearing some evenings, right before the dinner rush, no matter how busy we were. Now I was really alarmed. That was really out of character for John. We had been dating about six months at this point, and all the waitresses wondered out loud whether he had started seeing someone else. This made me nervous, scared even, knowing that if I were displaced, I had nowhere to go.

Despite all my suspicions, I remained too afraid to speak up. John always came back to the restaurant before I got off at midnight, sitting and reading while he waited for me to finish work. He no longer took me out for drinks or visited with his bar friends when they came in to eat. It was obvious to me that John had some secret that was making him act weird. I needed to find out what was going on.

After a few more weeks of his disappearing act, and all the gossip that came with it, I could take it no more. One day, as John was leaving the IHOP, I got the guts to step outside and ask him point blank, "What is going on with you lately, John?"

I expected a "shut up and get inside," which is what I got if I ventured too close to his personal life. But that's not what I got.

"Penny," he said, "I've been born again!"

16

The Family of God

I shuddered as John parked his car in a derelict Brooklyn neighborhood, in front of an ugly, squat one-story brick building that took up a whole city block. It was the kind of place where girls knew to never walk alone. I could see that the building had no windows, no steeple, and no welcoming entrance—nothing that suggested godliness. The sign above the door looked handmade. It said: "Brooklyn Bible Church." I was afraid to get out of the car.

When John had told me outside the IHOP that he had been born again, I hadn't known what he was talking about. I had never heard the term before. He saw my confusion and explained. He had been spending time with his good friend, Tony Ricciardella, whom I knew and liked a lot. Tony had taken him to a Bible Church, and John had been "saved."

I burst out laughing. John stopped me bluntly with an expression that registered hurt and seriousness. "This is not funny," he said.

I had to choke back laughter as John explained what had happened to make him change so dramatically. He said that he had been living a life of sin. That he had been unhappy. That he had known something was missing. That he had been squandering his life. And that God had both forgiven him and saved him.

I still thought this was all a joke because it just could not be true. I had not been back to church since my Communion, but I knew what was godly and what wasn't, and John was the least godly person I knew. He drank, smoked, cursed, and gambled. I knew that he had slept around. He could be mean to people, and gruff for no reason, and we had never gone to church before. He had always resisted talking about personal stuff, but still, I lived with him, and he had not seemed unhappy. He projected power, confidence, and control. He was not one to allow different perspectives to affect his thinking. In fact, he openly made fun of people whose ideas he didn't like. I was too young and inexperienced to imagine there was a side to him that I did not know. This big of a change was inconceivable to me.

Before we arrived, I had expected a more traditional building like the ones in my neighborhood—beautiful, large, majestic structures with stained glass, steeples, and crosses. This church looked like the converted warehouse it was. There was trash on the streets, and very few people about.

"Is this it?" I asked, not bothering to hide my disgust. Maybe he was pulling a prank on me. We stepped inside a big, bright room, with whitewashed walls. Laughing children were running around rows of flimsy folding chairs. In front of the room was a makeshift platform with a lectern, an upright piano, and a guitar. Immediately, people came up to us, and with voices that rang with warmth, they said, "Brother John, welcome back. Praise God, it's good to see you again, brother." They all hugged him and patted him on the back. Then they smiled at me and extended their hands.

"Welcome. Praise God."

"The Lord is good to bring you."

"Praise the Lord. Amen."

That was their way of saying hello. John thanked them for their support, saying things like, "Praise God, he gave me another day," and "Thank you, Jesus, for hearing my prayers."

It was as though I were seeing John for the first time. I looked around the room to get my bearings. People were milling about everywhere, young, old, Black, white, Latino. They looked happy, smiling, laughing, or chatting in groups, and clutching books that I later found out were Bibles. The men wore suits and ties, and the women were in skirts, with little makeup. I became self-conscious of my high heels, tight jeans, and dramatic eyeliner, shadow, and mascara.

John introduced me to more people. They talked about the last service, how the pastor had been "on fire." They mentioned what they had read in the Bible that week, or how God had been answering their prayers. Some talked about how "God was teaching them perseverance, but praise God, God is good."

It all seemed like a foreign language to me. I felt like I had gone back in time, to a Bible convention in a Third World country. Even though I was very uncomfortable, I noticed that people looked genuinely happy, even joyous. I glanced at John. He seemed happy and was animated, talking to another man about what he had read recently in the Bible, something about God being the God of love.

This was not the John I knew. The John I knew would have thrown a wad of bills on the table and would have said, "This is my God." The service was ready to begin. I kept waiting for the gimmick, the clue as to what was really going on, but I could not find it. Soon, a smiling man jumped onto the stage and started playing a hymn on his guitar. People filed into the seats and sang along:

I've got the joy, joy, joy, joy down in my heart.
Down in my heart.
Down in my heart.
I've got the joy, joy, joy, joy down in my heart.
Down in my heart to stay.

The room was packed on a Wednesday night, with about fifty to sixty people. On stage, Pastor Nico was tall, thin, and youngish, maybe thirty, very self-assured and charismatic. He had dark, wavy hair and piercing black eyes that seemed to see into your heart. He led a few rousing songs while people played tambourines and sang with an unbridled enthusiasm. It seemed more a cacophony than music to me, but people were into it, swaying and singing along. Not knowing any of the words, I just sat and observed.

After about fifteen minutes of singing, Pastor Nico started his sermon. He held up his black Bible to emphasize that these were not his words but God's word, written right here in the Bible for all to see. The audience was glued to his every syllable, nodding with the occasional "amen" or "praise God." Pastor Nico was full of passion and conviction, his voice rising to a near shout, or falling to a whisper. He pounded the lectern, slapped the leather-bound Bible, walked around the stage, and pleaded with us to hear the Word of God. Pastor Nico never took his eyes off the congregants. He did not read from notes. He did not open the Bible. It was as if his duty were not just to deliver the message but also to convince us of its truth. The audience was enraptured. To me, it all looked very much like worship, not of God but of him. I felt like I was at the theater, watching a performance rather than participating in it.

After Pastor Nico finished his sermon, he nodded to the

pianist, who at a funereal pace played the quiet, mournful hymn "Just As I Am."

> *Just as I am, without one plea,*
> *But that thy blood was shed for me,*
> *And that thou bid'st me come to thee,*
> *O Lamb of God, I come, I come.*

As the music played, Pastor Nico spoke over it. "Jesus died for you. He died for your sins. He wants you to be saved, to be born again. Come to Jesus now. Won't you come? He's calling you, brother. He's calling you, sister." He went on and on, pleading with those who did not know Jesus as their personal savior to come up toward the platform and be saved. "It's so simple. He's done it all for you. All you have to do is come. Come to Jesus."

Enough already, I thought, rolling my eyes. This went on for almost as long as the sermon, and I was ready to go home. But John had his eyes closed, as did most people, and he wasn't budging. To pass the time, I looked around the room to see who would go forward up the aisle. A few did. Once they got to the front, Pastor Nico touched their shoulder and passed them off to another person. I wasn't sure why.

It never occurred to me to go toward the platform, but after a while, I got the sense that the people up there were waiting for me. But I had no desire to be saved, as I did not feel lost. I had just saved myself by leaving home last year. Pastor Nico kept talking about the family of God, how great it was to belong to a forever family, and how I'd never be alone again. This was my opportunity to be forgiven for my sins, to have eternal life in heaven, and to escape burning in hell. The Hungarians I had been around were not overly religious, so I had no fear of hell.

None of it had any real meaning to me, except for the family part. I did not want to be alone. And I had always wanted to really belong to a family.

On the way back to John's place, I was quiet, just glad that the long service was over. At least I knew there was no one else in John's life, and I could relax a little. My goal was to settle back into my work routine and not bring up the church issue. But John would talk to me about the Bible when we were home. "God is love, and we were supposed to love others like God loved us," he'd say.

This started spilling over into our dealings at the IHOP too. Now when we ate together at the restaurant, he had us bow our heads—no matter who was around—to thank Jesus for the food we were eating. John started leaving little religious tracts at the waitress station, the time clock, and the busboy counter, with sayings on them like, "Do you know where you are going?" or "Eternity is forever." The waitresses all laughed at them and made jokes behind John's back. I was embarrassed and threw the tracts away when John wasn't around.

The next time John was ready to go to church, he asked me whether I wanted to come. I reluctantly said yes, mainly to not feel left out, and to figure out this other side of him that I still could not believe existed. Before long, I was visiting the church more and more often.

Each time I went, I was greeted with the same "Praise God, it's good to see you." "Thank you, Jesus, for bringing Penny back to us." Except now the church members had an additional refrain:

"Penny, have you accepted Jesus in your heart as your personal savior yet?"

"Have you been saved?"

"Penny, have you asked Jesus to forgive your sins?"

Each time, I would respond that I was just here with John and leave it at that. The more I went to church, the more I felt the pressure to be saved, to repent and to become born again. Sometimes it was the women who approached me about coming to Jesus, but sometimes it was John himself, or Pastor Nico. In those cases, I usually said, "No, not right now." But their questions steadily became more insistent.

"Don't you want to belong to a loving family that accepts you unconditionally?"

"Of course," I responded.

"Don't you want to feel God's love and unconditional acceptance?"

"Yes, I guess so. Who wouldn't?"

"Then accept Jesus into your heart, and you'll be saved."

I always stopped at that one. But after about a month of going to church a few times a week, I could not fight it anymore. *Why was I fighting it at all?* I wondered. I knew that if I didn't get saved, I would lose John, and probably my job too. And everyone at church sounded so sure, so happy. I gave in and walked the aisle, repeating the words that I was told to say, repenting of my sins, and accepting Jesus into my heart as my personal savior.

There, I did it. I was saved at last.

There were no fireworks inside me. I was just happy to get it over with, kind of like going to the dentist. But I did not feel any different. And I could not match the excitement of the church members, who kept grabbing my hand and hugging me.

"Praise God, Sister Penny! Hallelujah!"

"Praise Jesus, it's a miracle!"

"Praise Jesus, Sister Penny! I was praying for you."

After the service, Pastor Nico congratulated me. He was with his young wife, Rhonda, who was very open and genuine. I liked her right away. They both hugged me. Though it was nice to get so much attention and affection, I started crying from the pressure of it all. I knew it was a big decision, and I knew it was what the church people and John wanted. I went along with it, but it was as if it happened outside of me rather than to me.

At home that night, John asked me whether I knew we were living in sin. It had crossed my mind that living with him was wrong, but not because of my salvation. It was because all sex for me carried some amount of the illicit in it. I had the idea that we really weren't supposed to be having sex outside of marriage, but I did not consciously know it was sin, or had anything to do with God. Sin was a totally new concept to me. Before John came along, God, sin, and repentance had meant no more to me than quantum physics. Even after being saved, I felt more committed to my job at the IHOP—and my friends there—than to the concept of God.

I told John that I didn't see what the big deal was about our living arrangement. We could just stop having sex, I said. But that didn't fly with John. "I want to please God," he said. "You'll have to find your own place."

I started looking for an apartment. In the meantime, I continued working at the IHOP, but now I was scheduled off for every church meeting—regardless of whether I wanted to go or not, or how crowded the restaurant was. The other waitresses resented me getting off on Sunday mornings, the busiest day of the week. At one point, Irene pulled me aside and said, "What are you doing, luv? Why are you following him into this foolishness?" I didn't really have an answer, and she knew it. "You don't have to do this, you know, luv? You can say no to him." But I knew I couldn't, although I did not tell her that. Irene didn't understand that I'd lose John if I said no, and then where would I be?

Still, I resented being told I *had* to go to every service instead of having my own choice. All of a sudden, John had taken over managing my spiritual life like it was his job, not mine. Sunday morning service would go on till twelve or one, and evening service started again at six. Wednesday night was for prayer meetings and Thursday night for Bible study. Sometimes John would be reading the Bible and then talk to me about sin and death like it was right around the corner. Or he would read me passages from the Psalms, about the Lord's loving kindness. I really didn't get it all, but I played along.

A few weeks later, I found an unfinished basement apartment a few blocks from the IHOP on the other side of Northern Boulevard. It was a bare-bones place made up of a series of alcoves, underneath a fancy duplex, that you entered off the back alley. It had cement floors, no kitchen, a makeshift bathroom, and pipes running over the ceiling, but it was warm and cozy. My first apartment! People at work were happy about me moving out of John's place and gave me a cast-off carpet and a bed. Some of them had expressed their concern for me joining the church, and they thought moving out was a good idea. I bought sheets and towels at Alexander's and hung my clothing in a huge armoire that came with the place. The apartment also came with a large ornate dining table and chairs, which took up most of the space beside the bed.

I bought a cheap record player and put it and my growing record collection in the back alcove, so John would not see them when he picked me up for work or for church. He was starting to make noises about secular music being from the Devil, but I tuned him out. I had a ton of albums from Roger's mother, including James Taylor's *Sweet Baby James* and Cat Stevens's *Tea for the Tillerman*. I also had bought some Led Zeppelin, Elton John,

Chicago, Barry White, Al Green, and the Bee Gees—and was not willing to give them up.

It seems that salvation had come with a lot more do's and don'ts than was advertised in those first weeks. Some of it made sense. The people at church were convinced that I should read the Word of God for myself, so I would "understand" what God expected from me. They started sending me home with Bible passages to study. I loved to read, so reading the New Testament sounded attractive to me. Although it was not easy to understand, and certainly was not linear like a novel, none of it seemed overly rule-bound to me, but rather full of wise sayings or general suggestions on a good way to live. In the eyes of church members, though, the Bible was God's very word and needed to be obeyed verbatim. We were supposed to base our whole lives on the *literal* Word of God, and not question it.

But I did question it. I was being asked to change my whole life, at a time when I was finally coming into my own and blossoming as a grown-up. Every sermon seemed to be demanding more and more of us. Rhonda, the pastor's wife, told me that I would need to dress more modestly. As she made her pronouncement, she stood near me with a group of women in dowdy clothes, frumpy long skirts, and high-neck blouses. Rhonda was maybe in her mid-twenties, as were the other women, but they all looked and acted much older. They put no effort into their looks, and their outfits looked like they were bought at a thrift store. They said dressing modestly meant not wearing pants. Skirts had to cover your knees. You couldn't wear anything tight or revealing or show too much skin. Most of the women wore little to no makeup.

"That's just not me," I told them. "I don't like wearing skirts, and I don't own any." All I had were jeans. And I liked wearing makeup, although I did not toss that out at the time. Christian women don't wear jeans, they told me. They started quoting scripture about women dressing modestly, sensibly, respectfully, and not drawing attention to themselves. Rhonda explained that we women were supposed to be humble and dress accordingly, so that we could draw attention to God, "who lives in us," and to our husbands, who were in charge of us, as Jesus was in charge of the church.

Oh, brother, I thought to myself.

Each week, I was confronted with more rules. We were not supposed to smoke or drink, because our bodies were temples of God. We were not to associate with people who did smoke or drink, which was every person I knew. We were not allowed to dance, or listen to rock music, because it was of the Devil and would lead to sins of the flesh—lust, adultery, and fornication. Most church members did not go to movies or watch television for the same reasons. People of the opposite sex were not supposed to be alone together. We were supposed to abide by these rules to please God and "be a witness for Jesus."

For me, this was not part of the bargain. It felt like a classic bait and switch. I had not been told of these rules beforehand. I had seen the plain clothes on women when I first started coming to church but forgot about it, never thinking it would apply to me. It certainly did not occur to me that I would be *forced* to wear dowdy outfits. And I resented the reference to a husband overseeing a wife. I wasn't even married. Angry, I decided I wasn't going to follow all these rules. I was seventeen, and I had just started living. I loved finally being able to wear nice clothes. I got lots of compliments and attention for how I dressed, and I liked it. It was fun to shop on my few days off, being able to buy whatever I wanted.

Only a year earlier, I had left home, where I had no freedom whatsoever. No nice clothes, no choice, no free will. I had no desire to go back to living like that. I had my own life now, and I liked it the way it was. Yet I knew that I wanted to be with my boyfriend. I thought I loved him, and him me. So much of my life was tied up in him. I desperately wanted to belong. To be needed and to be wanted. To be part of something, instead of alone in the world.

Before long, Pastor Nico called John and me to his home. The pastor's place was a small, simple house, in a slightly nicer part of Brooklyn. We ascended two long sets of stairs into a spartan living room with a bare wooden floor, a few old chairs, a worn-looking couch, and lots of books, plants, and windows. Rhonda greeted us and took our coats before leaving to tend to their five young children, who were being noisy somewhere else in the house. Pastor Nico asked me to wait in the living room while he spoke with John in his office.

While I waited for them, I wondered what they would be talking about. I asked John to tell him I had moved out. I hoped there was not some new thing I was doing wrong or had to give up. I hoped it was not my record albums. And I hoped John did not tell him I still wore jeans when not in church.

When John came out, I tried to read his face. He looked resolute, as if he had just decided something big. He didn't beat around the bush. He looked me in the eye and asked, "Penny, will you marry me?"

17

Here Comes the Bride

The next time John and I attended church, people congratulated us and asked when our wedding would be. "Soon," we kept saying, although we had not set a date yet. Being engaged meant that we were the center of attention, which I enjoyed. But even better, all this marriage talk was an easy way to get the focus off the religious rules for a while. For now, no one was asking me about the clothes I wore or the music I played.

On Christmas Day, John's large family gave me a warm welcome and toasted our engagement. We gathered at his oldest brother Michael's place in New Jersey, as his was the largest house. Everyone was there: John's mother, his five siblings, and their spouses and six kids. John's mother, Rosa, was a sweet soul who looked like a wrinkled babushka from the old country. Because the family had done well since coming to the States ten years ago, she was adorned in gold rings and necklaces—tokens of her children's success. The family was a close one, comfortable and secure in their new world. Rosa was happy that John had met someone, and I think she liked me, although it was hard to tell because she spoke little English. The family mostly conversed in Polish, and John translated.

In the dining room, a formal table was set with a delicate lace tablecloth, crystal, and china. Like Hungarians, Poles liked to show off their success with fine things, and the house shone in the opulence of new wealth. In the living room was an enormous Christmas tree, over-decorated with elaborate ornaments and lights. Even more stunning was the pile of presents, almost waist-high, under the tree. I had never seen so many presents before. I felt in awe of this tight-knit family. It seemed they had all done well in their short time in America, and I could see myself fitting in here.

Once dinner was over, Vlad, John's younger brother, disappeared. Much to the delight of the round-faced, blue-eyed, blond nieces and nephews, he reappeared dressed as Santa Claus, with a hearty "Ho, Ho, Ho," to hand out presents. The kids, who looked more like siblings than cousins, all squealed in delight as they ran to hug Santa. Then they sat obediently to await their gifts in front of the tree, as the parents snapped pictures.

The children were adorable, giddy with excitement, all dressed for a magazine shoot, greedily comparing their gifts. I looked around me and felt lulled by the love, warmth, and the obvious prosperity. It had been a very long time since I'd felt this happy. At home, Christmases were always tense, with all of us nervously wondering whether my father would be sober enough to drive us to the extended family's Christmas Eve celebration. He hated having to rush home from work, change clothes and make the hour-long trip to Aunt Sári's in Yonkers. He grumbled the whole time, setting me on edge, not knowing when tempers would flare. Once at my aunt's, I could disappear with the kids, and maybe enjoy the food, but the night was inevitably a letdown. I couldn't help but notice how my siblings and cousins got many more gifts than me. Christmas was a constant reminder that I did not really belong.

Suddenly, all eyes at John's family Christmas were on me as Santa declared that he had found a present for Aunt Penny. He was holding up a tiny gift and making a big show of reading the name on the box. The women started clapping and calling my name as Santa stepped around the children to hand the gift to me. I did not expect it, as I had already gotten some expensive Chanel No. 5 perfume from John. I carefully removed the wrapping, discovering a blue velvet box. Inside was a ring—a large pear-shaped diamond surrounded by ten smaller ones in a showy starburst white-gold setting. It looked like something a queen would wear, and much too elaborate for the teenager that I still was. I was blown away and rushed to hug John as everyone gathered around to see my new jewels. All the women let out oohs and aahs and clamored to try on the heavy ring. I guess our engagement was official.

In those first few weeks, I was euphoric. But it didn't last long. John and I started fighting over little things, and now he was using the Bible to win every argument. Because we were officially engaged, he could use the "submit" clause. The Bible literally said, and our church taught, that wives had to *submit* to their husbands in everything (Ephesians 5:22–33). That the man was the head of the wife (as Christ was the head of the church) and that wives had to submit to their husbands.

Very quickly, John went from just being overbearing to having carte blanche to tell me what to do. And I had to do it, whether I liked it or not. If he didn't like what I wore, I had to change my clothes. If he didn't approve of the music I was playing, I had to turn it off. If I wanted to go somewhere, he could order me to stay home. And to top it off, his demands were all cloaked under the guise of being for my own good, for my protection, and his right and duty before God. How could I argue with that? I noticed that there were no church teachings about how a man should carry out these orders, "as God loved the church with gentleness, understanding, mercy, and compassion." But John's actions were harsh and abrupt. His mantra was: "Do it because God said to." This should have been another wake-up call to what I was getting myself into, but I did not wake up.

Pastor Nico insisted on meeting with engaged couples before he would marry them, and I was hopeful that these meetings would be an opportune time to discuss my issues with John, as I was certain that he was misinterpreting the Bible. On one of the first nights of couples counseling, Pastor Nico asked me about my parents and childhood. This was something that I rarely discussed with anyone, even John, so I hesitated. Eventually, though, I revealed bits and pieces of my family situation: my mother dying, my stepmother's meanness and wrath, my father's neglect, the daily cruelties, the beatings, and finally running away.

John and Pastor Nico didn't say a whole lot. Maybe they were shocked. I had remained ashamed of my childhood, as if it had been my fault. I was embarrassed that I did not come from a "normal" family like John's. Yet I was glad to finally unburden myself of my past. Family was a big deal in the church, and because Pastor Nico had five children of his own, I thought he would show me sympathy and understanding.

Instead, Pastor Nico quickly condemned me right in front of John. According to the pastor, God said children should honor and obey their parents. I was in *sin* for running away. It did not matter to God whether my parents were cruel, negligent, or even physically abusive. The scars on my forehead and heart were irrelevant. If I was mistreated—and that "if" told me the pastor did not really believe me—then it was God's will. And who are we to question God's will? God's will was always perfect. The greater concern to God, Pastor Nico said, was *me* not being obedient to my parents.

My stomach dropped and began to churn. I was speechless. How could he say that? I had not even told him the half of what I had been through. Surely, I reasoned, if I had given him more of the details, he would have reacted differently. But no, that was just wishful thinking. Nothing I had to say would have mattered. It all hinged on the Word of God—"Children, obey your parents"— to the exclusion of everything else.

John, who never questioned anything the pastor said, was just as resolute. Neither John nor Pastor Nico showed me any compassion for what I had been through. And both were calm as Pastor Nico pronounced that I needed to go back home and seek my parents' forgiveness for running away. That prospect was horrible enough, but there was more: if my parents wanted me to, I had to move back home!

I was incredulous. A year and a half ago, I had left home a meek, frightened waif. I was now a much different person, with my own mind (I thought), a job, an apartment, a fiancé, and my own money. I did not want to go back to my parents' place and could not even imagine how that could work. I no longer fit into the role of family servant and scapegoat. I had defied them and won. I was better off. I was stronger. I had finished my education. I was supporting myself and doing a better job of it than my father had. I was going places. But apparently none of that had changed "God's will." Going back to my parents was my burden to bear if I wanted to "do what was right" in the eyes of God and the church.

I was deflated, and I could feel the energy draining from my body. It was as though someone had died. On the way home from the meeting, John said he expected me to do the right thing, right away—the right thing being whatever the pastor said.

"John, I need some time," I pleaded. "This is hard for me to take. It does not feel right."

"Penny, feelings do not matter. What matters is that we obey God."

"Well, I want to obey God, but my parents are in the past."

"The pastor says you have to ask your parents' forgiveness, so you have to do it."

Tense conversations like this continued for weeks. I felt trapped, coerced, and miserable. But I could not see any way around it. People in the church were indoctrinated to do what the pastor said, regardless of their feelings, and John was trying to make sure that I kept in line. I was being brainwashed into thinking that I was the sinner for leaving home, not my parents for their abuse and neglect. I didn't believe it for one moment, but I knew that if I wanted to stay engaged to John, I had to go through with what Pastor Nico asked.

Shaking with fear, I capitulated. I dialed my parents' number and waited for my stepmother to answer. My stepmother picked up after a few rings and said, "Hello." My mouth was dry from fear, but I croaked out my greeting as best as I could. "Mama, this is Penny."

I felt like a mongrel dog, crawling back with its head and shoulders scraping the ground, after being beaten by its master. I had not forgotten how I'd left, my stepmother's anger when I'd seen her in the window, and the nasty note I'd written for her. Today I had all this to answer to, and I was not ready to grovel, even though that was my lot. I still hated her, and my family, for what they had done to me.

When I reached my parents' building, I trembled as I pressed the buzzer in the lobby, both from the cold and in fear of facing my stepmother again. Of course, John had insisted on coming with me, no doubt counseled by Pastor Nico to make sure I said all the right things.

My stepmother had chosen a time for us to come when she would be home alone, a Tuesday morning, when my brother and sister were both in school. John and I waited in silence for what seemed like hours for her to buzz us in the lobby door. We slowly climbed the marble stairs to the second landing, each step carrying more dread.

And there she was. My stepmother stood in the open apartment door, and once she saw me, she walked back inside, without so much as a greeting. By the time John and I entered the apartment, she had lowered herself back into her recliner.

"*Gyere be*," she said quietly in Hungarian. "Come in." "*Ülj le.*"— "Sit down." An eerie quiet filled the dank living room.

I immediately noticed how dirty the place had become. The floors and tabletops were dusty, and the living room was a mess. I couldn't help but feel guilty. My stepmother wore her usual downturned "U" frown, but this time she looked small, shrunken, and sad. She did not offer us the customary drink, I assumed because I did not qualify as a guest, or I was not worth the polite gesture that Hungarians usually offered visitors.

I sat on the edge of the plastic-covered sofa, timidly looking at my stepmother. I introduced John as my fiancé and stammered through my prepared speech as fast as I could. John sat back comfortably, unbuttoning his suit and crossing his legs as if he'd be there for a while.

"Mama, I am sorry I disobeyed you by running away," I said. "God tells children to obey their parents, so if you want me to move back home, I will."

She said nothing for a long time. I broke the silence by asking how Steven and Kitti were. She was terse: "Steven is fine." Then she asked why I was coming back now, which forced me to tell her about the church and my being born again. She was quiet and still as I spoke. She asked me nothing about my life, the church, or why I left home. Her only comment on my escape was that I had damaged my five-year-old sister by leaving. Her only question to my fiancé was asking what he was doing with such a young girl.

"She's a very good worker," he replied.

"Yes, she is a workhorse," my stepmother agreed.

They seemed to bond over that point, as if that was all there was to me. I mentioned that I had a job, an apartment, and that I was taking care of myself, but she wasn't interested. If she noticed that I had filled out and was dressing well and taking good care of myself, she didn't let on. It was as if she couldn't see the person I had become or didn't care to.

Our visit lasted less than half an hour. My stepmother didn't offer any words of forgiveness, but what mattered to the church was that I did my part. I didn't care about her forgiveness anyway. In the end, my stepmother said that she did not want me back. It was too late, she said, though she did not elaborate, other than to say that she didn't want to upset Kitti. Knowing that I wouldn't have to move back in, I almost cried tears of joy.

After we left, all my fiancé said was that she wasn't so bad. I shook my head. He really didn't get it, but I let it drop. I breathed a sigh of relief to be done with my stepmother. Yet escaping a prison sentence with my stepmother didn't mean that I no longer had issues with the church.

When John and I resumed our Friday night couple's classes with Pastor Nico, I spent the bulk of the time questioning everything the church taught. Why did we have to meet five times a week, and twice on Sundays? Why were movies wrong? Why do we have to be fruitful and multiply in current times? Why would the church have a stance against any type of birth control? Why couldn't we wear nicer clothes or high heels? Why couldn't we listen to whatever music we wanted outside of church? It seemed that whatever I wanted to do, it was forbidden. I was getting the sense that even the act of questioning the teachings was frowned upon.

At first, Pastor Nico welcomed my queries, assured that he and the Bible had an answer for anything I could ask. But after a while, I sensed him pushing back. He wanted me to ask fewer questions, and to just "trust God." I thought about that concept. That would be easy, I thought, if people weren't asking me to change my habits weekly, if I could just ease into the Christian life at my own pace. But that was not their way. The church was Fundamentalist, and Pastor Nico talked a lot about Bob Jones University, but I had no idea what any of that meant.

It seemed that people in the church showed their commitment and godliness by giving things up, and coming to more services, the external signaling the internal change. It looked to me like it meant giving up one's own life and thoughts. It felt like it meant giving up thinking.

One day, Pastor Nico, fed up with me challenging him and his teachings, said, "Penny, you have a rebellious spirit, and we are going to need to cure that."

Oh, please, I thought to myself. *The only cure is getting away from you.* I was surprised to learn that was exactly what he had in mind.

18

---◆---

The Word of Life

The Greyhound bus pulled up behind the small town's lone gas station, which also served as the bus stop and post office. I was exhausted and not a little carsick from the five-hour ride in the smoke-filled coach. As the bus driver got my bags, I looked around the deserted environs of Schroon Lake, New York, a far cry from Brooklyn. Panic began to rise in my throat. *Where in the world had they sent me?* But then a young man with short hair, wearing a white shirt and tie, lumbered over awkwardly.

"Are you here for Word of Life?" he asked, barely looking me in the eye.

The Word of Life Bible Institute was a small Bible school in upstate New York, in the Adirondack Mountains. It was associated with Bob Jones University, a staunchly conservative, evangelical college in South Carolina that Pastor Nico was connected to, and which supported Brooklyn Bible Church. The school was in Pottersville, New York, a town so tiny that the Greyhound bus didn't even make a stop there. Instead, a school van picked up arriving students in Schroon Lake, nine miles away.

Just a few weeks earlier, Pastor Nico had pronounced that I needed to get away to tame my "rebellious" spirit and learn what

Christianity was all about. As soon as I had been accepted into
the school, I'd given notice on my apartment, stored my few belongings at John's house, and said goodbye to the girls at the
IHOP, who all thought I was crazy for leaving, especially for Bible
college.

"How's that gonna help ye, eh, luv?" Irene asked me on my
last shift. "It's not gonna change 'im, luv."

I ignored her advice. What did a middle-aged woman with a
high school education know about college? Besides, I felt I had
no choice in the matter. I hugged all the IHOP girls goodbye, and
that was the last I ever saw of them.

On the drive to college, I prayed that the school would be a
nicer place than the church back home. As it turned out, Word of
Life was on a gorgeous campus, dotted with trees, flowers, and
streams, tucked in the deep woods. The air was redolent of pine,
moss, and baking bread. Even though I did not smoke any more,
I smelled of cigarettes from the bus ride. I arrived in stylish
"city" clothes, a striking contrast to everyone around me. I was
sure that the people in admissions thought they had a real sinner
on their hands—a sinner in need of conversion.

I was escorted through campus to one of the women's dorms,
where I would share a room with three young girls, all from the
surrounding area. They were there to prepare for their futures as
pastor's wives—probably the best a woman in these types of evangelical churches could hope for. The dorms were neat, clean, and
compact, with blue-gray carpet and lots of light from the many
windows. The rooms were divided into two equal sides, with bunk
beds, desks, and closets—and a common space in the middle.

The first person I met was Marlene, who was shy, reserved,
and anorexic skinny. She had cold hands and dark eyes that
seemed constantly watchful, as if she were guarding a secret.

Marlene averted her gaze, and her welcome felt like anything but. It made me worry that everyone would be reserved, but happily they weren't. Sarah was a pastor's daughter from Buffalo, a sturdy, confident girl with bright blue eyes and thick, waist-length blonde hair that she brushed religiously, one hundred strokes a night. She taught me the trick of only washing her bangs every night, as her hair was so voluminous that it took hours to dry. She played the guitar, and having already taught Sunday school, was Word of Life's top student.

Jenny was the most fun. She was from Burlington, Vermont, and although she came from a Christian family, she seemed the least religious, laughed more easily, and was more outgoing and inquisitive than the others. All the girls I met in the dorm—about twenty total, plus the hall monitor—had planned to come to Word of Life for years, thrilled to have been accepted when others in their churches hadn't. No one knew that I'd been more or less forced to attend, but judging from the girls' questions, they were figuring it out.

"What's it like to be engaged?"

"How did you become a waitress, Penny?"

"How were you able to manage in your own apartment?"

None of these girls had ever lived anywhere but home. Even though I was a year younger than most of them, I had seen a lot more life, and a lot less church, and it showed. For example, I did not yet know that complaining was a sin. So, when I grumbled that the food was too heavy, or the day too cold, both of which were true, a silence would fall on the room, until Jenny would laugh and say, "Oh, Penny means the Lord is helping her adjust to the weather." Or "Penny is learning about the Word of Life weight gain." I broke into a wide grin, thankful that she was one of my roommates.

The dorm monitor was probably told to keep a close watch over me, but there was no need. To my surprise, I liked the dorm setting, even if it was for only one year. Yet this was still Bible school, after all. The place was very concerned about modesty and morality. In order to ward off improper feelings between girls, something I did not know existed, we always had to be fully dressed, even in our dorm rooms. When it was time to get ready in the mornings, we had to be in a robe, tightly belted, and shower with the curtain completely closed. If we went into another dorm room, there had to be at least three people in the room at all times. No playing music unless it was Christian music, and only by approved Christian artists. Amy Grant did not make the cut at Word of Life. I was glad I had left my record albums behind.

The girls at the school were mostly fair, blonde, and plain looking. They all dressed in an updated version of *Little House on the Prairie*. Most did not wear makeup or walk around in heels, let alone have a sparkling engagement ring, which was hard to miss. With my slim pencil skirts, stylish blouses, and full-length brown suede coat and fur collar, I stuck out. I didn't own a robe, or modest pajamas that buttoned up to the neck, so they found me some in the lost and found until I could buy my own.

Many of the girls were ministers' daughters who had lived very sheltered lives. Most of them had never been to New York, or any city. They had never heard of Queen, The Who, or Led Zeppelin. They didn't listen to secular music at all. Most had never had a boyfriend, no one had admitted to having sex, and none of them had done anything as scandalous as running away.

Having been in New York City my entire life, I had naively assumed that the whole country went to movies, museums, and restaurants. I was surprised to learn it wasn't that way. These girls didn't even seem to appreciate the concept of shopping or eating out. The nearest clothing store was an hour away in Glens Falls, and no students at school went to restaurants, except if they were on the road. Although there were boys at the school, I saw them only in the lecture hall or dining room. I didn't interact with them, because it was not allowed.

Yet the beauty and tranquility of the school's setting took the edge off the rigor of the college's rules and heavy class schedule, which included courses like Theology, the Life of Christ, and Christian Conduct, which I got a D in, not because I was rebelling but because I did not know all the do's and don'ts yet. Throughout my life, I had never spent more than a few hours in such a rural setting. The air was sweet with the scent of forest, flowers, and peat. Birdsong guided you through the trees and around the pond to the dining hall. We walked to the lake after classes and sat on the rocks watching the birds, ducks, and boats ripple on the water. The winter was a picture-postcard of snow-covered trees and doorways cut out of snowbanks as tall as our dorms. The crisp crunching of snow under our feet was the only sound to break the icy silence.

Being a city girl, engaged, and a brand-new Christian made me a curiosity. Maybe because I was so different, they were kind to me. I was liked and popular right away, the exact opposite of my experience in high school. Before I knew it, I had fallen in love with this place. I was on my own, going to school somewhere new and beautiful, and not having to answer to John or Pastor Nico. I felt more accepted here than I did back home at church.

The achingly beautiful landscape enveloped me in a peace I had never felt before. Sometimes I could even forget what the church was asking me to give up. I walked to the antique store in town and bought old leather books. I wrote psalms and poems on the silver bark that we peeled from the local trees. I enjoyed the simple camaraderie of being with other girls my age, studying and doing homework. I barely missed John at all.

In many ways, the school was just as Fundamentalist as my church at home, though the rules here weren't as much in your face. What really set Word of Life apart was the kindness, acceptance, and love from everyone, from the kitchen help to the students, from the teachers to the staff wives. Most people seemed humble and modest. No one drove flashy cars. The men wore farming jackets and John Deere caps; the women dressed in skirts, even in the winter. The staff freely offered us little gifts, such as home-baked cookies, a drive to town for a dental appointment, or dinner after the Sunday service.

In addition to our studies, we all had chores, like cleaning up in the dining room, washing dishes, or scouring the dorm bathrooms. But compared to my duties as a child-servant at home, these tasks were easy, and I had fun doing them with my new friends. As part of our duties, we were also expected to so some sort of Christian ministry. On weekends, we got bused to nearby towns to knock on doors, mostly in poorer neighborhoods, to invite kids to Sunday school or to leave religious tracts for the residents. In the summer, we served as counselors for the college's Christian camp. I found that I liked helping people. It always made me feel good when I did things for others—the "gift of serving," as the Bible called it.

As I looked around at school, I saw people with varying degrees of faith. Some students constantly quoted scripture, leading Bible study or prayer groups as if it were part of their very being. Yet others never did. A few looked like they were just going through the motions. Several were rumored to be dating, a big no-no, while others slept during lectures, or even whispered to others during prayer meetings. When I visited Jenny's home in Vermont, she and her family never prayed at all, except before meals, and did not seem overly religious. I figured out that as long as I followed the rules, it didn't really matter what was going on inside me, even if I still had hesitations.

Oftentimes I would ask myself whether I was really saved. So, in an effort to do the right thing, I got baptized again at Word of Life, just to be sure. No one asked what I was feeling or thinking. Conformity was taken for internal belief at Word of Life. With hundreds of students and a ministry to run, no one had time to look too closely. As far as anyone knew, I was living the Christian life. And in many ways, I was.

During my year at Bible school, John visited only a few times, as he was very busy. He had given up his management job at IHOP to open his own restaurant. He called it the "New Creation," based on the Bible verse that said, "If any man be in Christ, he is a new creation. . ." (Galatians 2:20). He had used the knowledge from his years working at the pancake house to set up the business and recreate the menu, putting all his savings and time into it, and pausing only for church services. But within a year, his finances faced a brutal demise. The restaurant union—which the church urged him to oppose—picketed his storefront establishment in Flushing, keeping customers out and forcing him into bankruptcy.

During John's last visit at Word of Life, he looked weighed down and nervous as we sat outside in the common area, which was right outside the dining room, and in view of the office, so we were never alone.

"Penny, since I became a Christian, I wanted everything I do to be for God," he said, with a pleading tone in his voice. "I gave everything I had to create a restaurant that would please God, but now it's failed, and I have nothing left."

His shocking news was coming only weeks before my graduation—and our wedding.

"But I've been offered a new job managing an IHOP in Maryland," he said. "We'd have to move there and start over. It'll be hard work." John paused. He was still jittery. "Are you sure you still want to marry me?"

"Of course, I still want to marry you," I replied without hesitation. Hard work was all I knew, and John was all I had. And getting away from Brooklyn Bible Church was music to my ears, but no one had to hear that but me.

Shortly after I left Bible school, I called my stepmother, as a courtesy, and asked whether she wanted to be involved in the planning of my wedding. To my surprise, she did, and immediately took over deciding which of the extended family to invite. Still in the habit of trying to appease her, I offered to have both my brother and sister in the wedding party. My stepmother, ever eager to have them in the spotlight, accepted.

Having my stepmother involved in the preparations meant me having to go back home for visits. When I went my siblings were both happy to see me, but just walking in the door, I could feel the old instinctual apprehension creeping up my spine.

My stepmother still did not like me getting any attention and acted put out that the focus was on me. I was still not offered a drink or food when I came, and she more or less treated me the same as before: it was all about her kids and nothing about me. She didn't ask about my wedding dress, the all-important item for a bride-to-be, or where I was staying, or details about the ceremony. She did not ask where John and I would honeymoon.

Though we were talking more because of the wedding, my stepmother and I did not discuss any of the past issues between us, even though they were a shadow that followed us into every room.

I was surprised how good it was to hug my siblings. My brother had changed the most. In the two years since I had left, he had turned from boy to teenager, with a much lower voice, taller frame, and long hair and a protruding Adam's apple. He was almost unrecognizable from the boy I'd once played with. It was clear that he was still the Little Prince, deferred to by my stepmother. My sister had changed too, from toddler to kinder-gartner, more of a little girl but still clearly the baby of the family who sometimes spoke in a baby voice. No longer thinking of me as a mother figure, she seemed intent on trying to figure out who I was and how I fit in exactly. I did not know how my stepmother had explained my leaving to them. My hunch was that her story could not have been favorable to me, as she would never paint herself in a negative light to her children. As usual, my father was not home, but it was easier that way. Although my leaving had been an inconvenience for my stepmother, I knew he would have been most hurt by it. Even if he was partly to blame, I knew he would not see it that way. In his world, he was never at fault. Instead, the world had wronged him.

We decided that my brother would be an usher in the wedding, and my sister a flower girl. It pleased my stepmother to have her little girl all dressed up, her hair curled like Shirley Temple, scattering flower petals for all to see. Even though my stepmother didn't drink much, she was surprised when I mentioned that there would be no alcohol.

John and I got married in 1978, a month before my nine-teenth birthday, by Pastor Nico in a sanctuary that he borrowed from a friend in Saddle River, New Jersey. The wedding was a small affair. My father came only grudgingly, complaining that I was not having a Catholic wedding, about it being on a Friday night and in New Jersey, and about us not serving dinner or alcohol.

Despite his rants, I walked down the aisle on his arm in a gorgeous high-necked and high-waisted ivory dress.

My stepmother, in a place of honor as the mother of the bride, was escorted by my brother, looking very dashing in his tux. She wore her usual scowl and put-upon manner. She glanced around at the new family I had created, John's large clan, people from Word of Life, and the church. She saw me radiantly happy, with a promising future, but it was too much to expect her to be happy for me. Although she accepted her part, she was neither friendly nor kind. She didn't mingle with the other guests or compliment my attire. While I socialized with John's family and some church friends, she stood apart, with Nagyi, Nagyi-papa, and Aunt Sári and her family.

But my stepmother couldn't dampen my joy on this day. I was beginning a new life—and was too jubilant to care.

19

The Honeymoon

arried life suited me. I loved setting up our spacious new place in Marlow Heights, Maryland, in the suburbs of Washington, DC. We had rented a garden apartment, with a balcony and lots of windows. There was an open floor plan with a den, living room, and dining area connected by hardwood floors. Best of all was the compact, modern kitchen. The light-filled residence was a far cry from our drab digs in New York, and I took pleasure in organizing my kitchen with our new dishes and pans, all bought with wedding money. I was an eighteen-year-old bride finally getting to play house.

The IHOP on St. Barnaby Road was only a few blocks away, which was a good thing, because there were no buses, and I could not drive. The restaurant looked exactly the same as other IHOPs, albeit a bit newer, with more parking and surrounded by trees. The staff was much younger than in Jackson Heights, most in their early twenties, except for Suzie.

Suzie was tall, thin, and wiry, and looked about forty, which seemed ancient to me. She went out of her way to be nice to me, maybe out of fear for her future. It was unusual for managers' wives to work at an IHOP, and Suzie, who lived with her boyfriend and teenage son, might have been afraid that her job was on the line. She also didn't seem that happy with her boyfriend but took it in stride, as if it was the best she could expect, something I could not understand.

I was happy to be back waitressing, which was fun and didn't seem like work at all. Suzie befriended me right away and chattered to me throughout our shifts. She explained the differences in the menu when people ordered things I had never heard of before, including scrapple and grits, which looked too disgusting to even try. One day, she found out I could not drive.

"What do you mean you cannot drive?"

"Well, I never really needed to before," I said.

After work, she started teaching me how to drive. We started off in a large parking lot, just learning to start, stop, and drive a straight line. It seemed easy enough. Suzie was fun, cracking jokes, and was very patient, like a mother would be, I thought. She directed me while we listened to the radio and sang along. Often there was more laughing and talking than actual driving. Suzie knew that I was a Christian because John was open about our religious activities at work. But she tactfully avoided asking me about it, even though I could tell she sensed that John and I were not on the same wavelength. Suzie and some of our regular customers were vocal about their disdain for overly religious Christians, but I never mentioned that to John. When Suzie asked about my family, I kept it vague. Being the boss's wife, I didn't want people to know anything that would make me look bad. Besides, since the wedding, I had not spoken to my family. What was there to talk about? I knew that I would never be a real part of their lives.

John also took me on driving lessons, probably because he didn't like me spending so much time with a nonbeliever like Suzie. But he was not a patient teacher. I decided that because I did not like to be yelled at by John, or take up too much of Suzie's time, I would enroll myself in a driving school without asking permission. John did not object. Soon I was driving John's Cherry Bomb—a 1976 cherry-red Dodge Challenger with a black landau top—on my own. Because I did not get the concept of the horse-power under the hood, I would spin out constantly, burning rub-ber each time I left the IHOP parking lot. Everyone inside the restaurant could hear my tires squeal and would greet me with applause when I returned. They thought I was doing it on purpose, conferring a bit of coolness on the usually dreaded boss's wife, but I wasn't. It was just what happened when I barely touched the gas.

Life in Maryland was quite enjoyable. We had a good crew at work, and John and I could take time off. Business was growing—exactly what John was hired to do—which made his boss happy, and his paycheck higher. Soon enough, John had paid off all his debt, a big burden lifted off him.

We began shopping for a church and exploring the surround-ing area on our days off.

The churches in Maryland were quite different from our warehouse in Brooklyn. Maryland had real church buildings—some modest, some enormous—but most were modeled after more traditional structures, with nice altars, upholstered seats, stained glass, and pipe organs. The services were organized and orderly, with normal sermons that didn't last for hours, or drone on past the first invitation to salvation.

The congregants looked . . . normal. Most still carried Bibles but were dressed in stylish clothes and ready with a smile and friendly conversation. Things seemed less fervent. There was no talk of rules, music, or clothes. Some women even wore pants. There were choirs, potlucks, and laughter. I fit into this world nicely, but John thought that none of the churches were righteous enough.

Exploring Maryland opened new horizons to me. We met new people and took lots of day trips. My favorite was the Shenandoah Valley in Virginia, where we picked apples in the fall, when the air was crisp and cold but not yet frosty. When our bushel was full, we followed our noses to the smell of cider and doughnuts in a large metal barn, where a fire roared in a potbellied stove, apple cider simmered in a huge black vat, and cider doughnuts came out of the fryer. I did not want to leave. But the road back was just as glorious with the fall foliage and historic towns. Other times we visited DC or Old Town Alexandria.

When John and I weren't out exploring, we were going from church to church, never settling on one for too long. That was fine with me but left my husband wanting and restless. At one of these churches, which convened in a house, we met a young couple holding Bible studies in their home. John and I started attending.

Carl was in the Coast Guard reserves, and in his final year of college, studying for his degree in theology. He hoped to be ordained as a minister in the Baptist Church. He was of medium height and wore his blond hair in a military cut that set off his piercing blue eyes. He was a plain speaker and broke down biblical concepts into everyday terms, which people liked. Carl and his wife, Beth, had met in New Jersey and had moved to Maryland so Carl could attend seminary. They seemed down-to-earth, easygoing, and normal, not at all hard-core like Pastor Nico. Carl smiled a lot, and played the guitar, which I thought was cool.

Carl and Beth lived in a modest apartment with their one-year-old son, Tommy, barely scraping by on Carl's reserve salary. After the first Bible study, they had John and I over often, sometimes for dinner before the Bible study, or after services in the tiny living room. Despite the couple's limited means, Beth was a great host, and I liked being around her. She played piano and loved to cook, making great desserts like apple or chocolate cake. She spoke little, but what she said was always memorable, whether the topic was the power of listening, what it meant to be a Christian, or what we should want out of life. She was kind and welcoming, and generous with her time.

I adored baby Tommy and played with him every time I was there. Beth was a calm mother, unlike my stepmother, who watched my every move with Kitti as if I would hurt her dear daughter. I felt much more at ease being around Tommy. Beth was fine with whatever I did with him, trusting me to know how to feed him, or change him, and I grew very attached to the boy. I soon found out that Carl and Beth had another baby on the way, which was painful for me, because I had been trying unsuccessfully to get pregnant, and they were trying not to. It was hard to keep positive about a just God when something as natural as getting pregnant was seemingly withheld from me and granted to others who could less afford it. But Tommy helped soothe my desperation, at least for a while.

When the church gathered, we sat in a circle and sang, usually modern hymns of praise, with Carl on the guitar and Beth on the piano. It was an informal, happy gathering at their house. Fortunately, Carl wasn't concerned about what everyone wore or what music we listened to, as he himself was a big Eric Clapton fan and played Clapton on his guitar. John was surprised at first, but Carl emphasized that God cared more about what was inside us rather than outside, and that we were meant to enjoy life as part of our praise to God.

Often John and I stayed around afterward and shared a potluck meal as "community." According to Carl, sharing one's life with others was a big part of New Testament Christianity. I was content with our little group and told others about it. One, a young girl from our apartment building, joined us as well. The group grew. All of us became close, and our little group became our church. They were righteous, my husband thought.

During this time, Carl graduated from seminary and tried to get ordained, but because he would not agree to all the tenets of the Baptists' creed, they refused to ordain him. He was looking around for a denomination that would. None of us thought anything of it. Carl was just different, less traditional, and the organized church too caught up in tradition.

But little by little, I began to realize that perhaps the organized church had a point when it rejected Carl. His sermons were becoming more and more about how we were supposed to be selflessly devoted in our daily lives. He spoke constantly about our commitment to Jesus and to the church. The "church" was defined as the people we met with regularly . . . our little Bible study group of fifteen or so people. "Commitment" meant you were willing to give your all for them, and your level of commitment was measured by how much you'd be willing to give up, and how "open" you were to letting others into your lives and letting them partake in any decisions that you made.

I was not at all comfortable with the sound of that. By now, I had read the whole Bible—and was studying small portions of it almost daily—but nowhere did I find this kind of language, except when Jesus spoke to the twelve disciples. The truth was, I liked the comforts in my life, small as they were. I did not want to give everything away, or live only for the church, which at this point was only a handful of families. I did not want to be committed to the group in a way that made me "accountable," having to ask the group's permission before I made any major moves. And though

Carl seemed engaging—trying to interact with everyone—I could not figure out whether he was genuinely friendly or just playing the role of being pastor. I became leery of him. John, on the other hand, was completely enthralled and never questioned any of the dictates, because they came from Carl, his new Pastor Nico.

This caused friction in our marriage. I just could not buy into this constant push to give up more of myself when I felt I had been owned and subjugated my whole childhood. John thought by preaching to me, or reading me passages from the Bible, he could change my mind, but he didn't. In his view, it was their way, or I was in sin. No middle ground. After a while, I just went to Bible study because John expected it of me. I grew increasingly wary as I watched Carl spend even more time with John in Bible study and prayer, grooming him for who knew what. Carl and Beth would ask me questions about life, but I was reluctant to be honest with them. Any expression of personal needs or wants seemed unacceptable. To them, it was only what Jesus wanted that mattered.

Eventually, Carl found a sect of the Baptist Convention that was willing to ordain him, and because he was a new pastor with no real experience, he applied to many open positions before he found one that would have him. Carl and Beth eventually got hired in a tiny, rural nondenominational church in southern Michigan. Built in 1862, the church had been maintained and run by the local ladies' aid society, all women over sixty—and Carl and Beth's new bosses.

I was elated to learn that Carl and Beth would be moving away soon, and that I would be free from their controlling influence. John seemed to be bereaved, but we did not discuss it. We ambled on, living out our comfortable Christian lives but never really settling into a church that he felt was home. We continued to see the sights in the area, business at the IHOP continued to improve, and all seemed reasonably well. Except that John missed Carl and Beth, and so after they'd been gone a year, he convinced me to drive to Michigan with him for a visit.

I was shocked at how rural it was. When we turned north off Interstate 90 in Holiday, Ohio, we drove on two-lane back roads for more than thirty miles. There was not a town in sight—only cornfields, farms, and a feed and tractor shop. When we finally arrived in Mosherville, population two hundred, it was nothing more than a post office, the church, and a cemetery, flanked by cornfields on every side. Not a soul was around. Next to the modest, white church building, Carl and Beth lived in a small trailer home. Beth ran out to greet us with a hug, baby Abby on her hip.

"You made it!" she said. "Welcome to Mosherville. How was the drive?"

I was too shocked to answer, because I'd never been anywhere so completely devoid of commerce or life of any kind. I asked to use the bathroom, a plausible enough excuse for an escape.

The church was sparsely attended. A few old ladies, who were part of the ladies' aid society, had gone there for ages, and several new families had joined since Carl and Beth had arrived. The congregation totaled about thirty people. The old New England–style church building featured a bell tower, a wood-paneled interior, and uncomfortable wooden pews. It was a lot like the churches we'd seen in historical sites like Mount Vernon, Virginia.

During our visit to Michigan, John and I attended Sunday services, participated in Bible study, and saw parishioners for dinners or lunches. The members were nice enough. All were older than thirty and had lots of kids. Since John and I didn't, the parishioners didn't seem to know what to say to us. I could not wait to leave.

When John and I got home, I forgot about Michigan and threw myself into my role as a "helpmeet," as the Bible directs wives to center their lives on their husbands. I learned how to bake, kept an immaculate house, and did everything at IHOP to make John happy. I took a sewing class, bought new plants for the apartment, and began riding the new Peugeot ten-speed bicycle that John bought me. We renewed our search for the right church, and even found one we seemed to settle on.

Unbeknownst to me, though, John had been talking to Carl and Beth about moving to join them in Michigan. Without consulting me, Beth was looking for apartments for us, and after a few months, she called to say that she had found a place in the neighboring town of Jonesville, with two thousand residents and a real downtown, six miles away.

I was blindsided by John's unwavering devotion to them. What would we live on? John did not have a job. It was a depressed area, and there were no IHOPs. When I protested to John that I did not want to go to such a desolate place, he ignored me. In his mind, moving to Michigan was synonymous with being a serious, committed Christian, and by default, not moving meant you weren't. He did not force me to go, but it was clear that he was heading off there, one way or the other.

Beth was waiting for the okay to put a deposit down on the apartment. I was feeling pressure from all sides. I knew I did not belong in Michigan. But divorce was a big sin, and remaining on my own would be too. John said it was up to me to make peace with God about it. I had enjoyed our life in Maryland, my new friends, and John's family in New Jersey a few hours away. But before I knew it, I was in a U-Haul, headed for Michigan.

20

Michigan

On the way to Michigan, I was too despondent to eat, drive, or take in the scenery. John was oblivious to my gloomy mood, remaining upbeat throughout the trip and acting as if we were on a grand adventure. At twenty-one, I felt like my life was over.

But my outlook brightened a bit when we arrived in the town of Jonesville and turned into the driveway of a large, elegant white house. It had a huge lawn and a wraparound porch and looked like a miniature Victorian mansion. At the end of the driveway, nestled in the trees, sat a cute, remodeled carriage house.

Our new home.

I didn't notice the beat-up Ford pickup parked behind the mansion until the door opened and a tall, lanky man and an attractive woman ambled out. They were Don and Lucy, part of Carl's church. They had been alerted as to our general time of arrival and had come by to help. Lucy provided hugs and a few bottles of cold pop—that's what they called soda in Michigan. Don towered over us at six foot five, looking older than he was with glasses and salt-and-pepper hair.

Don gazed at the U-Haul and then pointed to the small house. "You plan on getting all that in there?"

"I hope so," I said sheepishly, not wanting to lose any more of myself than I had to.

"Well . . . we'll give 'er a try, we will. Lucy, why don't you go round up a few more guys, and let Carl and Beth know they're here."

I was shocked when Lucy hopped into the driver's seat of the pickup and did a perfect U-turn in the small parking lot. I'd never seen a woman driving a truck.

Before long, the U-Haul was empty and our belongings packed into our tiny apartment in the carriage house. The men seemed awkward around me as I tried to direct the flow of boxes and furniture, and they hightailed it downstairs as soon as they unloaded. Women's faces appeared at the top of the stairs, saying hello, and offering casseroles, a whole cake, cookies, and even homegrown bouquets.

Beth, Pastor Carl's wife, appeared with baby Abby and greeted me with a big hug. I was too overwhelmed with all the kindness to hold on to my sadness. I had never received a welcome like this before.

"Welcome to the church!" Beth beamed. "This is what we mean by community."

"Part of it, at least," chimed in Jeanne, a stout older woman with kind blue eyes. "There is more to come, but you'll have to wait for the rest."

Jeanne had grown up in the area, so she explained the history of the property. The front house was a classical Queen Anne built in 1900 for the mayor, but it now belonged to the school principal, his wife, and their four kids. The carriage house had been remodeled into four efficiency apartments.

"They're nice people, your landlords," Jeanne said. "From a big city, like you, and one of the daughters acts in the community theater."

Community theater? Maybe this place wouldn't be so bad after all.

John left me alone to unpack. It had been a long day, and the emotion of it had left me drained. I sat by the back window and gathered my thoughts. Like it or not, I was in Michigan. That was not going to change. But after this kind of welcome, what did I have to fear? And what was I fighting against, really? I tried praying, but I was too tired to know what to say or what to ask for. As night fell, I concluded that the only thing I could do was make the best of it.

A few days later, the ladies of the church gave me a "pounding." It was a Michigan custom that when people moved into a house, you helped them out by bringing over a pound of flour, sugar, or butter, or a pound of vegetables, apples, or berries, whatever you had. Because most people in the area hunted, gardened, and canned, John and I got frozen venison, homemade jam, and jars of beans, pickles, and tomatoes. There was so much food, we didn't have room for it all, and had to store it in a bureau in the hallway. This kind of love was difficult to resist.

True to Jeanne's word, the landlords welcomed us heartily and told me that I could put in a garden next to theirs. I was still not used to all this generosity. Back in the city, no one gave things away. People here—even those who could least afford it— gave whatever they had, from garden produce to bits of the hog they had butchered.

John got a job delivering office supplies to factories and businesses in the area, and although there were restaurants in town, he did not want me to work. We were still trying to have a baby, and he assumed that because I had come around to being in the church, I'd get pregnant right away, so no sense starting a job.

The women in the church showed me around and schooled me on how things were done. We picked strawberries in early June, and they taught me to make freezer jam out of them. Eggs were bought from Miller's farm down the road—fifty cents for a flat, which was thirty eggs. On my first trip to the farm, I was so revolted by the strong urine smell of the fertilizer and chicken dung that my eyes watered, and I had to cover my nose. The flats of eggs were left by one of the barn doors, with an old coffee can half full of quarters for payment.

The women also showed me how to put in my first garden, suggesting that I start small, because the garden rows were about twenty-five feet long. I had nary planted a seed before, but the soil was dark and rich, and my tomatoes, cucumbers, peppers, and beans sprouted in no time at all. I liked the physical challenges of gardening, which was fun and rewarding, although being a city girl, I did not always know which end was up. One November, as it was snowing outside, I proudly told my dinner guests that I had grown the string beans I was serving. My friends asked how the rest of my garden did. I listed the usual—tomatoes, cucumbers, squash—but said I didn't know what had gone wrong with the potatoes.

"One day, they were thick, tall, healthy-looking plants, and the next day, they were limp and dead on the ground," I explained. "I could not revive them."

"Did you dig them up?" someone asked.

"Dig them up?"

I ran downstairs in the falling snow and grabbed my shovel, and sure enough, right there in my backyard were bunches of potatoes that I had not known existed under those wilted plants.

We all got a good laugh out of that. These salt-of-the-earth people were softening my tough city veneer.

But because I had too much energy, I was always looking for something more to do. It was too hot to be outside long in the summer, and too cold in the winter. Most people at church—the only folks I associated with—barely scraped by and didn't do much beyond day-to-day living. No one had a pool, and there were no lakes around to cool off in. There were no book clubs, nights out, or weekend trips, as we were in church every Sunday.

I started volunteering in the church. The "community" part of the church meant that we all helped each other out, and since I had a lot of time on my hands, I helped a lot. Pastor Carl's sermons weren't as bad as I'd expected, and my faith grew. I relaxed more and threw myself into the life of the church, which made me surprisingly happy. I had the "gift" of serving, while John had the "gift" of giving. I took meals to people who were sick or had just had babies. I helped by babysitting or doing laundry when it was needed. I did my own Bible reading and prayers and invited people I met to the church. John got involved in the men's Bible study and was being trained for leadership of some kind.

Sometimes, John's "gift" of giving would get on my nerves. Anytime he heard that anyone needed anything, even if these people had more than we did, he wanted to give them every spare dime we had. To John, giving our money away somehow redeemed him. I wasn't greedy, but I liked having savings in the bank for emergencies. But as soon as we had any extra money, John wanted to give it all away, and Carl, of course, encouraged him. Usually, John helped out if someone's car broke down, or if someone got laid off, which was common in an area so dependent on the auto industry. If I asked for anything even as minor as a new pair of jeans, I got turned down, while John gave freely—no questions asked—to everyone else. Even though I was devoted to the church, I felt like I didn't have a say in much of anything.

Then, about a year later, came an unexpected announcement from Carl. He told the congregation that the ladies' aid society had voted not to renew his contract with the church. The old ladies were noticeably absent from the service. According to Carl, they were looking for a more traditional pastor who would deliver the simple sermons they were used to, wear a suit and tie, and not try to change things like he did.

The congregation was silent for a long time. Finally, someone stood up and asked, "Where will you go?"

"Well," Carl said slowly, "we can start our own church, and I could be your pastor."

Carl described how churches started in Jesus's day, when people just gathered in homes, and as the gatherings grew, they became a church. He said there was space for rent in the old Jonesville Hotel, which had been empty for years. It was our chance, he said, to really live how Jesus wanted us to live, without any interference from a committee or denomination. We could live our values by being self-sustaining. We'd all have to give more, but we could do it.

Give more than we were already giving? We already tithed ten percent, and John gave much more on top of that. Carl said that if we decided to go ahead with his plan, we could pool our resources, pay his salary, rent a space, and try to make a go of it. After a few months and many meetings, everyone in the congregation, except the old women, voted to leave, and New Testament Fellowship was born.

Life moved along, my faith seemed to grow, and over the years, I became an integral part of the church. I brought a few women my age into the church and started leading weekly Bible studies with the new converts, something I loved doing. One of the newbies was Lea, who worked at her father's hardware store in Hillsdale, had been to college, and played the cello. Lea was vivacious and fun, and lived with her boyfriend, Saul, the only Black person around. Lea's mom, stepfather, and sister also lived in the area, and soon the whole family was coming to church. Lea's mom was very loving and grateful in her faith. Donna, another new member, was a petite, dark-eyed beauty who was newly married. She was very pregnant with her first child, and went into labor in my living room, naming her baby Joy. She was quiet and observant, eager to please God. Before I knew it, the church and my friends in it had become my life, and I had my own tiny group of students.

Still unable to get pregnant, I persuaded John to let me work part-time. I began waitressing at House of Flavors, an ice cream parlor/café in nearby Hillsdale, which had delicious ice cream and great fish fries on a Friday night. I loved being back at work and got to know a cross section of the locals, including town folks, farmers, and professors and their wives from Hillsdale College. One of the café regulars, Ryan, told me his story. He had married his childhood sweetheart, and they had a daughter. But she died in her crib when she was only five days old. Since then, he could not stand to be alone in the house, so he came to the café for coffee, and worked till his wife got home. Many of the customers were elderly and tottered in alone to the café when their spouses died. They cried openly at the table, while other customers and I held their hands and paid our respects. These moments always moved me.

Even though I enjoyed the job, the pregnancy issue was weighing even more heavily on me. I loved children and felt unmoored without them. Motherhood was so highly valued in the church, and most of my "sisters" did not work outside the home, because they cared for their many children. I couldn't help but wonder whether I was being punished for something, or if it meant that I wouldn't be a good mother. I finally got John to agree to go to a fertility doctor. After a few tests, I was told that my fallopian tubes were blocked and there was little to no chance of me ever getting pregnant, even with an expensive operation. The doctor suggested that we look into adoption.

Our part of rural Michigan in the 1980s was a very white place, and the only kids available for adoption in the state were Korean. I rarely saw anyone in the area who was not white besides Saul, and it wasn't unusual for locals to make ugly racist remarks. I could not bear the prospect of an Asian child suffering in this insular place. From an early age, I had known what it felt like to be an outsider in my own home, and I wasn't about to have such pain inflicted on my own child. Yet knowing at twenty-four that I could never be a mother was almost too much to bear. I was crushed inside but could not show it. Because everyone believed everything was "God's will," there was no one I could go to for solace. My heartbreak was not discussed at all. No one comforted me. I was utterly alone in my loss.

During this time, I had little contact with my family, except for my brief, annual phone call at Christmas. They never called or wrote, and I rarely thought of them. One day, I was surprised to receive a wedding invitation from my cousin Stella, Aunt Sári's eldest daughter. I hadn't been in touch with anyone in the extended family since my ceremony six years before. The idea of attending a lavish, fun-filled wedding sounded great. Although I had adjusted to church life, every week was the same. There were no trips or events to change things up. I asked my husband whether we could drive back East for the festivities.

"Why would you want to go?" John asked. "They're nonbe-lievers, and you're not close to them."

"I don't know why," I said. "It just sounds fun, and it's a chance to get out of here and do something interesting and dif-ferent."

My answer did not sit well with him, and the next time he met with Pastor Carl, he told him about my request. They thought it was unusual that I would want to go back East and see my family. Soon, Pastor Carl came out to our apartment, asking me whether I had prayed about going to the wedding and whether I thought God wanted me to go.

I looked over at John, then answered: "No, I hadn't prayed about it, but why would He not want me to go? It's just a wedding— it's not as if I'm asking to move back."

Carl smiled his canned smile. "I think you do know, Penny."

A chill started to creep up my spine. "No, I don't," I answered.

Carl paused, staring at me. I did not understand what was going on. They were treating me like I had done something wrong when all I asked was to go to a family wedding. What business was it of theirs, anyway? We'd only be gone four days or so. Didn't John and I do enough for the church?

Finally, Carl sighed dramatically and said in a pedantic voice, "We do not think you should go. We think you'll want to stay back East. We think you've always wanted to move back. You need to pray and ask God if you should go. If He tells you it is okay to go, we are okay with that."

When Pastor Carl left, I could feel a fury building inside of me. This is just what I had resisted in Maryland, and now here it was at my door again. Yet I knew better than to let John see my anger. Hadn't I shown my commitment to Jesus and the church? Hadn't I done everything they asked me to? Wasn't I the model

Christian, doing a lot more than most people in the church? Sure, I had been gloomy at times in the early days and had even asked John whether we could move back to Maryland. But it had been years since I had made such a request, and I had adjusted quite nicely since then. Besides, it was just a stupid wedding! John told me that he would support whatever God told me to do.

I prayed about it but heard no answer either way. So off we went to Connecticut, and I felt no guilt about going. Hungarians liked parties, and this one did not let me down. My cousin was radiant, my aunt and uncle proud and happy, and the wedding was great fun. There were so many people there that I hardly had to interact with my stepmother. After the expected Hungarian greeting, "*Csókolom*," and a polite peck on the cheek, I was able to avoid her at every turn. I was a married woman now, so mingling with my husband, away from her, was considered acceptable behavior.

It was nice to see my brother, Steven, though we didn't have a lot to say to each other. I was a religious woman, and he was a cocky college boy. He now attended Harvard on a scholarship, and Nagyi told everyone in earshot how senators and presidents came from the school, implying that Steven might rise to that level. It reminded me how my stepmother had seen unlimited potential in Steven, and nothing in me. That he got all the benefits, while I was forced into a secretarial course and keeping house for the family. He got to go to his dream college, and I was serving ice cream. My sister, Kitti, meanwhile, was not a little girl anymore—she was your typical teenager. She pretty much ignored me, joining her younger cousins to check out the eligible boys.

All in all, it was a wonderful trip, and I was glad I decided to go. John seemed to have fun too. He liked parties, good food and drink, and looked at ease and happy at the reception. I felt relaxed and invigorated on the drive and refreshed by the food, music, and people I saw at the reception. I completely forgot about Pastor Carl's concerns.

But he didn't. When John and I returned home, I received a call from one of the elders, asking me to meet with them early the next morning before John left for work. After I hung up, I gazed at John. He would not look me in the eye.

21

---◆---

The Knock on the Door

T he next morning, the knock on my apartment door
sounded louder than usual, and my uneasiness made me
jump. I had lain awake most of the night wondering what
the church elders would have to say.

"Good morning," Carl said, with his usual canned smile. Another elder, Richard, a quiet, bearded man, followed Carl into
the living room. Richard barely nodded at me, but he managed a
"How are you doing, brother?" to my husband John.

I served tea to Carl and coffee to Richard. I had no desire to eat
or drink. John didn't either, and seemed to have forgotten how to
speak English. As we sat down on the couch, Carl's friendly airs
quickly gave way to a threatening, prosecutorial tone.

"Penny, tell us about the wedding trip."

Where was I supposed to go with such a question, when he
was asking it in such an ominous way?

"I did what you asked," I said. "I prayed, and although God
did not tell me to go, He did not tell me not to, so we went. We
had a great time, and we came back. What more is there to tell?"

"You had a great time, Penny? Really?" Carl asked, as if I
were a hostile witness on the stand. Elder Richard sat watching
me silently.

"Yes, we both had a great time." I looked to John for support but got none. He stared at the floor.

"Are you sure you weren't just *trying* to have a good time?" Carl asked.

I did not understand what he was getting at, but I knew it couldn't be good. My mind replayed the events of the weekend wedding, but I could find no fault in anything that I had done.

"Penny, we think you knew God did not want you to go to the wedding, and you went anyway," Carl said sternly. "The elders don't care that you went to a wedding, although we were surprised that you wanted to go. What we are concerned about is you lying about it."

Suddenly, the room was too hot. My palms became sweaty, my tongue thick. I was dumbfounded and could not figure out where all this was coming from. I gazed from face to face, hoping for some signal. Nothing.

"No, that's not true," I insisted. "God did not tell me not to go to the wedding. God did not tell me anything about it. I wanted to go, and that's it."

The room was silent. Carl and Richard looked at me, then at each other. A knowing glance passed between them. "We don't believe you, Penny," Carl announced. "We think you are lying."

I sat stunned. I started to stutter. "No . . . no . . . that's not true."

They offered no proof of their allegation. It was just a hunch and a feeling from a church member who during prayers had gotten a "message" that someone in the church was lying. Carl did not reveal the recipient of this message, or exactly what the church member had said. I had no way to defend myself—it was their belief against my word. I felt trapped, even though I had done nothing wrong. And I could tell from the distant look on John's face that it was three against one. Knowing Pastor Carl's hold over John and the church, I had no recourse, and could not think of a way out of this interrogation.

After an hour or so of back and forth, Carl and Richard hugged me woodenly and left. On the way out, they told me that I was still their sister in Christ, and that they were concerned for my soul but also could not let sin permeate the church. They would discuss the matter at the elders' meeting next week, but in the meantime, I was to stay away from people in the church. I was numb with an unknown fear.

The next week was very difficult. John was distant and cold, left early for work, and went to elder meetings afterward, leaving me home alone with my distress. I kept replaying in my mind what I could have done wrong by visiting Connecticut. It was just a wedding, and God had not "spoken" to me on the matter. In fact, I had never actually "heard" God's voice. Sometimes I got hunches, or felt a direction or an idea while praying, but a direct order was not my experience, although I'd heard of people who had. If God had told me that attending the wedding was wrong, there was no way on earth that I would have gone. The last thing I wanted to do was go against God.

Not knowing what would happen with the church was sheer torture. The church was my life, and I felt isolated—with John no comfort at all. I hardly slept and couldn't eat. Word traveled among the elders' wives that I was off-limits, but a few of the younger sisters were startled when I told them that the elders would not allow me to get together with them. I was their role model. I had brought them into the church. They all loved me. Now the elders considered me a pariah. I desperately wanted to tell everyone my side of the story, but the elders had sworn me to secrecy. I was allowed only to say that the elders had forbidden me to meet with anyone.

On one of these agonizing nights alone, my sweet sister-in-law, Caren, called me. At the sound of her voice, I burst into tears, and against the elders' warnings, I told her the whole story. Caren was a Christian, married to John's youngest brother, and attended a megachurch in New Jersey. She had been saved for years, yet she was still a free thinker. She took opera singing lessons, had her own thoughts about food and health, and had decided she did not want children, a rare stance in an evangelical church. I looked up to her as a mature Christian, stable and secure in her faith. During the phone call, Caren comforted me and told me not to worry.

"Penny, we're all in sin, all the time. We're all sinners. That's why Christ had to die for us. There was no other way to be redeemed."

She agreed that the wedding issue was being blown out of proportion.

"This is no big deal, Penny. I think you should just confess to it. Tell them you lied. That you know you shouldn't have gone and be done with it. They'll welcome you back to the church, and it'll be all over."

A weight was lifted off my shoulders. Suddenly, it was clear what I needed to do, and I wondered why I hadn't thought of it myself.

My next meeting with the elders was short. I did as Caren suggested, and they forgave me. Each of them hugged me and welcomed me back into the fold, even though in my mind, I had never left. As the elders filed out of the session, I thought the incident was finally behind me. But then Carl turned to me and said, "Just to let you know, at Sunday service we'll be telling the church what happened. You are totally forgiven, as Jesus forgave us, but many people with the gift of dreams or prophecy have had dreams that someone was in sin. This is just to let them know it's been dealt with, okay?"

This was the first time that Carl had mentioned "dreams," and I did not know what to make of it. But I nodded in agreement because I really didn't have a choice. Besides, it felt good to know I was forgiven. I was relieved, and I looked forward to being with everyone on Sunday.

Our services were open forums, usually joyous occasions of singing, clapping, and thanksgiving. Because we had a large meeting space, we sat in a huge circle with everyone facing each other. One of the elders usually gave a short sermon, but anyone was allowed to share scripture, a prophecy, or a teaching to build the church up.

On my first day back from exile, Carl quoted Luke 15:7 from the New Testament.

"I tell you that in the same way, there will be *more* joy in heaven over one sinner who repents than over ninety-nine righteous people who have no need of repentance."

Flashing his typical canned smile, he went on to say that it was a day of rejoicing. That one of us had been in sin, and in fact had been under the elders' discipline for a week.

"But praise God," Carl intoned, "our sister Penny has repented and come back to the fold. We are to welcome her back as God had welcomed us into His fold, and it should be as if it never happened."

The congregation was silent. After a while, Steve, one of the newer members, looked at me tenderly, and then with a somber expression whispered something to his wife. She nodded her head. Steve and his wife, Bonnie, were gentle souls, longtime Christians but new to the church. I did not know them well, but Steve came across as a very thoughtful person. He seemed to reason things out thoroughly when discussing scripture. Steve worked with Lea, one of the girls in my Bible study group, at the hardware store.

"That's just not right, and we can't be part of this," Steve announced. And with that, he and Bonnie got up and walked out of the church. They never came back, and I never got to speak to them again. I was shocked but grateful for their love. Deep down, though, I feared that I would be blamed for their leaving the church.

I had hoped things would get back to normal, but they didn't. The elders had told the church that I had lied to them but did not say what I had lied about. Church members did not know how to respond to me. Even though Carl and Beth and the elders demonstrated forgiveness by hugging me or having us over for dinner, the church members acted differently around me. It didn't help that I was from New York and had not lived in rural Michigan all my life. Many of the churchgoers had never quite gotten used to me to begin with, and this incident seemed to add to their wariness of me. Nevertheless, I got back into teaching classes, and the new converts remained loyal. My marriage got back to a semblance of a routine, but I wasn't sure whether things with John would ever be the same.

The inquisition and its aftermath had shaken me to the core. My life of faith and joy had become one of uncertainty. Because the incident was so random, and I did not know how or why it happened, I was never quite sure whether I was doing something wrong or not. In any church activity, I started to doubt and second-guess everything I said or did, even the simplest things, like answering "How are you doing, Penny?" I over-explained myself to people to make sure no one misunderstood me. I called people back to clarify things, to make sure I did not inadvertently "lie," which made me look worse. I could not tell anyone the real truth, not even John. If I said I hadn't lied in the first place, then the admission itself had been a lie. I could not go there.

Being falsely accused of lying left me living in fear, just as I had as a child, never knowing when I'd displease my stepmother and face her retribution. But I would never bring up such a matter to the elders. Because my childhood was "God's will," it was not something that was talked about at all, not even between John and me, but certainly not with Carl, Beth, or any of the church members. I got the sense that like Pastor Nico back in Brooklyn, they never quite believed me. I got the impression they believed that discussing such painful matters would diminish God's providence and weaken their belief that everything was His will. Coupled with my ongoing unhappiness at not being able to get pregnant, and wondering whether it was punishment from God, I came across as scared and nervous most of the time. I could never quite get back to my old upbeat self, although I tried to. The elders always told me, "Penny, if you did nothing wrong, you have nothing to be afraid of." I did not find that to be true.

This state of uneasiness plagued me over the next few years. Even though I was no longer considered to be in sin or in need of church discipline, I was chronically depressed about my life and simply going through the motions. Where was the joyous person who loved to sing, clap, and praise God from the top of her lungs? She was nowhere to be found.

Then one day when I was more depressed than usual, the doorbell rang. I looked out the front window to see who it was, because most people would have walked right upstairs without ringing. Downstairs was my long-haired brother and two of his college friends. I ran downstairs and hugged Steven tightly. I had not seen or spoken to him since my cousin's wedding years earlier.

"Happy birthday," he said, swinging me around.

"How did you remember?"

I had completely forgotten that it was my birthday. Steven and his friends were driving across the country from Boston during summer recess to visit my parents, who had moved to Desert Hot Springs in California. The young men looked like they had slept in their clothes for days, which they had.

My brother seemed less like the Little Prince than I remembered. He jostled comfortably with his friends and discussed life with me in a mature way. We talked about his college experience, our parents' move to the desert for my stepmother's worsening arthritis, and Kitti going to high school. We spoke in English, not Hungarian, and avoided some of the messier topics, like my running away, joining the church, or my stepmother's abuses. He seemed mature, grown-up, normal. Steven didn't know all of what had happened to me when we were growing up, or if he did, he wasn't letting on.

But for now, I could set that aside. I was used to the family acting like it had never happened. I was just happy that he had come to visit me. As Steven and his friends stretched their legs, they kicked around a "hacky sack," a weird crocheted bag with beans in it. Steven asked how married life was, and I gave a canned answer: "Fine." He tactfully steered clear of the Christian topic—it had never been his thing. He told me about his classes at Harvard: English lit, world history, and Sanskrit, which I had never heard of. He told me what a blast that college was, with lots of music, films, and groups to join. He raved about the girls and the parties—stuff I could not relate to, but it was still fun to hear his stories.

As we chatted and laughed, I felt at ease with my brother for the first time since we were both adults. We went shopping and picked up food for him to make dinner—he was cooking now! He made ginger beef, something I had never had, and was not quite sure I liked, but it didn't matter. I was happy to have him there. When we were alone getting his bag from the car, I had to ask him a question.

"How did you know I needed something just now?"

"I just knew that I needed to see you," he said.

I got so choked up—he had really gone out of his way to visit me—that I could not tell him how much it really meant. Steven and his friends could only spend the night, as they had a schedule to keep. One of them slept on the couch, the other two crowded on the floor, as we had nowhere else to put them. I was truly happy for the first time in years, which made Steven's early morning departure so much more painful. I cried as I watched him turn out of the driveway, not knowing why I was crying, or when I'd see him again.

Afterward, I continued to try to stay out of trouble with the elders. A few others in the church were disciplined, under similar, secretive circumstances. I thought those who were punished were good, committed Christians. One was a deacon's wife, who in her despair had moved back East to live with her parents, leaving her two children behind. Another was someone whom I had known from Brooklyn Bible Church and had moved to Michigan to join Carl's church after John and I had. None of these people seemed bad or rebellious, yet the elders were convinced that these folks were guilty of a lie that they would not admit to, even with the threat of church discipline. Instead of making me feel less alone, these events made me more frightened that I might make another unwitting mistake.

Then came an especially cryptic Sunday service. More than one person shared with the church that they had experienced dreams from God, telling them that there was still someone in the church living in sin. Everyone in church, including me, looked around, wondering whom this sinful person could be. A heavy pall fell on the room—and on my heart. We sat silently, our heads down in prayer, until Carl ended the service, reminding us that God was still in control and that he was a loving God, willing to forgive those who repented. We all quietly shuffled out of the joyless room.

That afternoon, I heard an unexpected knock on the door. It was louder than usual, similar to the one I had heard years before. In the second I looked over at John, I knew. They had come for me.

22

The Lost Years

"Are you in sin, Penny?"

The question sounded eerily familiar. I was in an utter state of confusion, just as I had been during the first interrogation years before.

"Tell me!"

Carl, who had stopped by unannounced, had raised his voice, something he had never done before. With my husband John and Elder Richard at his side in my living room, the pastor glared at me. His tone and expression were menacing, and I could feel myself shaking. How could this be happening—again?

"One of the sisters told the elders that she thought God was referring to you in her dreams," Carl continued. "What do you have to say to that?"

I didn't have anything to say to that. How could I refute someone's dream? I tried to say I was not in any sin that I knew of, but Carl seemed to have already decided that I was guilty of something. So had John.

"Penny, did you mean to hurt Rose?"

Rose? I barely knew the woman, and we almost never spoke, except to exchange pleasantries at church. Yet I could feel Pastor

Carl building up to some unspeakable offense that I had committed against her. My tongue was thick, and it hurt to speak.

"No," I finally said, as emphatically as I could. "I would never hurt anyone on purpose."

"She seems to think you did."

Then it hit me. The previous week, I had bumped into Rose at the Market House grocery store. Rose was not someone I spent a lot of time with, and she had never been warm or welcoming. We didn't have much in common. She was at least ten years older than me and had a large family to take care of. She had never left Michigan and still talked about high school like it was the best time of her life. She had married her childhood sweetheart in her teens. They had four children and lived in a small house in nearby Jonesville. It was odd that I noticed this, but she was the same size and shape as my stepmother, average height, rotund, and with a full face. The one time she got into my small car with me to carpool to an event, I had involuntarily started trembling around her, just as I had around my stepmother.

That day in the market, Rose had told me that she thought she had been pregnant and might have had a miscarriage, and that she was not feeling the best. I told her that I was sorry for her, and that I had been trying to get pregnant for some time, and that maybe God would give her baby to me. Though I had meant the remark to be taken in an oddly comforting way, I could see now that it was a stupid thing to say. I was always nervous around Rose for some reason, and I was depressed and sad about not being able to get pregnant. In that moment at the store, I did not comprehend how insensitive my words had come across. We said goodbye, and I thought that had been the end of it.

"Why would you say that, Penny, that God would give her baby to you?"

"I don't know," I said, facing my accusers. "I've been trying to get pregnant for years, and she has four kids already. It was not the right thing to say, but I just said it, casually. I did not mean to hurt her."

Carl and Elder Richard stared at me in silence, and then they looked at each other and back at me.

"We don't believe you."

I sat in stunned silence. I glanced at John, who looked down at the table. I could tell that the elders were waiting for me to further defend myself.

"I don't have anything else to say. I did say those things, but I did not mean to hurt her. Why would I hurt her? I did not plan to see her at the store. I barely have a relationship with her."

"Penny, we think you wanted to hurt her because she is one of the people in the church with the gift of prophesy," Carl said. "We think the Devil is using you to silence her."

My body went cold. I was in utter shock. I was being accused of working with the Devil, a very real force of evil in our lives, and a big part of the salvation story that we all knew, taught, and clung to. We talked about the Devil often in our church. He was the reason we needed God. Jesus had saved us from the very clutches of the Devil, who was out to trick people, to steal souls and imprison them in the burning fires of hell forever. The Devil was the King of Darkness. That someone would accuse me of this was like a swinging anvil hitting me in the chest. I was literally gasping for air, physically crushed. I could not speak and started to cry.

"Why would someone cry if they are innocent?" Carl asked. He was merciless, using my own despair against me. "We believe you are being used by the Devil," he said. "Your lies are giving the Devil a foothold in our church. Maybe you are even working with the Devil now."

"No," I said, but I could barely utter a word, as I felt the oxygen sucked out of my heart and lungs. "I will apologize to her. I am not working with the Devil."

"We don't believe you, Penny."

We went on like this for hour after excruciating hour: me being ganged up on, and no one coming to my defense. I felt exhausted and beaten up. I was being accused of the worst thing possible for a Christian. Their charge did not seem reasonable. I had never hurt anyone in the church. I helped everyone I could. But these men did not seem to hear me. They were basing their charge on someone's dream, and I could not even face my accuser! Eventually, after trying everything they could to get me to admit that I was working with the Devil, the elders left. They ordered me to stay away from everyone at the church, especially Rose. They would allow me to think about it and return in a week. John left with them. I sat for a long time—trembling, crying, and despairing. John didn't come home until dark, and he went straight to bed.

The next week was miserable. I slept poorly and had terrible dreams. My appetite was gone, and since I did not want to bump into anyone, I stayed in the tiny apartment, confused and scared. John dealt with me in a perfunctory sort of way, not mean but not kind either. He barely spoke to me and left every night after dinner and returned in time for bed. Hour after hour, I mulled over what I had said to Rose, and what the elders were accusing me of. But I kept coming back to the same conclusion: my encounter with Rose had been an accident. I had not known she was pregnant. I had not meant to hurt her. I felt cornered and abandoned, and I could not see a solution. I assumed I could reason or pray my way out of it, but prayer did not help. I had lost my connection to God and had no idea how to get it back.

When the elders returned the following Sunday, they seemed in a more jovial mood and treated me with perfunctory kindness, which gave me hope. They asked me what I had been doing and how I was feeling—as if this were a normal meeting—and then paused, waiting for me to take over.

I swallowed and told them that I had been thinking and praying, and that although I missed the church, I could not confess to something I did not do. I was not changing my story. I never intended to hurt Rose or anyone, and that was the truth.

The elders shook their heads and looked toward John, whose eyes started to tear up. I tried to take his hand, but he pulled way. Then, in a despotic tone, Carl declared, "Penny, you leave us no choice. We believe you are working with the Devil. We cannot let the Devil have victory in our church. We know you are in sin, and until you repent of your sin by confessing your lie, you are ex-communicated from New Testament Fellowship. The elders and the church will pray for you. You are not to have any communication with anyone in the church at all. Do not contact anyone. Do not call us. If you want to get a message to us, you can tell John. When we believe you are repentant, we will call you."

Carl stared at me with malevolent eyes that chilled me to the bone. They all left, and I fell to the floor, sobbing. My heart was seizing in my chest like a stroke. I felt more alone and forsaken than I had ever felt, even during some of the darkest hours of my childhood. Without Christ and the church, I was alone. They were my life.

Many months passed, and I deteriorated in my lonely cell. My faith, hope, and emotions declined. John and I lived by rote, going about our lives in our home without feeling or warmth. Because John had bought into the elders' claim that I was of the Devil, he would not tell me much about the church, or how people were doing. Even my closest friends at the church could have nothing to do with me.

John went to work, and I did all the house chores, as wives were supposed to do. We kept up with our "family time," watching *Hill Street Blues* on Thursday nights, but it was painful for us both. At one point, I saw tears in John's eyes. His only comment was that this was not a life. He did not ask me why I refused to confess. He did not try to get me to repent. I asked him whether we could just leave and go to another church or move back to Maryland. He shook his head and said no. That was not the answer, he said, yet he offered no other solution. Christian husbands are supposed to love their wives as Christ loved the church and give themselves up for her (Ephesians 5:25), but those teachings never seemed to apply in our church. The rules always went in favor of the husbands.

Every night, I walked alone for miles in the dark of winter to escape the lonely confines of my home. I started in the woods behind our house and kept going. The frigid cold numbed my body, and sometimes my mind. No one else was out. The only sound was my footsteps breaking through the deep, icy snow. The stars and the moon lit my way, past the houses of town, past the last of the farms, out into the white fields.

During one of these walks, I harkened back to the wedding incident, which had given me so much stress. Yet that dispute had been minor compared to being called a pawn of the Devil. The Bible was full of stories of how the Devil was expelled from heaven, how he was the Prince of Darkness, and how Jesus came to destroy the work of the Devil. In my desperate state, I began to think the Devil *was* out to destroy me. But I had no means of escape because I was already saved. Or was I? If I was already saved, which I knew I was, why was this happening to me? Why were the elders being so hostile? Was the Devil after me? Was this some sort of test? Hadn't Jesus already won that battle for me? Maybe I was in sin after all. Maybe I did mean to harm Rose. No, I never wanted that! And around and around it went, until I thought I'd go mad.

Every moment, I lived in a state of apprehension, fear, and turmoil. My stomach churned with anxiety, and I was becoming stick-thin, because I could not eat. Even on the rare occasions that I could sleep, the Devil occupied my dreams. He was laughing at me, gnashing his teeth at me. Coming for me. And then I woke up choking, my hands on my neck, to face another tortuous day.

I tried to work as many hours as possible at the ice cream parlor to pass the time. When my boss, Elaine, saw me crying at work, and repeatedly asked what was wrong, I finally told her. Elaine, a devout Christian, said that my church was wrong, and that no matter what I did, they had no right to treat me this way. She urged me to speak to another minister. But I knew that if I took such a step, my church would never take me back. So I soldiered on, praying for a miracle.

At one point, I thought about suicide—by mixing some rat poison from work into a milkshake—just to get it over with. But I couldn't go through with it, even if I felt dead, because I was afraid the Devil was on the other side, laughing at me.

I missed being in the church. I missed my friends. I heard that Lea had gotten married, and that it had been a beautiful wedding. I thought long and hard about what my sister-in-law Caren had told me to do the last time the elders went after me: to confess and be done with it. But I could not go through with that either. Taking her advice had been a mistake.

From time to time, John would ask me whether I was ready to confess to the elders, and my answer was always the same. I had nothing to confess. Then he would turn away. We eventually stopped talking because he did not believe anything I said. The house echoed, dead and quiet. It was an untenable situation.

Finally, John announced that we were going to see the elders after services the next day. He told me that I had better be ready to repent of my sins. I said nothing but started shaking.

We met the elders at the church, in a small room with high ceilings and a large table, behind the main meeting area. Carl and two of the elders were there. They said hello to me and asked me to be seated. They got straight to business.

"Penny, we want you to confess your sin right now, or pack your bags and get out," Carl said.

I didn't quite know what he meant.

"Do you mean leave the church?" I was momentarily heartened. Perhaps John and I could leave and join another church after all.

Carl was furious. "Did you not hear what I said? We want you to admit that you lied or pack up and leave. Leave your house. Leave John. Leave the church. Leave the state."

I was dumbfounded. I had never considered going to a new church on my own, let alone divorcing John, which would be a sin in the church.

I looked around the room. Time slowed to a stop. I was vividly aware that I was deciding what to do with the rest of my life, when I had always assumed that the rest of my life would be here, with John and these people. My only two options were to confess to a sin I did not do, or to leave my husband and the only life I knew. I realized that even if I confessed again, the elders would never stop attacking me. And regardless of what I did, my church friends were never going to treat me the same again. And what about John? The truth was, I no longer loved or respected him. He did not defend me. And he was not asking me to stay. In that moment, things became frighteningly clear. My marriage was dead. I no longer belonged in the church. They had completely broken me.

I took a breath. "I'm leaving," I said.

Minutes later, I walked out of the church for the last time. The sun was bright and warm, but I was shivering. I got into the car with John, who looked just as devastated as I did.

"Thank you for everything," I said. "For the beautiful engagement ring, and all the great vacations and fun we used to have."

"Penny, there's a lot more of that out there in the world," he said. "I have to hand it to you. You tried. You tried to be a good Christian."

We both wiped away tears and said nothing more on the drive home. Once we got home, he packed a bag and told me that he would be staying with Carl and Beth. And just like that, John was gone.

After a while, an unexpected fury began to overwhelm me. I paced from room to room, screaming at the top of my lungs. It was a lie! It was all a lie! They promised me unconditional love and acceptance, but it was not true. John promised to love me forever, and that was not true either. I banged my fists against the wall, not caring who heard me. I had never felt such violent anger in my life. I hated Michigan and everything about it. I hated John, the elders, and the church.

I tore our wedding portraits off the walls and dresser and stuffed them into trash bags. I tossed in our wedding album, and all the photographs, cards, and mementos that I had saved over the years. I jammed my precious wedding dress into a trash bag. I loaded all the bags into the car and dropped them into a restaurant dumpster filled with rotten scraps. Back in my car, I just sat there. I was unable to move.

Days later, when I returned home from an errand, I sensed that John had been there. I walked through the empty rooms looking for clues. His clothes were missing, and a few more books were gone. I checked the desk. The checkbook and credit card were gone. I laughed out loud. All this time, he had never trusted me with our pitiful savings.

I plopped down on the couch that John and I had picked out together so many years ago, in happier times. Our marriage was truly over. I was unwanted, just as I was with my family. I was thirty-one. I had given half my life to John and to God. And for what?

It was now dark outside. I picked up the phone and slowly dialed the number. A voice answered on the other end.

"Hello."

"Hi, Steven," I said. "It's Penny."

23

——

New Beginning

My first day in San Francisco was a far cry from rural Michigan or even New York. The city was foggy and drizzly, cold, and damp. I walked down to the Creamery on Valencia Street for breakfast. The girl behind the counter had a buzz cut, dyed green, with several piercings in her eyebrow, nose, lip, and chin. I felt like I had landed on Mars. I clutched my croissant and coffee, shuffled nervously back to my new apartment, and locked the door.

Steven was already at school for the day, so I was on my own. When the church forced me to pull up my roots and leave, I had called my brother to ask whether he'd let me room with him in California. It was a long shot: He lived with a woman who was supposedly just a roommate, and he had hated my religion to the point of ridicule. We hadn't lived under the same roof since we were kids. Much to my surprise, though, Steven said he was sorry that my marriage had fallen apart, and instantly agreed to share an apartment. But he had conditions:

"I do not need anyone to mother me."

"I smoke pot, so you have to get used to it."

"I am a busy grad student, so I can't be there for you all the time. I'll help, but you have to figure things out on your own."

I paused only for a second. Despite the years of distance and the trauma that had transpired, my brother felt like a soulmate, the only one I had. I could tell that he liked things his way, and I'd have to fit into that. I hadn't been around pot smokers in years, but I had nowhere else to go, and no one else I could call.

"Sure, Steven, I can live with all of that." In short order, I packed four suitcases and left my life in Michigan behind, flying to San Francisco and arriving to a Victorian duplex in the city's Mission District. The neighborhood was a mix of students, Latino immigrants, bohemians, and people displaced two years earlier by the 1989 Loma Prieta earthquake. At thirty-one, I felt like a refugee, with little left of my life and faith.

Steven found us a place in the Mission because it was cheaper than most of the city's other neighborhoods. It was also close to his many grad school friends, and a supposedly fun place to be. When I arrived, the apartment was cold and empty, except for Steven's bed and a small table and chairs. I slept in a sleeping bag on the floor until I could buy a cheap mattress on Mission Street, and a used sofa at the Community Thrift Store on Valencia. The rent was four times what it was in Michigan, and my breakfast cost at least twice as much, which scared me. I needed to find a job, and fast. I had come with $1,200, and half of that I paid Steven in rent.

Because I had no college degree and no skills except waitressing, that's where I started. One of my cousins suggested that I go to North Beach, an Italian neighborhood that would be more like what I was used to in New York. It was a good call. People looked more normal there. I got a job right away—weekend nights in a tiny Tunisian place called Dar Tunis on Broadway and Columbus. The joint was near gaudy strip clubs—another shock to my prudish mind. I had never heard of Tunisia and had to look up where it was. Eventually, I took some additional shifts at the Hilton, catering banquets. That gig was great money, and great fun, with amazing food thrown in to boot.

But I still had to fight with the demons of my past. I had arrived in San Francisco a completely broken person. Everything I had believed in and cherished had been ripped away from me. I had to figure out what I believed, and how to live day to day. Previously, my Christian faith had dictated every aspect of my life. In order to make sense of my unspeakable loss, I had to acknowledge to myself that my faith was gone. This took time, and was painful to ponder. I no longer believed in God, salvation, or the Bible, and was sorry I ever had. Yet I was more sad than angry. I came to the conclusion that there was really no heaven or hell, and there never had been. I wondered whether I had ever been a Christian, but the answer didn't matter anymore.

Thursday nights were an immersion by fire into secular life. My brother had invested in a large television and stereo, and his friends gathered every week in our living room to watch *The Simpsons* and *Liquid Television*, both new to my deprived senses. The young, twentysomething males were confident and boister-ous—typical grad school males. The witty jokes flew as we sat shoulder to shoulder on the floor. They drank beer and smoked joints, things I hadn't done in fourteen years and was not quite ready to partake in.

The casualness of it all surprised me. Steven even had a gay friend, Raph, who was so sweet and good-looking that it was hard to stop staring at him. I had never known an out gay person before, let alone hung out with one. The Bible might have con-sidered these gatherings drunkenness and debauchery, but they didn't seem that bad to me. The guys were all Ivy Leaguers, like my brother, or kids whom he'd known from the Bronx High

School of Science. They were fun but cocky, each a master of debate, trying to outdo each other in coolness and intellect. No one was drunk or out of control, but they were loud and laughed a lot. I mostly smiled and kept quiet. At first, I felt so out of place. I did not have their vocabulary or cultural references—things that had passed me by during my dark years in the church. I watched and took it all in, eventually becoming part of the gang. Now when Raph came over, I easily discussed him growing up gay in Kansas, his Syrian heritage, or what he thought of law, which he was thinking of going into. Soon we had gay neighbors, James and Ronny, move in upstairs, and it felt so natural. They became part of my tribe.

Now that my whole immediate family was in California, I joined them for Thanksgiving and Christmas gatherings for the first time since I had left home at sixteen. It was uncomfortable being around them again, although I desperately wanted it to feel like a "normal" family. No one mentioned anything about the past and their part in it. It was as if my childhood had never happened. But I always felt the weight of it when I was around my parents. I also felt sheepish about my failed marriage and my discarded faith, which I had once defended so strongly.

My parents now lived in a small, neglected house in Desert Hot Springs. Seeing the place triggered my old guilt, as if it were still my job to make the house clean. It was obvious that no one was doing any cleaning beyond dishwashing. There was dust everywhere, and things accumulated in piles rather than put away. There was no carpet, and the bare floor was filthy. My father, who was grayer than I'd last seen him, was his usual gruff self, not wanting to be bothered with anything.

"Hello, Papa, how are you?"

"Fine, Chicken, I'm fine. We've been fine," he said tersely, though clearly they weren't. I sensed that he was still resentful of me leaving like I did, although he would not admit it.

My sister, Kitti, was nineteen, and in the blossom of womanhood, vivacious and carefree, and off with her friends after a casual hello. She had nary a thought about where I'd been for the last sixteen years, and why would she?

Of everyone in the family, my stepmother had changed the most. She seemed smaller and subdued toward me somehow. She still deferred to my brother, offering him food that she was clearly too frail to make, and asking him many questions about school, his girlfriend, and money. He clearly enjoyed the attention, as if it were the natural order of things. One day, she asked me what I planned to do now that I was divorced. Still infected by evangelical doctrine, I was ashamed of my crumbled marriage and embarrassed that my faith had been so easy for me to expunge. I hung my head, waiting for my stepmother's typically harsh judgment, but I got none. Instead, she offered me something close to praise.

"Penny, you can do anything you want now."

I didn't know exactly what she meant. I was still grappling with the regrets and sorrows of my past. But my stepmother saw me as free, something that she wasn't. I didn't feel free, though. Even if I had left Michigan behind, my problems had not left me. I was scared and downcast most of the time, and lonely, but technically still married, as the divorce was not yet final. I was not sure how to date, or whether I should. I thought of myself as probably too old to love again. I did not miss John at all but missed the belonging that marriage entailed. Still, when he served me divorce papers, it hurt. Marriage had been a sacred thing in the church. We had agreed on a small divorce settlement before I left Michigan, and that's the last I heard of him.

Because I did not use the Bible as my guide anymore, I had to decide what I believed about dating or sex, drugs, and alcohol, even dancing. I loved dancing. Since church prohibitions against external beauty no longer applied, maybe I could get acrylic nails? The possibilities were endless, but lacking a compass, I was stuck, unable to escape the belief that my life had been a failure.

I cried often and was not sleeping well. I started running in the wee hours, which gave me some relief—but not for long. Sometimes I would call my brother at work, despite his prohibition, but I could not help myself. The turmoil—wondering why all this had happened to me—would not stop. One day when I called, he told me: "Penny, I love you, but you can't keep calling me. Go get a pen and write down this number."

I did as he told me. "I am going to hang up now," Steven said. "Make the call."

The number was for the Marina Counseling Center. I had never been to therapy and was not sure what it was supposed to do. But I called and made an appointment.

My therapist, Mavash, was a beautiful, young East Indian woman. In her office, I started at the beginning, pouring out my history to her.

"Mavash, why did all these things happen to me? Why did my mother die? Why did my stepmother hate me so much and beat me? Why did my dad not care?"

"Penny, I cannot tell you why."

That was not the answer that I had wanted. But her next words would stay with me.

"I can only agree that you were treated horribly. You did not deserve to be treated that way. You have been terribly abused, but it's not your fault. It is *not* your fault."

I cried and cried. It was the first time in my life that someone had truly validated my pain. I was thirty-two.

Mavash and I started meeting regularly. And although the
pain would get worse before it got better, I kept going.

I started to get out of my bubble and see what the world offered
me in San Francisco. I made my first friend on the J-Church
trolley line, which I rode to my job at the Hilton. Hilary seemed
about my age but was actually much younger and lived with her
sister a half a block from us. She was dating a man named Wally,
who was from New York, our instant connection. She was a recent
college graduate and was doing something in finance that I did
not quite understand. Soon, she and her sister joined our Thursday night soirees, or I went to their place when Hilary made a
quiche for dinner. I started going out occasionally for drinks,
meeting friends at the Lone Palm, a tiny bar on Twenty-Second
Street. Hilary even took me rafting on the Sacramento River.

Hilary was a solid friend, but her presence in my life, and my
brother's friends, reminded me of the wrong turns I had taken. I
constantly felt that I did not have what other people seemed to
have. The people in my orbit reeked of confidence, promise, and
future. They had coveted degrees and set their sights on exciting
careers. I was a waitress. No one belittled me, because I was
Steven's sister, and he was a smart grad student. But the disparity
between us was obvious. Steven and his friends talked about
jobs, money, and trips to exotic places. They knew what engineers
made versus developers, and they discussed the ranks of various
grad schools with ease. I wanted to be like these people, but I had
no idea how to pick a career. And I had never had a chance to go
to the schools they had. I was determined to go to college too.

One of the real estate developers my brother worked for had
an office on a houseboat in Sausalito, a gorgeous hillside town

just north of the Golden Gate Bridge. The guy desperately needed a receptionist, and although I hated "office" work, Steven convinced me to go see him. The guy promised me more money than I made waitressing, which made the jump easy. But seeing an opportunity to save up money, I hung on to waitressing on weekends. I never wanted to be so close to being homeless and broke again.

I really liked the office—real estate foreclosure investing—and was treated very well despite barely being able to type or spell legal terms. The only bad thing was being on a houseboat when it stormed. I would get severe motion sickness. But work was work, and I managed to stick it out while learning about the world of business. A year or so later, the investment firm that Hilary worked for was hiring, and she told me to submit my résumé. I could not believe it. Hilary worked in the Financial District, where people dressed in smart suits hurried around looking like they had important things to do.

Hilary had never known want, having gone to prep school and gotten a prestigious degree. Although she was whip-smart, she never treated me differently because of my lack of education or worldliness. When I hesitated about applying at her firm, she said, "Penny, you are very smart. They won't care that you don't have a degree, because they want someone they can train. Go for it!"

So I did, and to my great surprise, they hired me, over the stack of résumés that I saw on the desk. It seemed that others were seeing things in me that I could not yet see. I knew nothing about finance or investing, and had to learn about things like futures, options, indexes, and shorts. It was a steep learning curve, and sometimes everything seemed so foreign. But now I was working downtown, in a landmark high-rise, and I had my own office. It was hard work and long hours, but I was part of a team, and treated as such, which felt good. I made lots of mistakes, which didn't feel good, but my coworkers were patient, which I was not used to. I learned that when handling other people's money, everything had to be very precise.

I started college that fall, taking the subway to City College at night. I loved my office job, but I loved school even more. Learning new things like economics and Beat poetry was water to my parched soul. Even though I got home after ten and left at five in the morning to get to the office by six, I was thrilled to finally be on a path. Life was starting to look up, even if I was still struggling with loneliness and the past.

With my time suddenly my own, I had to *think* about what to do for fun, because the church had imposed such limits on what we were allowed to do. On one of my early morning runs, I spotted a run-down club on Mission Street called Cesar's Latin Palace, which offered free salsa lessons on Thursday nights. Despite having two left feet, I loved it. Because I was not dating, I went alone, and because I didn't drink, I was able to have good, cheap fun. On Fridays, the club had a live band and women got in free, so it became my routine. Most of the men were Latin, spoke little English—and were great dancers. I fell into the world of Celia Cruz and Ruben Blades, the sound reminding me of my early days in the Bronx. I discovered a bar a few doors down, El Rio, which had world beat dance on Sunday nights. Then I dabbled in the South of Market dance scene at the DNA Lounge and the Holy Cow. The Financial District had salsa dancing at Sol y Luna, a different crowd, but great DJs. My world opened up, and being single in San Francisco started to be fun.

On the other hand, living with my brother was not. When I first moved out to California, we were good together. We shared expenses, chores, and meals, and grew closer because of it.

His friends became my friends when I had none, and I learned from a safe, protected place what the real world was like outside the church. I was able to shed some of my fears and become cheerier and less rigid. I was also there for him, during hard times in school and when Yvette, a gorgeous Greek grad student whom Steven was in love with, left him. We constantly discussed what we each wanted out of life, and trips we wanted to take.

Late one night, he heard me crying in my room and came in to see what was up.

"Steven, I'm too stupid for college," I said.

"Penny, what do you mean? You just started. It hasn't even been a semester."

"Mama told me I was too stupid for college, and she was right," I sobbed. I was upset because I had received an eighty on a math test.

"What do you mean, Mama said you were too stupid?" he asked.

It was hard for me to believe that he didn't know this, because my stepmother's refusal to send me to college had been such a pivotal moment in my life. I told him the story, and how she had laughed in my face when I wanted to continue my education. Still in tears, I confessed how I hated that he got to go to Harvard, when I never got to go to college at all.

Steven hung his head and seemed genuinely shaken. "I am so sorry, Penny. It is terrible that this happened to you."

"You did not know?" I asked, still incredulous. Steven and my stepmother were very close. They talked all the time. How could he not know? "Steven, did you ever ask Mama why she was so mean to me? Why she hated me so much?"

After a pause, Steven replied, "Yes, I asked her, many times, but she never had an answer for me. She always said she did not know. I felt bad about how she treated you."

I could not stop crying. He held me for a long time.

We talked until early morning. Steven was very kind and sympathetic to me that night, but it didn't last. Maybe he wanted to forget that it ever happened. Or avoid upsetting the memories of his privileged childhood. Maybe he was just too caught up in his own life. I wasn't sure.

I started seeing a side of Steven that I had not noticed at first. At first, he was good to me, setting me up with his friends and a job. But Steven was very busy with school, and accustomed as I was to the servant's role, I tried to do everything around the house to make his life easier, despite being a working student myself. Sometimes he came home in a foul mood, and had a condescending or sharp tone with me, or stayed in his room for days, ignoring me without explanation. He was hot or cold, nothing in between. Everything about our life had to be his way, even though I paid my share of expenses. He would question who I could have over and when. He would reject what I wanted to put on the walls or windows. It was the Little Prince all over again.

The last straw came when I bought some material to hand-stitch curtains for the bathroom window. I could never relax in front of a bare window, so I made simple lace curtains that let in light while obscuring the view.

"Those are coming down. You should have asked me before you put them up," Steven admonished, his tone lawyerly.

"But you're never home, and I hate going to the bathroom with no privacy."

"Well, that's tough," he said, retreating into his office. "Take them down."

I knew that the curtains were not worth fighting over, but

something in Steven's tone woke me up. I could not articulate why, but something inside me told me that I needed to stand up for myself. Or else I would forever be that broken little girl.

It was time to move out.

24

Family Matters

My sister and stepmother flew up from Desert Hot Springs to San Francisco for a rare visit. On the drive from the airport, I promised my stepmother that I would make *csirkepaprikas*, paprika chicken, her favorite Hungarian meal, while she was here. We were en route to the Hilton, where Steven was treating us to a pricey brunch. Though everyone was in good spirits for the visit, I was more nervous around my stepmother than usual.

Today I hoped to get some answers.

I had always wanted an explanation from her. *Why? Why did you treat me the way you did? What would make a person be that cruel to a child? Why did my father choose to look the other way?* Yet for twenty years, these questions had been forbidden territory in my family. Everyone pretended that nothing had happened, and I had been too traumatized by it to bring it out into the open. I had played along with the happy domestic routine, despite the fact that the falseness of it only deepened my pain.

But that wasn't going to cut it anymore. I was not the same person that I was when I had moved to San Francisco. I had been forced to come to grips with my faith and my failed marriage. That crisis had changed me for the better because I had learned to face my mistakes, to stand on my own two feet, and to rebuild my life on my terms. But I still had not addressed my family history. Until now it had never occurred to me that I could even do so.

"Look, Mama, they have *dobos torte* and *kifli!*" I said, sharing my stepmother's love of Hungarian pastries. The Hilton had a great buffet, and the mountain of food and gorgeous desserts made us all giddy.

To make conversation and calm my nerves, I asked my stepmother how Papa was.

"Your father is your father. He never changes," my mother replied acerbically.

"How is your apartment?" she asked me, changing the subject. A few months earlier, I had found my own place near Golden Gate Park, which displeased my brother to no end, and he let me know constantly.

"It's very small, just one room and a kitchen, but I like it," I said.

"When are you going to give up your shenanigans and move back in with me?" my brother asked, pretending to be joking. "It's so foggy out there."

The truth was, I cherished my newly found independence, and for the first time in my life, I felt like I was coming into my own. I loved having my own place and being away from his dominating influence. But Steven was not ready to hear that, so I did not say it.

As we ate ourselves silly at the buffet, we discussed the rest of the extended family, what each cousin was doing, who was getting married, who had bought a house, who was saying what about who. There was always drama in the family at large, and everyone felt free to chime in on everyone else's business. I was quite surprised that I had not heard from any of my cousins since my divorce.

Kitti told us about her boyfriend, Luke, and about her plans to transfer from her community college to San Jose State. I sat back and observed my siblings interacting with my stepmother. Both, usually self-absorbed, were more solicitous toward her, I thought. I wondered what was going on.

When Steven and Kitti left for the bathroom, I saw a window of opportunity to talk directly to my stepmother. I found myself shaking as I tried to get up the nerve to ask serious questions.

"Mama, why did you marry my father?" I finally asked, way more timidly than I had planned. Burning on my tongue was, "Why did you hate me so much?" but I could not muster up the courage to get the words out. Inexplicably, I was still clinging to the belief that I was to blame for her meanness, which justified her behavior somehow. Asking her about why she married my father—whom we both considered a loser—seemed to be the safest entry point to the sensitive issue that mattered the most.

My stepmother hesitated, as if pondering her every word. "I hated living at home," she said slowly, keeping her eyes glued to her plate. "Hungarian girls do not leave home until they are married. My mother was very strict, and I wanted out. He was Hungarian, a refugee like us. He was good-looking and charming, so I accepted his proposal."

She did not look up at me as she continued. "He said he had Swiss bank accounts." The idea of my father having any money was laughable. "My parents hated him. They saw through him," my stepmother said. "They knew he was a liar and a fast talker. They did not like that he had been married before. They begged me not to marry him, but I did not listen."

These revelations shocked me and explained some of the animus from Nagyi and Nagyi-papa toward my dad. But they still didn't answer why my stepmother had abused me. I wanted her to continue her story—to tell me what I really needed to know—but she hung her head silently until my brother and sister returned. The rest of the meal was small talk. We never got back to what really mattered.

Later that night, as I lay awake in bed, I rehashed my stepmother's story. I had no idea that she, too, had wanted to escape her home life. To this day, Nagyi and Nagyi-papa were always doting on her. Were they mean as parents? That was hard to imagine. They were firm but loving and generous to the grandkids. It did not make sense. Did my stepmother's cruelty have anything to do with my father? Was he to blame? Did it justify why she had mistreated me so? Over and over, I replayed her words, as I grappled with my own still-raw grief and my need for answers. I fought against the notion that she might be a victim too. But somehow she was. My father had let both of us down. Maybe it was not about me at all. Around in circles I went as I drifted off.

After my stepmother and Kitti left, I tried to avoid letting these thoughts consume me, and sometimes I succeeded. My first semester at City College was winding down. I was more than passing my courses, and I had received compliments on my class contributions from my teachers, which was a huge shot in the arm to me. Much to my surprise, I was making new friends all the time.

Hilary and her cohorts sought me out for dinners and drinks whenever I was not in class. I was starting to date—men I met at salsa clubs or on Tele-personals, a voicemail dating service in *The Guardian*, San Francisco's fringe newspaper. These lifestyle changes, a far cry from my repressed experience in Michigan, let me see myself in a new light. I was feeling more confident, and less like damaged goods. I cried less and laughed more. Through work, school, and dancing, I was finding a community that was my own. It felt good, even if I could not completely escape feeling the weight of being flawed.

Christmas was coming, and the city glowed with parties, lights, and good cheer. Most of my friends left town for Christmas until after the New Year. When our semesters ended, Steven and I flew down to Desert Hot Springs to be with the family. The shabby little house seemed festive, with all the decorations I grew up with: fancy glass ornaments, a small Nativity scene, and *szaloncukor*, a traditional Hungarian Christmas candy that was wrapped in colorful paper and hung on the tree. There was an abundance of presents under the tree, way more than I expected, and even my father seemed more upbeat.

"How you doing, Chicken? How is school?" he asked as I gave him a hug, reminding me of our old routine. I wasn't sure how to react to my father these days.

"It's fine, Dad," I said. "I like school a lot."

I hid my little presents around the tree and joined Steven and Kitti in the kitchen to help with a quick dinner that we had picked up on the way from the airport. My brother and I had gone in together on a space heater for Mama, which he would drive to the store to get in the morning. Later that night, Kitti and I drove to a dance club in Cathedral City, where we met up with her young friends. We talked about clothes, school, and dating. For the first time, I felt like we were normal sisters.

Hungarians traditionally open presents on Christmas Eve, after a light meal, usually consisting of fish. We ate in the living room so Mama could stay in her recliner, as she seemed more tired than usual. We all sat around the tree, playing Christmas music on the old stereo. As usual, Steven was the self-appointed emcee, handing out the presents, one at a time, with great flourish and ceremony. After that, we would all pause to watch each person open their gift. My stepmother pointed out a large package that she wanted Steven to start with. Steven read the tag and announced it was for me. Surprised, I looked up at my stepmother to see whether it was a mistake. She nodded silently. I took the parcel, surprised at its weight.

"What could this be?" I asked, looking at my sister and brother, neither of whom had much money for something this heavy.

I tore off the paper, discovering a box from Ohrbach's, a high-end department store in Southern California that I had heard about but had never been to. Inside the box was a gorgeous cashmere sweater. I had never received anything so soft and lovely before.

"Who's this from?" I asked, looking around.

"It's from me," my stepmother said quietly, in almost a baby-talk voice. She didn't bother to include my father in the giving, even though his was the only income that she had.

I did not know what to say. I usually received sale items from Alexander's, the cheapest department store in Queens, which Nagyi or Aunt Sári picked up for my stepmother so that I'd have something under the tree. The gifts were usually coarse, off-color, or outdated. One time, my stepmother even gave me a pair of slippers that she returned for the refund after Christmas, just to appear to be giving me something.

But the cashmere sweater in my hand was sumptuous, stylish, and expensive. I looked quizzically at my brother and sister, who were smiling at me and in a hurry to get to the rest of the gifts.

"Let's go, let's go, there's more presents here," Kitti implored.

"Thank you," I mumbled quietly as I hugged my stepmother loosely.

When my brother continued distributing the presents, my

name came up again. I thought Steven was playing a joke on me. Seemingly, every other gift was for me, and from my stepmother. If I was surprised by the first gift, the rest of them genuinely perplexed me. There was an elegant leather wallet, an angora sweater, a bottle of perfume, and a beautiful shoulder bag for books that Kitti must have picked out, judging by her grin.

I appeared to get as many, if not more, gifts than my siblings, but oddly they did not seem surprised. Kitti loved her Sony Discman that Steven and I gave her, and Steven loved the rare Grateful Dead T-shirt that I got him from Amoeba Music, a store on Haight Street. Finally, I had to speak up.

"Mama, this is too much for me. We should take some of this back. How can you afford all this? I really don't need all this."

"*Nem, nem veszem vissza őket*. No, we're not taking them back. I wanted to buy you those things. Kitti helped me pick them out."

Steven and Kitti were smiling at me as if they were in on it. I gazed at my stepmother. I was quiet for a moment, still at a loss as to what to say.

"*Gyerünk, együnk, éhes vagyok*. Come on, let's eat, I am hungry," my father interrupted, saving me from saying anything else.

The next day, as I was preparing to go back home, my stepmother asked Kitti to get the ornate silver tray stored in the vitrine, the display case that housed her treasured porcelain. Kitti ran to get it and handed it to me in a velvet case.

"Mama, what is this for?" I asked, bewildered.

"I want you to have it," she said quietly, almost sheepishly, barely holding my eye for a second.

"But why? This is too fancy; I'll never use this."

"That's okay, I want you to have it. You'll use it someday." She glanced at me and then quickly looked away. "Put it in your suitcase so you don't lose it. It came from Hungary."

I was confused by these acts of kindness, but they did not diminish my desire to ultimately confront her about the pain she had inflicted on me. This was the holidays, though, and the time was not right. I vowed to myself that I would summon the courage on the next visit.

I bent over to hug my stepmother in her recliner, thanking her for the gifts, unable to articulate my feelings about her generosity. Kitti, who was driving my brother and me to the airport, hurried me along.

"Let's go, I don't want to hit traffic," she said jokingly. There was no traffic in that part of the desert.

During the drive to the airport, the conversation seemed deliberately light. We discussed the pop songs my sister was into, like "Someday" by Mariah Carey, versus the "serious" music my brother and I favored, including R.E.M., Lenny Kravitz, and Prince. On the short flight home, Steven and I talked about how happy Kitti seemed, about her boyfriend, who was tall and good-looking, and loved dancing as much as she did. Soon enough we were home and thrown again back into the hectic world of work, school, and a new semester.

One late afternoon, as I was going over a long list of tedious interest payments at work, the phone rang. It jolted me because I never got calls at the office after the markets closed. I was hoping that it was Ricardo, a guy I had recently met at a tango class at Harry Denton's in the Financial District. He had asked me for my number. He was handsome and a great dancer. I picked up with a smile in my voice, planning on playing it coy.

"Hello, this is Penny, who's calling?"

"Penny, it's Steven. You need to get on a plane right away. Mama is dying, and she may not last the night."

25

Eulogy for a Mother

I arrived late at night to a house already in the palls of death. I had known that my stepmother had been ill, but not that she was this close to gone. She had previously been diagnosed with breast cancer, but it had been in remission. Until now, my brother had never mentioned that she might be dying, and the issue never came up during my recent holiday visit. Had my siblings been hiding her condition from me? Or did they not see a need to tell me everything, since I had been away for so long?

During the flight to Desert Hot Springs, I realized that I did not know how I felt about my stepmother's impending death. Kitti was somber when she picked me up from the airport, my first time seeing my carefree sister remotely serious. We hugged briefly, and I told her I was sorry for her that Mama was this sick. Kitti nodded her gratitude, with upturned hands that said, "What can you do?" She explained in a stoic voice that although Mama's cancer had abated steadily since last summer, she had suddenly gotten sicker after the New Year, and she had been going downhill since. She had been spending most of her days in bed, with Kitti cleaning her up and feeding her each day after returning home from school.

"Is Papa helping?" I asked, wondering how he was dealing

with this. My father had never so much as changed a diaper or made a meal in his life.

Kitti shook her head. "He is useless. He can't manage to do the simplest things, yet he complains all the time about how hard he has it."

"How bad is it?" I asked timidly, knowing that this was her mother, and no matter how I felt about her, this had to be hard for Kitti.

"It's bad," Kitti said. "The hospice people came this morning and said it was only a matter of time. There was nothing we could do. She is fading fast."

I looked over at Kitti as she drove. She was not crying. She seemed composed and businesslike. I could not help but wonder what she was thinking.

The house was dark and quiet when we arrived, smelling of decay and soiled sheets. Nagyi and Nagyi-papa were there, having flown in from Florida the day before. They sat in the dark on the sofa, their faces frozen in grief. My father rose from his chair to greet me.

"Hello, Chicken," he said. "Steven is in with your mother. You better go see her before it's too late."

I walked down the dimly lit hallway, thinking about the sadness on Nagyi's face. When I entered Mama's room, I was not prepared for what I saw.

My stepmother was unrecognizable. In just a few months since I had last visited, she had wasted away to half her size. Her scalp showed through the patchy tufts of white hair. Her hands were blotched black-and-blue from the IV needles. Her skull was shrunken, her temples protruding over bloated cheeks. My brother sat hunched over her bed, holding her hand. He wore dark circles under his eyes and looked like he had not slept in days.

Steven stood to greet me and explained the situation in a whisper. My stepmother's body had simply given up. After years of radiation and chemotherapy, on top of the cortisone she'd taken for decades, her liver could no longer function. The best that doctors could do was put her on morphine to dull the pain. Hospice said it was a matter of days.

As Steven and I sat in silence, I continued to grapple with my emotions. I looked at Steven and wondered how he could assume I felt the same way about his mother as he did, but I could see that it did not occur to him that it was otherwise. I looked around the room, which was small, dark, and decrepit. The smell of rotten flesh was unbearable, but I did not dare leave. I felt sorry for my brother, whose calm belied his pain. Yet somehow I was unable to share that pain. The shell of the woman in the bed had ruined my life and had never acknowledged it. She was dying young, at fifty-two, in squalor, and that was sad. Though I did not wish for her to suffer this fate, I still did not feel much of anything—not sadness, not even anger.

After a few hours of this quiet vigil, my brother suggested that I get some sleep so I could relieve him in the morning. I placed a hand on his shoulder, not knowing what else to say. Then I left, found a spare cot in Kitti's room, and fell into a deep sleep.

A few hours later, my father shook me awake.

"*Penniké, Penniké, az anyád meghalt. Menj el most meglátogatni.*"—"Penny, your mother is dead. Go see her."

It took a few moments to comprehend what he was saying. Still groggy, I stood on weak legs and walked to her room. The door was open, and Nagyi and Nagyi-papa sat by her bed in tears. Nagyi held a rosary in one hand; Nagyi-papa held her other one. My brother sat on the other side of the bed and moved aside for me.

"What happened?" I asked quietly.

"She never woke up," Steven said. "I stayed with her all night. She passed about ten minutes ago."

I stood frozen in my place as I stared at the corpse on the bed. I was numb. No sadness. No grief. Just empty. I looked up to see Nagyi crying as she touched the body.

"*Szegényke, annyira szenvedett.*"—"Poor thing, she suffered so much," Nagyi said through her tears.

"*Egy szülő, akinek nem szabad temetnie a gyermekét.*"—"A parent should not have to bury their child," Nagyi-papa said sadly.

My brother moved aside, motioning for me to take his place near the head of the bed. I hesitated but took his position on the bed. Steven went over to hug Kitti, who cried on his shoulder. I just stared at the body, not knowing what to do.

My grandmother broke the silence.

"*Jó von, felhívhatod a temetkezési vállalkozást?*"—"Okay, Steven, can you call the funeral home, please?"

Steven nodded, and I followed him out of the room.

The rest of the week was a blur of exhaustion and activity in the crowded house. Aunt Sári arrived at the airport and needed to get picked up. Steven and my grandparents met with the funeral people and the priest at the local Catholic church. My father was in and out but did not say much, and curiously was not part of the planning. I helped with cooking and tidied the house as best as I could. I felt like a fly on the wall, seeing the actors on a stage, not quite being a part of the story. Everyone looked to my brother to lead them.

I felt sympathy for my emotionally frail grandparents, who clung to each other as they moved wordlessly through the days. But on some level, I was relieved about the death of my stepmother. In the war between us, I had survived, and she was gone.

I knew that this was a terrible way to think—people all around me were grieving, and I hurt for them.

On the day of the funeral, I tried to muster something, anything, for my stepmother, but it was of no use. I rode to the church with Kitti, Steven, and my father in Kitti's car. Aunt Sári and our grandparents had a rental. At the church, there were maybe half a dozen people besides us, some who rose to greet my father, who played his part of the grieving widower. It seemed that my parents did not have many friends. The family shuffled into the first pew, but there was not enough room for me, so I sat in the back. No one seemed to notice.

This was my first funeral, so I did not know what to expect. Although my grandparents were not comfortable with the service being in English, there was no Hungarian priest anywhere near us. An organist played some gentle hymns as a few more people wandered in. A priest in a purple robe said a few words before my brother stepped up to say the eulogy. He had not mentioned that he was writing one. I wondered where he had found the time, as the small house had been full of people night and day. Despite his grief, Steven stood tall and looked scholarly in his glasses and suit.

"We are here to celebrate the life of my mother, who was a great woman," he began with an orator's confidence and cadence. At his words, my heart stopped beating, and I felt myself leave my body to observe the room from above.

"She was a wonderful, loving mother to her children, Kitti, Penny, and myself."

Did he really just say that?

"She was cultured and well-read. She loved music, opera, and theater. She was warm, generous, and loving."

On and on he went. As I watched him, the casket, and the

people in the room, some wiping their eyes, I wondered: Who was Steven talking about? The mother I had known was cold, bitter, and mean. She had read embossed novels and watched daytime soaps. I hadn't ever heard opera in the house since we moved to New York and knew my parents hadn't been out in many years. It was as though he was talking about a completely different person.

Then it dawned on me. This version of my stepmother was the one my brother and the family wanted to remember. My father knew better, and I knew better, and maybe everyone else did too, but my family sat politely, quietly morose. My father was burying his second wife, which had to hurt more than he was allowed to say in front of her family. When the service was over, my grandparents and aunt praised my brother and hugged him.

"Steven, that was wonderful. You wrote a beautiful eulogy. Thank you," said my grandmother before she broke into tears.

They seemed to ignore me. Maybe my presence was a reminder of a darker truth that they did not want to face.

During the burial, I remained silent. My brother's portrayal of my stepmother as a saint had been a jolt. How could he say all these glowing things about her when he knew it was not true? The only thing I felt was a growing disgust at how the family had chosen to remember her—at my expense. It was as if I had not been sitting there with them. As if they did not remember the beatings, the plainly visible scars, the black eyes, and the downcast face I wore throughout my childhood.

For years, I had been trying to figure out why my stepmother had been so unspeakably mean to me. I had just wanted her to tell me why, so I could understand. I vowed I could live with whatever she told me. Since childhood, I had gone from angry and vengeful to broken and weeping, then to energized but sad.

My life was better, much better than it ever was, but I felt the weight of *why* on my shoulders. It was hard to have peace or know for certain it was not my fault. I had missed my chance to ask my stepmother directly—I had thought there would be more time to get the answers. Yet I could not imagine her ever truly telling me why she was so hard on me, let alone apologizing for what she had done. She would have never told me the truth. And now, in the wake of her passing, the family narrative was firmly entrenched: she had been a normal, loving mother who died of cancer. I shook my head.

I could not be complicit in this lie. No matter what the cost.

26

Good Night, Father

My brother and I sat down in his sunny living room with the burritos I had picked up at Pancho Villa's on Sixteenth Street, our favorite taqueria. The apartment was eerily quiet, a contrast to the bustle of the streets. Steven put on some soft background music before he sat down heavily. I gazed at him. He seemed down—again.

"How are you doing, Steven?" I asked gently, already knowing the answer.

"I just miss her so much," he said. "She was my best friend. No matter what, she was always there for me. I just cannot believe she is gone."

I remained quiet, listening and making eye contact, touching his hand, letting my burrito grow cold. I did not know what to say, so I said nothing. I knew that empty clichés would not help.

My brother had been calling me more lately since Mama's funeral, wanting to hang out. Most of his friends were still in school and busy with their studies. None of them had been through a death, and after expressing sympathy and drinking a beer with us, they had little time or energy for his grief. His grief and his need for support seemed endless.

I spent as much time with Steven as I could, just being there for him, despite my gnawing feelings about the family whitewashing Mama's past. My brother had no idea that I was suffering too. He never asked how I felt about it all, but I never expected otherwise. I was becoming conscious of the fact that my family expected me to stoically handle whatever was dished out to me, whether it was my stepmother's abuse or everyone's obliviousness to the pain it had caused. My feelings really did not count. My family assumed that it was my role to comfort my brother in his mourning, even if his mother had left me scarred.

It had been about three months since the funeral. My brother was studying for his professional exams. I was working, going to school, and dating. Whenever Steven called, I came over. Sometimes during these visits, we would call Kitti to see how she was doing. She had not shown much emotion at the funeral.

My sister seemed to be having an easier time of it. She was getting on with her life. Although she missed Mama, she was able to quickly resume her routines of school and work. I wondered why. Maybe it was because she had watched my stepmother suffer so much. Maybe because she was only nineteen, and just wanted to do what young people do. Maybe she just wanted to be happy and unencumbered.

Steven and I hadn't heard from our father since the funeral. He was never around when we called. I didn't think much of it— he was never around much during my childhood—until we got a panicked call from Kitti. She had come home from a weekend outing with friends to find all her things packed up and moved into the garage. When she confronted our father, he said that he was getting married, and that Aranka, his fiancée, wanted to use Kitti's bedroom as her sewing room.

Huddled by the phone, Steven and I stared at each other in

disbelief. Neither of us knew that Dad had been seeing someone. We had never even heard of Aranka.

"I cannot believe he is seeing someone only three months after Mama died," an incredulous Steven told Kitti.

"I didn't know either," she answered. "When I asked him, he said she was a Hungarian woman he knew from the coffee shop in town."

"Kitti, did you ask him if he told Aranka you still lived there?" Steven asked, his tone back to in charge.

"Steven, I did not know what to say. He just said Aranka wants the room, and that was that. What am I going to do?"

"Did he tell you he was getting married before today?" I asked.

"No, he didn't. But he is never home anymore, and between work and school, neither am I."

It was clear that Kitti was shocked and lost—and looking for us to figure out what to do. We asked her whether she could stay with a friend or her boyfriend until she found her own place. Steven and I also told her to keep going to school, that we would drive down on the weekend to talk to Papa and help move her stuff. It did not make sense for Steven to try to reason with my father over the phone. I was furious at my father, but I shouldn't have been surprised. Since the day he whisked me away from Aunt Charlotte's, I could not remember a single time when he had put his family first. He went hunting on holiday weekends, leaving us home alone with no cash or transportation. He always found money for drinking at the bar when there was no food at home. He had cash for new rifles but not for my school clothes.

Since the funeral, my grandmother had been more vocal about her disdain for my father. Nagyi called me numerous times to check on how Steven was handling things, but mainly to rant to me about my father. She never asked how I was doing.

"*Penniké, Tudod, milyen senkiházi vagy, mint apa?*"—"Penny, do you know what a nobody your father is?" She would yell these things at me in a fit of rage, as if I were to blame.

"*Egy dollárt sem adott a felesége temetésére.*"—"He did not give a single dollar for his wife's funeral."

"*Még virágot sem vett neki.*"—"He didn't even buy her flowers."

"*Ki csinálja ezt? Miféle ember nem vásárol legalább virágot temetésre?*"—"Who does that? What kind of person does not at least buy flowers for a funeral?"

On and on she went, bringing up all the ways that my father had slighted the family over the years. How he had lied about having Swiss bank accounts. How there were times when he didn't make enough to buy food, which I knew, but also how she had to buy my stepmother medicine and pay for her doctors' visits, which I didn't. How he never remembered my stepmother's birthday (or mine, but Nagyi never mentioned that). How Nagyi had to buy my parents a new stove and a washer for Desert Hot Springs because my father could not. How she had told my step-mother not to marry him.

I bit my tongue. I did not know what to say. I was as disgusted with him as she was. How could my father throw my sister out of the house? It was a good thing that Nagyi did not know about Aranka.

On the drive down to Southern California, Steven and I had our first opportunity to discuss the situation at length. My brother took charge and had called our father repeatedly until he finally caught him at home. As usual, Papa was short and defensive. He said he had done his part. He had stayed with Mama while she was sick and now wanted his own happiness. He told Steven that he did not know that Aranka had moved Kitti's things to the garage, but that Kitti was never home anyway. He said he had assumed that Kitti was living somewhere else. In the end, he grudgingly agreed to be home the night that Steven and I arrived.

"How can Papa be so clueless?" I asked Steven in the car. "Is he really so out of touch, or does he just not care about Kitti, like he did not care about me?"

My brother did not have an answer. He had never said anything bad about our father, even with this latest act of absenteeism. Steven, too, had been on the receiving end of Nagyi's fury over Papa's deficiencies, but my brother was taking a softer, more lenient approach. It's as if he understood my father's weakness and did not hold it against him. Or maybe, because he had a loving mother, Papa's neglect affected him less.

This time, though, I was not going to sit by and let Steven whitewash the situation, like he had done with my stepmother. In blunt terms, I complained to him about the choices that our father had made. I could never understand how Papa could spend money on drinks at the bar when we needed things at home, and had to borrow money from Nagyi constantly. How he never thought of our future. Why he had not thought about what I would do when I graduated high school. How could he even think of remarrying so soon? And why would anyone want to be with him anyway?

"I don't know what he is thinking," Steven said, "but he is who he is, Penny."

I said nothing. In my silence, I was hoping that Steven would sense that his answer was not good enough.

Finally, he said, "I don't know what to tell you, but if you think he is such a bad father, you should tell him yourself."

I thought about it for a few moments. He was right. I had lost my opportunity to get answers from my stepmother, but glaring at me was the *one* opportunity I did have left. Yes, I would sit down with my father and ask him tough questions about my childhood, including why he took me from Aunt Charlotte.

Throughout the years, my father had always claimed innocence. It was someone else's fault that Kitti was being thrown out of her home so soon after she had lost her mother. Just like he pretended not to know I was being abused all my life, even though he was living under the same roof with us. I finally saw it: he just would not accept blame for anything. I was tired of him getting away with it.

"You're right, Steven. I'm going to tell him this weekend."

We spent the rest of the drive discussing the logistics about how to help Kitti. We would pack up her stuff and move it into storage. We'd help her look at some shared apartments near her school. Papa had done nothing to help Kitti himself. He had a small pickup truck and could have offered to move her stuff, but he didn't.

We arrived in Desert Hot Springs at dusk, just as the sun washed the horizon in an orange glow, and the clouds turned purple. We met Kitti at her friend's place. Steven and I hugged her and asked how she was bearing up.

"I'm fine. I was shocked and mad at Dad, but I'm over it now," she said. "I just want to get my stuff into storage and get on with my life. I'm going to finish school, and I'm going to be happy. I think that's what Mama would have wanted."

We agreed.

Then the three of us drove over together to my father's house. Papa came out to greet each of us as if it were a routine family visit.

"Hello, Chicken, how is school?"

"Fine, Papa, but it was a long drive. I need to use the bathroom."

When I came out, Steven and Kitti were sitting at the kitchen table with our father. He looked well, like in the days before my mother got sick. He seemed happy. The house had had some work done to it. It was cleaner and had fresh curtains on the windows.

My brother and sister politely asked about his coming marriage, and about Kitti moving out, but I barely heard them. I was focused on my father, unable to reconcile his jovial demeanor with the recent events. His second wife had suffered for years and had died a painful death. He was broke and, as far as we knew, did not have work. He had effectively kicked his grieving daughter out of the house while she was still in school. I studied my brother and sister. They seemed calm. I heard my brother gently saying something was not fair to Kitti. I was seething with anger.

"Dad, I want to tell you something." Everyone stopped talking and looked at me. My stomach clenched. I looked Papa in the eye and took a breath.

"You have been a terrible father. You never think of what your kids need. You sat around and did nothing while Mama abused me for years. Everyone knew she was mean to me. You knew she hated me, because she complained about me all the time, but you didn't do anything about it. And the one time I asked you to help me, on the drive back from Hicksville when I ran away, I begged you to let me live somewhere else. You said you'd take care of it, but you didn't. You made me stay and suffer some more even though you knew. You cannot say you didn't."

The words just came out. Never in my life had I spoken so directly to him, or to anyone in my family. When I was finished, we could all hear the clock ticking on the wall, the refrigerator humming. No one spoke for a long time. Finally, my father mustered a response.

"You think I was a bad father?"

"Yes, I think you were a terrible father," I said forcefully. "I would have been better off with no father at all."

My father did not answer me. He got up from his chair and left the room. My brother and sister sat in silence. I went outside for some air and then sat in the car.

I never saw my father again.

27

The Dark Prince

T he platform shook as I closed my eyes and waited for the train. It was a Thursday night, and I was spent after three nights of classes after work.

"Hey, Penny!" my friend Eloise called, jolting me awake. I knew better than to fall asleep on the train platform at night.

"Hello, you," I called back. I liked Eloise, who was also a night student at City College. After working ten years on cruise ships, she had decided to follow her passion and study creative writing. We were both single. Eloise was free-spirited and way more fun than me.

"Let's go to Café Du Nord and listen to this great jazz singer," she'd say, referring to a club in the city that I had never heard of. Or "Let's go to the film noir festival at the Roxie," before I knew what film noir was. We would often discuss work, school, books, or dating.

Tonight was no exception.

"I am so glad I found you!" Eloise exclaimed. "I found this ad for a cool bike club. I think we should swear off guys and take up mountain biking."

That sounded like a great idea. I wasn't having any luck in the dating world. Because of my divorce, I had a long list of things I was looking for in a relationship, and a commitment was at the top of the list. Finding someone who fit the bill wasn't easy.

The ad for the bike club said its rides were on Sundays, which worked for my school schedule. The flier listed a name and a number to call, which I wrote down.

"All right, I'm in," I said.

Since my confrontation with Papa, my brother had thrown himself into his studies, and I was finishing up a hard semester of school. I was lonely. My friend Hilary had met someone serious and was scarce on the weekends.

I was spending less and less time with Steven—and not just because we were both busy. He was changing somehow. He had been my soulmate, but now it was hard being in his presence. He was getting downright mean and hurtful to those around him.

Before I moved in with him, Aunt Sári had warned me that he could be moody and would not be easy to live with, but I hadn't thought much of it at the time. Even Nagyi asked me occasionally, *"Penniké, Penny, hogy boldogulsz Stevenlal?"*—"How are you getting along with Steven?"

Right after my divorce, Steven had been very gentle and understanding. But since Mama's funeral, he had become strident, demanding, and harsh. The kind, thoughtful person he had been was gone. He had to dominate every situation. The last time I had hung out with him and his girlfriend, Abby, he had berated her in front of me. Apparently, Abby had forgotten to bring something that Steven had asked her to pick up, thereby "spoiling" the evening. She apologized profusely and offered to make the lengthy trip to get the item, but he sharply told her it was too late—the evening was already beyond repair. Feeling bad for her, I made an excuse and left. Abby was a sweet, kind person, and did not deserve this mental abuse. I did not have the appetite to be around Steven, or his anger.

Maybe joining a bike club was exactly what I needed.

The voice on the answering machine for the Parnassus Bike Club had a charming British accent, which I had a thing for. I smiled to myself as I waited to leave a message. In the days that followed, I completely forgot about the message. I had too many other things to think about.

On Saturday afternoon, the ringing jolted me awake. I had fallen asleep on my thrift store couch while studying for a final.

"Hullo there, is this Penny?"

I had no idea who this was. I hoped it wasn't an annoying sales call.

"This is Charles Bain from the Parnassus Bike Club. You called about a bike ride."

That accent again.

"Oh, hello. Yes, that's me," I said, now awake and smiling.

The first ride, he said, would be in Marin, on a trail called Railroad Grade, which went up a mountain called Tamalpais, or Tam for short. I got directions from Charles and agreed to come the next day. Earlier, I had purchased a beautiful, dark green Gary Fisher bike. Finally, I would get out of the city and ride on a real mountain. I called Eloise to tell her that the plan was in place, but she still hadn't bought her bike and told me to go alone.

"I'll miss you," I said, knowing that I'd have more fun with her along.

For me, the shocking thing about mountain biking was that it involved actually *climbing* mountains, which turned out to be quite difficult. I met Charles and the rest of the club members at the bend of a heavily wooded road. There were gorgeous, tall redwoods and a stream that ran alongside a trail. There were ten to twelve people, all looking very fit and prepared with gloves, special shoes, and water, none of which I had. Charles handed us maps, describing the shady trail and the rules. Wait at each junction. Don't ride ahead. I fretted to myself that I might not be able to keep up with these folks.

Sensing my nervousness, Charles encouraged me in his polished accent: "I have extra water, and I'll stay with you on the ride up."

The riding was tough—rocky, hot, and dusty. What had I gotten myself into? I was dead last, but everyone was nice and told me not to worry. "It's how we all started," they said, but I did not believe them. The scenery made up for it, and once we stopped for lunch at the peak, the view of San Francisco Bay and the city made the arduous journey worthwhile. True to his word, Charles had stayed with me.

I had never done a sport before and had not known what to expect. During lunch, the bike club members asked me about my job, my schooling, where I lived, and whether I'd seen *Wallace and Gromit*, a new animation movie that had just come out. There was a scientist, an accountant, two architects, a few people in tech. One was a vegetarian and lived in Oakland; most lived in the city. Everyone was around my age and seemed easygoing and fun. Despite the grueling exercise, dirt, and sweat, I liked these people and was having fun. I fit in.

I couldn't wait to tell Steven. Maybe he could join too, I thought, hoping that the workouts and fresh air might make him less tense.

As the weeks rolled on, my riding improved, and I joined the club for midweek rides when I did not have class, on top of the regular Sunday rides. Steven did not want to join, and he joked that I was getting carried away. But his "jokes" always carried a derisive tone.

"What, all of a sudden, you're a *biciklista* (a cyclist)?"

I felt like I was defending myself for having a good time. I explained to him that Eloise had suggested that I try something new. "And I met this guy at the club."

"Oh, that's it!" Steven said, mocking me in a singsong voice. "Now I get it. You have a boyfriend."

I tried to ignore these put-downs and focus on my new friends. After riding with the club a few weeks, I found out that Charles also did volunteer work with underprivileged kids. That caught my attention. In the world of finance—where I still worked—the men I met were arrogant and self-absorbed. It was all about them. They boasted about their vacations, big trades, and fast cars. These guys were all undatable in my mind. Yet here was someone obviously smart and well employed but who also cared about other people enough to give his time. How refreshing. Volunteering was something I wanted to do, but I never had enough time. I had liked helping others in the church, and I missed it. I asked Charles whether he wanted to have coffee to discuss his charity work. He quickly agreed.

A few months after I joined the bike club, I started dating Charles, and we began to grow close. But I knew that if I wanted to take things to the next level, I would have to reveal my "secrets"— namely, my dysfunctional family and my inability to conceive. I felt vulnerable when talking about them, fearing he might reject me. If, on the other hand, Charles made light of my past—or did not understand the gravity of it—I could not go on dating him. When I decided to bring it up, I was nervous and scared, but he completely got it. He waited and listened, and held my hand as I slowly, haltingly, recounted my broken childhood. I was still angry with my stepmother and father. I was still coming to terms with the role that my brother and the rest of the family had played in it. Charles and I cried and talked into the night, huddled in the cove of my bed in the closet. He, too, had had a less than perfect childhood. That night brought us closer.

On Memorial Day weekend, I grudgingly went on a camping trip with Steven and Abby, only because the excursion had been planned for months. I had gotten used to biking with the group every weekend and was loath to miss a ride, but I had committed to my brother. By now, I was firmly part of a subgroup within the club: we were eating out after rides, seeing movies together, and exchanging calls to plan the next weekend.

The only upside of the camping trip was spending time with Abby, who I loved being around. She was a beautiful soul, an elementary school teacher, smart, well-read, fluent in Spanish and French. She always asked about my schooling and was full of encouragement for all that I was doing.

The road approaching the Sierras was a gorgeous drive. The mood in the car was light as we sang along with the radio and joked about what to do if we encountered a bear while camping. But throughout the drive, I couldn't help but wonder how my bike friends were doing.

We arrived at the campsite. Steven, Abby, and I found our spot and began clearing the ground and pitching our tents. We put food in the bear box, and I gathered kindling for the evening fire. Soon, I heard voices rising from their tent.

Complaining to Abby in a pedantic voice, as if speaking to an insolent child, Steven said, "Why would you talk to Wayne about me? Why would you tell him anything about what I was going through?"

"We were just chatting, and he asked about you," said Abby,

sounding nervous—and almost afraid. "I didn't think anything of it. Wayne and I talk all the time."

Wayne was a hairdresser for Steven, Abby, and a few of our close friends. I had met him at one of our house parties. Fun guy. Never took anything too seriously. He was a hairdresser, for God's sake, so he heard everyone's business. I was sure that Wayne didn't think twice about what Abby said. Steven was blowing things way out of proportion.

Steven and Abby emerged abruptly from the tent. I occupied myself with the kindling, pretending not to have heard anything. But after a minute of dead silence, Steven launched into another tirade against Abby.

"I was looking forward to a relaxing weekend, but now you've ruined it! Now I have to worry about what you say about me to people."

"Steven, I am sorry. I won't do it again," Abby begged. "Let's just forget it and have a good time."

"No, I'm not going to forget it!" Steven ranted. "And neither should you, if you want to be with me."

I walked away from them. I could not believe how Steven was speaking to her. He was being domineering and downright rude. Abby did not deserve this, even if she had been out of line, which she hadn't. Why was my brother making such a big deal of it? Why was he being so controlling? It made me nervous to be around him. It seemed there was no pleasing him. Months ago, before I had joined the bike club, I had mentioned the possibility of us buying a duplex or triplex where he, Kitti, and I could live together. He had upbraided me harshly for assuming that he would want to live in one house with us. "What if I want to do my own thing?" he had countered pointedly. Yet he had recently been chiding me about how much time I was spending with the bike club. He always had to be the boss. He had to have the upper hand and show that he had it. It did not make sense. Something was going on with him. And it unsettled me.

The rest of the weekend was miserable. Abby continued to apologize and kowtow to Steven, and he made sure to ignore her or bring up other slights from their relationship. I stayed far away from them during our hike, and after a frosty dinner, I went to sleep early. I could not wait to get home. I suggested that we leave early Monday morning to avoid the traffic, and I drove as fast as I could to put them and the weekend behind me. On the ride home, Steven tried to make jokes to lighten the mood, but the weekend was already ruined. I knew that his relationship was none of my business, but I felt sorry for Abby. I knew that if I sided with her, I would feel even more of Steven's wrath. So I did nothing.

The summer was a whirlwind in the bike club, and since I was dating the club leader, it was doubly fun. Charles was a respected architect, working in a big firm in San Francisco, designing cancer research hospitals. He had come to the United States on a scholarship and had decided to stay once his student visa expired. As a Brit, he was much more reserved than me, and naturally quiet as a person, which took some getting used to. He was very supportive of my education, and never pressured me for more time. I asked a lot about England, which seemed like such a romantic place to me. He told me about the beauty of the Lake District, of the ancient Roman wall that crossed the northern part of the country, and the "New" castle that his hometown was named after, which was built in 1063. Charles and I were good together. He helped me become a better rider and widened my view of the world. I had now become a strong enough cyclist to master Mount Diablo in the East Bay, and I was no longer trailing behind others during the rides. I was truly part of the gang.

That fall, I started my last year of college and got a new job as a clerk in a prestigious investment bank. Steven had passed his exams and was working as an engineer in a large firm. With my free time booked with bike outings, I was in motion nonstop—and loved it. It seemed whenever my brother called to do something, I already had plans.

"Penny, let's meet in Golden Gate Park on Sunday and hear some music."

"Sorry, Steven. I'd love to, but I am riding that day."

"You are spending too much time with your boyfriend."

How was I supposed to respond to that? And why did he so clearly resent me for finally being in a good place? I had made my own friends, and we were having meaningful conversations about books, travel, and life. Everything we did was fun, a far cry from the drama that I got from Steven. I still sympathized with my brother for the loss of his mother, but his behavior didn't seem to have anything to do with mourning. He had admonished me for trying to build a life around him by buying a duplex, but now he resented that I had built a life with others. He seemed almost intent on stopping me from moving on with my life. It made me edgy around him. I was always on alert, wondering whether I would be attacked, just like I had been with my step-mother.

No matter what Steven said, I was not about to give up my relationship with Charles or the bike club, even if I didn't know exactly how to tell my brother that. Yet I was afraid of how Steven would react if I told him the truth: I had found a new family—one that treated me like I belonged. Like an equal.

The holidays came, and my brother and I shared the load.

Thanksgiving was at his house with Charles, Abby, and Kitti, who was now in school much closer in San Jose; Christmas was at my place, where I over-decorated my first tree. As always, my brother had to be the master of ceremonies. Though Kitti and I were used to it, Charles saw it another way. From his vantage point, my brother had an unhealthy desire to be in charge. Preeminent. He had to have people beholden to him.

Charles's observations gave me fresh insights into my brother. Steven needed the attention. He had to dominate. He needed praise, which Abby had learned to shower on him.

"Steven, your dinner was so delicious. The stuffing was perfect, the turkey so moist," she would coo to him. This dynamic seemed rather one-sided. But it was the holidays, so I let it go.

January brought my last semester of college. I also began studying for the entry-level brokerage exam, which would qualify me for a job with Merrill Lynch, a big-time Wall Street firm. Brokers there had promised me a job once I got my degree. I longed to work on a real trading floor and do million-dollar security trades.

I was writing flash cards for the exam late one night when the phone rang. It was Steven.

"Penny, I never see you anymore."

I was surprised that he was calling so late. "How are you?"

"Well, I am not okay, actually."

My stomach dropped. "What's wrong? Are you sick? Is Kitti all right?"

"No, I am not sick. I assume Kitti is fine. But I am not happy with you."

He was obviously in one of his moods. Again.

"Me?" I asked. I scanned my brain for anything I could have done but came up blank. I hadn't seen or talked to Steven in many weeks. I was working and going to school. I was riding on Sundays. The days were blending into each other.

"You are not familial enough," Steven stated with a tone like he was telling me I had cancer.

"What does that mean?" I asked.

"You spend too much time with your friends, the bike club, and your silly boyfriend," he said with a sneer. "You don't spend enough time with me."

"Steven," I began timidly, "I am so busy. I have to see my boyfriend," I said pleadingly.

"Those are just excuses."

I paused, not knowing what to say.

"I want you to stop spending so much time with them," he said, his anger building. "As your brother, I demand it!" He spoke like someone with a right to demand it, to whom my compliance was a forgone conclusion.

My body became chilled to the bone. I hung up without saying a word. I had nothing to say.

28

———◆———

Last Call

On the night of the Merrill Lynch Christmas party at the Coppola Winery, I decided to throw caution to the wind. It must have been the wine, which kept being generously refilled. "Charles," I said, "let's quit our jobs and travel the world for a year."

I had shocked myself. Being so security based, and fearful of being homeless or without income, I had no idea where this impulsive idea had come from. As the seconds ticked by without a response, I thought that Charles hadn't heard me.

Charles sat up and, straightening his back, sized me up. Then he took my hand. "Deal," he said emphatically. "You're on."

We spent the rest of the evening at the Napa Valley winery giggling about what we had done. And we spent the next few months discussing and planning the details. We decided to sublet our rent-controlled apartment so I would know that I had a home to come back to. We saved money by eating in and renting movies at Le Video rather than going out.

The planning, and the trip, proved to be a good testing ground for our future. Each of us had needs to check off. Charles wanted to see the United States because most Europeans have a fascination with America. But I had been here my whole life and thought it would be boring. I wanted the exotic, but not on the tourist route. I wanted to meet people I wouldn't otherwise encounter in places like the Middle East and Africa.

We compromised. The plan was to start off the trip and the new millennium in Scotland, and then fly to Egypt, and backpack counterclockwise around the Mediterranean, following the path of Paul Theroux in *The Pillars of Hercules*. Then we would travel around North America, hitting national parks and cycling with friends we had met online in the mountain biking community.

In late December of 1999, off we went. We journeyed to Egypt, Jordan, Syria, Israel, and Turkey, and we added Western Europe so I could see Paris, Athens, Venice, and Rome. After four months abroad, Charles and I found ourselves on the East Coast before having to fly back to the U.K. for a wedding. We had been invited to a huge pool party at my cousin's place in Connecticut. Nagyi and Aunt Sári and the whole clan would be there, giving Charles a chance to meet the rest of my family. It was much hotter in the East in the summer than we were used to in foggy San Francisco. Thirsty, I ventured to the drink cooler, where I bumped into my brother.

"Hey, Steven, how are you?"

It was my first time seeing him since Charles and I had left on our trip. Our only communication had been emails when I could find Internet service, still rare in most parts of the world. I hugged Steven fiercely. Despite our differences, I loved my brother dearly, and kept hoping that his off-putting antics were just part of his grief.

"Hey, world traveler," he said, hugging me back.

"Is Abby here?"

"No, just me, Abby could not get away."

We chatted for a moment as I bent over the huge cooler

looking for a craft beer, which Charles and I favored back home. No one we knew drank Budweiser or Coors, which was all I could see. Fortunately, I found a Sierra Nevada hidden in the bottom and grabbed it.

"Ooh good," I said, "this will work."

Steven stared at me and laughed slightly. But he was not amused.

"Penny, you barely drink. Why are you giving that to your boyfriend? You should give it to me."

His sneering tone made me ill at ease. The last thing I wanted was for him to make a scene, so I plotted a quick exit strategy.

"Charles and I will share this one, "I offered. "I'm sure there's another one in there. Have a good time."

And with that, I walked away to make the rounds with Charles.

Seeing all my relatives reminded me how far I had come since joining the bike club a few years earlier. I was less fearful than the tortured soul who had left the church. I had graduated college with a business degree. Contrary to my stepmother's denouncements, I had earned straight As, and was runner-up for valedictorian. Merrill Lynch had hired me as a sales assistant, and I had done multimillion-dollar trades, a far cry from being a waitress at the International House of Pancakes. I was still honing my skills and accumulating the financial licenses needed to advance in the industry. More important, everything I was doing was because I had decided to, not to please my stepmother, the church, or anyone else.

Yet if I was being honest, Steven still had an uncanny ability to put a damper on everything I had achieved. Like my stepmother, he had this hold over me that I could not quite explain. My past, it seemed, was never really past. It always lurked in the shadows.

Despite my brother's best efforts, I soldiered forward.

Charles and I had grown closer and fallen in love, ironing out the differences that my damaged family history and his reserved culture had brought out in us. He had convinced me it was time to live together, something I had been petrified to do because of my divorce. We were moving forward together.

After the pool party, Charles and I flew to England. It did not disappoint. We were there for the wedding of his best friend. As a groomsman, Charles looked so handsome in his high-collared dress shirt, embroidered waistcoat, and gold cravat. Being tall and thin, with a ginger goatee, he carried his morning suit well. The reception was at the beautiful fourteenth-century Langley Castle in Hexham, which had worn stone walls, stained glass, and enormous ceilings. It was a magical setting, and as church bells rang in the distant green valley, I soaked it all in, as if I were in a fairy tale.

It was a large wedding, full of old relatives and a small crowd of people our age seated together. Many of them were cyclists like us, or people whom Charles had known since childhood. I was listening carefully to a joke being told across the table—the accent forcing me to pay close attention—when a movement caught my eye to the right. The raucous table suddenly became quiet, and all time stopped.

Charles got down on one knee and took my hand. "Penny Alexandria . . ."

I waited for what felt like an eternity and thought in my excitement that I had missed the moment.

"Yes. Yes, Charles Bain, I will marry you."

The table broke out into a loud cheer.

"Well, you could've waited for me to ask you properly," Charles joked, getting up from the ground, as I threw my arms around his neck. Our friends rose to congratulate us and pat

Charles on the back. The groom came over with a bottle of champagne and stemmed glasses.

At this point, I was crying and laughing and grinning from ear to ear, all at the same time. What could be better for an avowed Anglophile than being proposed to in an ancient English castle by a handsome Brit? I was over the moon.

After the castle wedding, Charles and I crisscrossed England to visit with Charles's family and friends to share our news. His family was very pleased to hear of our engagement and welcomed me into the family with open arms. They showered us with toasts and gifts: a sterling spoon set from his grandma, a crystal glass set from his aunt and uncle. I was so pleased to be part of what I considered to be a "normal" family. I asked Charles's aunt whether I could call her "Auntie Beatrice," as Charles did.

"Darling, you may call me whatever you want," she answered with a laugh. Not knowing my story, she did not understand what it meant to me to be part of a real family, but I basked in her warm welcome anyway.

Charles and I called my siblings and friends back home to announce our engagement. We promised to celebrate in person when we finished our travels and returned to San Francisco. My girlfriends were ecstatic, wanting every detail. Their boyfriends, less so. They knew now that Charles had "fallen," as they called it, there would be more pressure on them to propose to their girlfriends. Steven and my family barely said a word.

During the next two months, Charles and I drove across the United States, visiting places like Yellowstone and Wind Cave National Park. We discussed what kind of wedding we wanted. Neither of us had much money left, and we knew that weddings were expensive. Charles suggested that we elope to Las Vegas for an Elvis wedding, a piece of Americana that he loved.

"Charles, there is no way I am going to elope. This is a big deal for me. This is more important to me than my first wedding. I earned this. I worked for it. I want to celebrate it with all our friends."

"Okay, I agree," he said. "But if we have a wedding, we have to start planning it right away."

When I had gotten married the first time at the age of eighteen, I had been too immature and too influenced by the church to make an informed, wholehearted decision. I had lived with the shame of that decision, and its aftermath, for years. This time around, I wanted to get it right, thereby overcoming and healing that part of my past.

I was not motived by fear or loneliness but was in this relationship with my whole heart and mind, for all the right reasons. Finding Charles was something to celebrate. We agreed that as soon as we got home, I would call our friends James and Ronny to ask for wedding planning assistance. James was a chef and restaurateur and was well connected in the industry.

After nine months of travel, we finally returned to our little apartment. I called James and Ronny right away. They would come over the next evening, after securing a promise that I'd cook up some Hungarian food that James loved. I was making *töltött káposzta*, stuffed cabbage. I decided to invite my brother and make a party of it. I called him next.

"Hey, Steven! We're home! We're having James and Ronny over tomorrow to help plan our wedding, and I am making *töltött káposzta*. Do you want to come? We'd love to see you."

Dead silence.

"Steven, are you there?"

"Yes, I am here, and no, I do not want to come over tomorrow," he said icily.

"Why?" I wondered whether he was okay.

"Because I am offended that you would call James and Ronny before you called me."

I had barely unpacked my bags, and he was starting already.

"And besides," Steven scoffed, "I am still offended by what you did at the pool party."

"The pool party?" I strained to think of what I could have done at the party.

"Yes, at the pool party. You gave your *boyfriend* the good beer instead of giving it to me. I haven't forgotten that. And I am insulted that you called friends instead of me when you got home. I am your brother, and I deserve more than that."

I held the phone to my ear in disbelief. In only a few seconds, my mood had transformed from euphoric to hurt and confused. It was a familiar pattern, but this time I felt something new: profound anger. Since coming to California with my broken life, I had striven to do everything right. I no longer depended on him or anyone else in the family for my well-being or happiness. I was fulfilling my own goals, and getting married was *my* dream. Yet he had to dominate it. He had to squash it in service of his need for eminence.

Quite suddenly, as if I had stepped over a threshold, something in me changed. I could not let Steven steal the joy that I had earned. Otherwise, I would be forever in his thrall. In a microsecond, I felt a power . . . a strength in my physical being. My soul shifted. I would never stand down to him, or anyone, ever again. I waited until Steven finished speaking.

"Are you done?" I asked with a new authority in my voice.

"Yes, I am done."

I hung up the phone. We never spoke again.

"Penniké, miért nem beszélsz a bátyáddal?"—"Penny, why aren't you speaking with your brother?" Nagyi asked in a pleading tone.

"Because he is a bully, and he is mean to me, and to Kitti. It's hurtful, Nagyi. He always has to make us feel small."

"Igazad van, igazad van, de ó a testvéred, és szüksége van rád."— "You're right, you're right, but he is your brother, and he needs you."

"Well, Nagyi, he can come to me if he wants to talk."

Since our phone call, Steven and I had not spoken. Now he was leaning on Kitti in the same way he had with me, belittling her needs and demanding more from her. She ignored him by not answering his calls anymore but told me about it when we talked.

Fortunately, I had many other things to occupy me. I was consumed with an exciting new job at Bloomberg, a cutting-edge software company where I finally got my own book of business instead of being someone's assistant. And I was planning a fabulous wedding at Fort Mason, a historic army base in San Francisco, overlooking the Golden Gate Bridge and Alcatraz. The family would stay on the base and be close to some of the Bay Area's most famous attractions. Charles and I mailed out the invitations before the end of the year, so that people could save the date.

As soon as she received her invitation, my grandmother called me again. This time, her tone was markedly different.

"Penniké, is Steven coming to the wedding?" It was a demand, not a question.

"No, Nagyi, he is not. We haven't spoken," I answered as gently as I could.

"*De meg kell hívnod, "ő a bátyád*," she said emphatically. "You have to invite him; he is your brother."

The next day, I received an email from Steven stating that "if I gave up my shenanigans, he would *allow* me to come to his house for Thanksgiving dinner," which had become our tradition since my stepmother had died. He still did not get it, but regardless I would not subject myself to his bullying again. I wrote back that I would be open to talking with him before Thanksgiving to discuss our issues, but that because he was verbally abusive and berated me constantly, I did not feel safe around him. I wanted a third person present when we talked. I asked him to pick the time and place and decide who he wanted to join us. I named some mutual friends who I knew were fair-minded and clear thinking and told Steven that I looked forward to hearing from him.

I never heard back.

But Nagyi was not giving up her fight. She called again a few weeks later.

"Penniké, if Steven is not coming to the wedding, then neither am I."

I paused, surprised that I had not considered that it might come to this. Nagyi either did not get it or refused to acknowledge what I had been through in the family because of her daughter—my stepmother. I realized that I would always be the victim of their family cover-up, of their lies about my stepmother and their complicity in her abuse—unless I stopped letting my brother repeat the pattern. I loved Steven, but I would not let myself be abused by anyone ever again.

"*Jo von, Nagyi, ha így érzed magad.*"—"Okay, Grandma, if that's how you feel, that's the way it's going to be."

That call was the end of my long, twisted relationship with

my stepfamily, which had started when Nagyi-papa had accompanied my father to take me away from the loving home I had with Aunt Charlotte. The people who had been my grandparents, aunts, uncles, and cousins, and who had always told me I was treated like one of them, were shunning me for not bowing down to my brother, even though they knew in essence that I was right. He was a bully.

As the wedding preparations moved forward, not one of my relatives bothered to RSVP. When I called my closest cousin, Bitsy, to ask whether she planned to come, she offered a weak excuse: "We bought a summer house on the lake, and we're going to be busy with that."

I knew I had to stand up to my family's maladjusted ways in order to heal from the childhood abuse and the wounds it had left on me. I suspected that they would punish me. No one came to my wedding. No one sent a gift. All phone calls and Christmas cards stopped. Yet deep down, I believed I was doing the right thing.

My strong convictions, however, did not eliminate the nagging doubts about whether my horrible upbringing had somehow been my fault. Why had no one in my family ever wanted me? Was there something wrong with me? In ways I never imagined, I was finally about to get the answers.

29

Homecoming

One early spring evening, long after holiday cards had stopped arriving in the mail, a curious hand-addressed envelope waited for me on the kitchen counter. I let it sit as I changed out of my work clothes and began preparing dinner.

"Are you going to open that card or what?" Charles asked, dying to know what it could be.

"Yeah, I'll get to it." I didn't exactly share his urgency. I never got any real mail except for Christmas cards. And the postmark read "Syracuse, New York," where I knew no one.

"Okay, okay," he said. "It's probably just a solicitation disguised as a real card."

After dinner, I finally opened the linen card, ready to toss it in the trash. But to my surprise, it was not a solicitation. In handwritten cursive, the note said:

Dear Miss Lane,
My mother's name is Charlotte. She had a younger sister
named Patricia, who had a daughter named Penny before
she passed away. If you are that Penny, and would like to
reconnect, you have cousins who would love to talk to you.
Signed,
Alex

My heart stopped in my chest, and my legs started to shake. Charles could tell that something was up.

"What is it?" he asked.

"It's from my cousin, my aunt Charlotte's son. I have not heard from them since my father took me from them when I was four. I had lost contact with them. I cannot believe he found me."

I sat down to think as I showed Charles the card. He agreed that it appeared to be real.

"What are you going to do?" he asked.

Fifty years had passed since I last saw Aunt Charlotte on that frightening day when my father took me away from her. Since then, he and my stepfamily had never mentioned her. It had been practically forbidden for me to bring up the topic. Over the decades, there had been no contact with Charlotte: I knew only her first name and had no address. Was she even alive?

I responded to my cousin's email, provided at the bottom of the note. As it turned out, Aunt Charlotte was alive! A few weeks later, I flew to upstate New York.

Maneuvering my rental car onto I-90 toward Syracuse, I trembled with both excitement and apprehension. Would they consider me "real" family? Would this little reunion open up wounds that I had worked so hard to heal? My cousins Alex and George had been young boys when I left Aunt Charlotte's place. I didn't know them anymore. They were mature men now, with grown children, and I was a middle-aged woman, with a family of my own. Would this be awkward or, worse, painful? Would they make me feel unwanted all over again? My biggest fear was Aunt Charlotte herself. She was over ninety years old. Would she even remember me?

I pulled up to a brick Colonial with a massive front yard bordered with trees. I took a few deep breaths. Maybe this was a mistake. But no sooner had I opened the car door than relatives poured out of the house to greet me. I was overwhelmed. I felt just like a long-lost relative finally being reunited with her loving family. I recognized Alex and George right away, taking me back to their boyhood faces. Their wives, Angela and Mary, greeted me warmly, as did George's daughter, Gretchen, and Ana and Nissa, Alex's girls. After the introductions, they ushered me into the house.

And within seconds, I felt something that I hadn't felt in half a century—that I was truly a treasured part of someone's family.

"My Precious! Is that my Precious who's come to see me?"

Tears ran down my face. I staggered toward Aunt Charlotte, seated at the dining room table. I embraced her with all I had, trying to erase the years that had come between us. She patted my back as I cried.

Everyone gathered around us. They were eager to hear my life story, and I was eager to hear theirs. They had made up the guest room with flowers and planned a whole weekend around my visit. Gretchen had driven five hours from Newport, Rhode Island, to meet me. Ana and Nissa had taken off work to be there.

Angela, Alex's wife, told me that they had been looking for me for at least three years. They finally found me when my maiden name, which I used as my middle name, turned up on the deed to a house that Charles and I had bought a few years before. Angela was a researcher at a local teaching hospital and had used her skills and access to multiple databases to track me down.

Soon after my arrival, we all sat down for lunch, where I looked around the table in awe. At the table, Aunt Charlotte kept calling me "Precious." That was what I called Charles, my son, Jake, and those I loved dearly, although I had never known why I had landed on that particular word. Now I did. Over lunch, the family caught me up on their lives and careers. George had been a computer programmer at Dell. Mary had been a nurse and a nursing supervisor, often bringing her two girls to work after school when there was no childcare. Gretchen was a photographer. Alex worked in construction.

I waited to go last, still uneasy about revealing my story to these loving, normal people. I did not want to spoil the wonderful moments of our reunion. But after taking a breath, I told them how my stepmother had never wanted me, and consequently made my life miserable. I told them about my absent father, who had died recently—and how we hadn't seen each other in the years before he passed away. My relatives sat in stunned silence, hanging on my every word. I could tell that they believed me, and that they could feel my pain.

After the dishes were cleared, I sat down again with Aunt Charlotte, and the family sat with us. I still had so many questions. What was my mother like? How did she meet my father?

We spoke for hours. My aunt showed me photos. I saw my mother as a young girl, in white anklet socks and black patent leather shoes, at her First Holy Communion, and at a birthday party. There was a photo of her at the age of fourteen with her mother, Olive, in a smart coat and hat during a trip to DC.

I saw many of my parents' wedding photos, and pictures of me as a baby, as a toddler and as a young girl. There was one of me at my own birthday party when I turned three, with a cake, balloons, and presents. As Aunt Charlotte spoke, it was clear that she had loved my mother. She referred to her as "my sweet, adorable sister." My mother had been a light in their lives, vivacious and outgoing, and everyone had adored her.

My grandmother Olive had been involved in the Hungarian Catholic Church, which sponsored the refugees after the revolution in 1956, including my father. He had moved in with them when Patricia, my mother, was sixteen. Charlotte said he was very good-looking and charming but a bit of a storyteller, and the family was not sure he could be trusted, even back then. But people married young in those days, so they got married, and Patricia was very happy, according to my aunt.

Then Charlotte uncovered a photo that took my breath away. It was of an older man with what looked like a Jewish prayer shawl around his neck. All my life I had been a "closet" Jew. My stepfamily was Catholic in name, but I had always liked and felt drawn to Jewish people, and secretly wanted to be one. I had never said a word about this to my stepfamily, as the grown-ups were all virulent anti-Semites.

"Who is this?" I asked.

"That's your grandpa," Charlotte said. "Grandma Olive's husband."

"Is he Jewish?" I asked, hoping that he was.

"Yes, but he is not your *real* grandfather."

I looked at her, confused.

"Your mother was a love child."

A love child?

"Your mother was born when I was seventeen," Aunt Charlotte explained. "Your Grandma Olive, our mother, was older. She was having an affair with Tom, a guy who owned the Greek restaurant next to our church, when she got pregnant with your mom. She thought she was done with all that. It was a big scandal in that day. But your grandfather loved her so much. He forgave her and adopted your mother as his own. She was quite a surprise. But we all loved her because she brought so much joy to our lives."

This story blew me away. For about thirty seconds, I had thought I was part Jewish. But knowing that my mother was a love child was even more shocking.

"How did my mother feel about having me?" I asked timidly.

Aunt Charlotte said my mom was thrilled to be pregnant and loved being a mother. My parents had a big fancy baby stroller that someone in the church had given them, and they loved to promenade around the East Side, where they lived, and show me off to everyone. There was a photo of me on my mother's lap, sitting on a park bench, my father behind her, looking over her shoulder. My mom was looking into the camera, overflowing with pride as she held me.

Not long after that picture was taken, my mother suddenly got sick and was hospitalized. I was four months old. It turned out to be cervical cancer, seldom heard of at the time. No one could believe that she was so ill. She had been the very picture of health—buxom, strong, and energetic—and had easily given birth to me with no complications. Grandma Olive, widowed by then, was wracked by worry about how I would be cared for. Aunt Charlotte was married at the time and living in New Jersey with her husband and two sons. She took me in while my father worked and visited my mother at night. My mother never left the hospital. She died one month after her twentieth birthday.

The room fell silent as the afternoon light turned to night. I was exhausted from the emotion of it all, and imagined that Aunt Charlotte was too. I was happy, and grateful. But I still had a delicate issue that I wanted to bring up.

"Aunt Charlotte, why did you let my father take me?"

I was afraid of how she might react. My aunt paused as a tear slid down her face.

"I wanted to keep you," she said, as if the event had happened yesterday. "You were an easy child. Your father never even came to visit you. But we had no formal agreement. He was your father. By law, you belonged with him. Our lawyer said we could not stop him. We had no rights. If he wanted to take you, there was nothing we could do."

"So you would have kept me?"

"Of course, I would have kept you. I loved you."

I hugged her, even tighter than before. In that moment, the years of hurt and pain peeled off me. I had finally found my way back home. I had always been loved and wanted after all.

The next day, before hitting the road, I stopped at a local florist, ordering a large, colorful arrangement.

On the card, I wrote:

Dear Aunt Charlotte,
Happy Mother's Day.
Love, Penny

Epilogue

Over the years, my feelings toward my family have softened, although I cannot say I forgive them. I can now view their behavior through a more mature lens. I can understand *intellectually* how my stepmother may have felt as a young woman barely out of her teens, with a crippling disease, her dreams dashed, robbed of the marriage and life she had wanted. I can see that she was unable to vent her anger on the real perpetrator of her demise—herself for marrying my father. I can see how in her immaturity, frustration, and anger, she could take it out on the easiest victim and the least likely to call her on it. And I can see how the extended family depended on me to do all her housework and childcare, looking the other way so they did not have to do it themselves. I can see how my father just gave up, drinking to numb the disappointment of losing country and family, losing his first wife, and coming home daily to a cold and bitter spouse who brought him no joy, for whom he was never good enough. Even though my stepmother did the most damage, I now hold my father more responsible for not protecting me. This is how I make sense of my senseless story. It has helped me heal and move on.

Even though I have a remarkably successful life by most measures, my trauma remains. I am still driven by fear to this day: fear of failure, fear of being found "stupid," fear of being fired, fear of being homeless and broke on the street, even though I am far from any of those things. My husband is all the things my father wasn't, and more, and yet I still have trouble with trust. I can be defensive, judgmental, and self-protective when there is no need to be. I need everything defined, orderly, neat, and wrapped with a perfect bow before I can relax. I worry about "making it" when I already have. I hoard food and money when we have enough. I sometimes forget that there is no one to punish me anymore, and that my goal should be simply to be happy.

In 2019, I got a shocking surprise. I was heading home on the commuter bus when I received an instant message. It took a few seconds to realize who it was. My heart stopped.

Donna had been a young, newly married woman when I brought her into the church in Michigan. We studied the Bible and spent a lot of time with each other. She had gone into labor in my living room before delivering a beautiful daughter named Joy. Donna and I had been good friends, but because the church had made me persona non grata, I never got to say goodbye. It had been nearly thirty years.

I sat in my bus seat, stunned. I had never expected to hear from anyone in the church again. But Donna had been looking for me for years, to thank me for showing her so much love when she was a new Christian. As soon as I got home, I called her.

"Donna, I can't believe it's you. How in the world did you find me?"

"John told me your new last name, and as soon as I saw your picture on Facebook, I knew it was you."

For a few seconds, I didn't know whom she was talking about.

"John, as in my ex-husband? You talked to John?"

"Yes, we've kept in touch."

"Oh my. He must hate me. I know he thinks I am a terrible

sinner," I said, lapsing into the vernacular of the church. I had not heard from him since I'd left Michigan in 1991.

"Just the opposite, Penny. He said losing you was the biggest regret of his life. He recently told me what the elders did to you."

I could barely take it all in. I sat in shock as Donna explained that the church had disciplined many others—including John—all for vague, unsubstantiated reasons. Eventually, Donna and countless others had left the church of their own accord because they knew what it was doing was not right.

"Penny, I never felt right about how you were treated. You were wronged, and I am so sorry it happened to you."

I started to cry.

"Donna, I was suicidal. They told me I was working with the Devil," I said.

"I can believe that, Penny. I am so glad I found you. You were always so loving to me. I am so grateful to you."

Then she gently added, "John said you were the love of his life. He is sorry he lost you."

I felt like a death-row prisoner who'd finally been declared not guilty. As it turned out, church members besides me knew that I had not been in sin. I had done the right thing by not confessing to something I didn't do. Overjoyed, I thanked Donna for validating what I had always known to be true. That day in 2019, one of the most impactful in my life, I finally put the horrors of my church past behind me forever, and I reconnected with a friend who loves me and will remain a friend for life.

Two years later, in 2021, I took another big step. After years of Hebrew lessons, studying the Torah, and endless hours of memorization, I became "bat mitzvah," an important rite of passage that signifies becoming a full-fledged member of the Jewish community.

I had always wanted to be Jewish. Mostly because the nice kids at school in Jackson Heights, the kids who did not make fun of me, who were smart, calm, and bookish, were always the Jewish kids. They looked confident and loved; they didn't brag or demand attention. One day, I caught myself thinking that if anything happened to my husband, I would convert. But why, I asked myself, was I thinking that when he was not the one holding me back?

And so I did. In 2012, at the age of fifty-three, I started studying Judaism with an amazing rabbi who understood that I did not believe in a supreme God-being, and that I did not agree with everything Israel did, but that I still wanted to be Jewish. He assured me that I was in good standing with my beliefs and that being a Jew was not about believing in God per se but about living a Jewish life.

At my first Shabbat service at the temple, where I knew no one, tears fell uncontrollably. Even though I did not understand many of the Hebrew songs, I knew that I had found my people. Twenty-five years after I had left the church, in a mikvah ceremony with my husband and closest friends, I became a Jew, giving voice to my spiritual side and finding a home for my soul.

I have come so far that sometimes I do not believe it myself. My husband has to remind me. But on some level, some wounds never go away—you just learn to deal with them. One nagging regret is that I will never know who I would have been, who I *could* have been, if I had not been crushed as a child. If I had had a normal family. If I had not been abused. If I had not been controlled by fear. On the other hand, my childhood forced me to work harder for what I do have, appreciating it more. It's not the same, but it's something.

Acknowledgments

More than fifty years in the making means many, many people contributed to this book's writing and my journey. It will be impossible to remember them all, but I will try. A special thank-you to those who loved and helped me along the way: my husband and son, Chris and Jack Lane, my cousins Alex and George and their families, the ladies at the IHOP in Jackson Heights, Aunt Maria, the Sykes family, Deanna Shaw, Dr. Zoltan Horache, wherever you are, to Aaron Weidner for telling me I needed to write this book, along with Kevin Delaney and Scott Shute for your generous support. To Irene Graham for teaching me to write memoir. To my gracious first readers, Amy Hunter, Dana Park, Erica Filanc Tanamachi, and Michael Harrowwood. To my amazing editor, David Lewis; proofreader, Beth A. Bazar; and the friends who encouraged me along the way: Julian Guthrie, Emily Bouch, Joanne Green, John J. Geoghegan, Rebecca Woolf, and all the women who believed in me—Lisha Driscoll, Marian Maher, Penny Harwood, and Andrea DeRochi. And to Brooke, Lauren, Shannon, and all my writer-sisters at SWP. I am eternally grateful.

About the Author

photo credit: Dave Zahrobsky

Penny Lane is a writer, wife, mother, and woman with an insatiable passion for life. Originally from Jackson Heights, Queens, she loves being outdoors—cycling, hiking, traveling, and connecting to, and inspiring people. She has a BS in business and management from the University of Phoenix and an MA in industrial/organizational psychology from Golden Gate University. In her spare time, she helps under-served youth learn to read, apply to college, and find jobs once they graduate, and in food pantries and other nonprofits near her home in Mill Valley, California. You can reach Penny through her website: www.pennylanewriter.com.

SELECTED TITLES FROM SHE WRITES PRESS

She Writes Press is an independent publishing company founded to serve
women writers everywhere. Visit us at www.shewritespress.com.

Seeing Eye Girl: A Memoir of Madness, Resilience, and Hope by Beverly J. Armento.
$16.95, 978-1-64742-391-9. Written for the invisible walking wounded among
us who hide their pain behind smile—and for the educators and mentors who
sometimes doubt the power of their influence—*Seeing Eye Girl* is an inspiring
story of one girl's search for hope in an abusive, dysfunctional home, and of the
teachers who empowered her.

*Baffled by Love: Stories of the Lasting Impact of Childhood Trauma Inflicted by Loved
Ones* by Laurie Kahn. $16.95, 978-1-63152-226-0. For three decades, Laurie
Kahn has treated clients who were abused as children—people who were injured
by someone who professed to love them. Here, she shares stories from her own
rocky childhood along with those of her clients, weaving a textured tale of the
all-too-human search for the "good kind of love."

Being Mean: A Memoir of Sexual Abuse and Survival by Patricia Eagle. $16.95, 978-
1-63152-519-3. Patricia is thirteen when her sexual relationship with her father,
which began at age four, finally ends. As a young woman she dreams of love but
it's not until later in life that she's able to find the strength to see what was before
unseeable, rise above her shame and depression, and speak the unspeakable to
help herself and others.

Fourteen: A Daughter's Memoir of Adventure, Sailing, and Survival by Leslie Johansen
Nack. $16.95, 978-1-63152-941-2. A coming-of-age adventure story about a
young girl who comes into her own power, fights back against abuse, becomes
an accomplished sailor, and falls in love with the ocean and the natural world.

*Now I Can See the Moon: A Story of a Social Panic, False Memories, and a Life Cut
Short* by Alice Tallmadge. $16.95, 978-1-63152-330-4. A first-person account
from inside the bizarre and life-shattering social panic over child sex abuse
that swept through the US in the 1980s—and affected Alice Tallmadge's family
in a personal, devastating way.

Raising Myself: A Memoir of Neglect, Shame, and Growing Up Too Soon by Beverly
Engel. $16.95, 978-1-63152-367-0. A powerfully inspiring and unflinchingly
honest story of how best-selling author and abuse recovery expert Beverly Engel
made her way in the world—in spite of her mother's neglect and constant criti-
cism, undergoing sexual abuse at nine, and being raped at twelve.